Catch Me
If You Can

Catch Me

If You Can

Frank W. Abagnale, Jr.
with Stan Redding

GROSSET & DUNLAP
A FILMWAYS COMPANY
Publishers • New York

This book is based on the true-life exploits of Frank Abagnale. To protect the rights of those whose paths have crossed the author's, all of the characters and some of the events have been altered, and all names, dates, and places have been changed.

To my dad

Contents

1 The Fledgling   1

2 The Pilot   19

3 Fly a Crooked Sky   40

4 If I'm a Kid Doctor, Where's My Jar of Lollipops?   59

5 A Law Degree Is Just an Illegal Technicality   86

6 Paperhanger in a Rolls-Royce   102

7 How to Tour Europe on a Felony a Day   135

8 A Small Crew Will Do—It's Just a Paper Airplane   162

9 Does This Tab Include the Tip?   191

10 Put Out an APB—Frank Abagnale Has Escaped!   221

Epilogue   247

Catch Me

If You Can

CHAPTER ONE

The Fledgling

A man's alter ego is nothing more than his favorite image of himself. The mirror in my room in the Windsor Hotel in Paris reflected my favorite image of me—a darkly handsome young airline pilot, smooth-skinned, bull-shouldered and immaculately groomed. Modesty is not one of my virtues. At the time, virtue was not one of my virtues.

Satisfied with my appearance, I picked up my bag, left the room and two minutes later was standing in front of the cashier's cage.

"Good morning, Captain," said the cashier in warm tones. The markings on my uniform identified me as a first officer, a co-pilot, but the French are like that. They tend to overestimate everything save their women, wine and art.

I signed the hotel bill she slid across the counter, started to turn away, then wheeled back, taking a payroll check from the inside pocket of my jacket. "Oh, can you cash this for me? Your Paris night life nearly wiped me out and it'll be another week before I'm home." I smiled ruefully.

She picked up the Pan American World Airways check and looked at the amount. "I'm sure we can, Captain, but I must get the manager to approve a check this large," she said. She stepped into an office behind her and was back in a moment, displaying a pleased smile. She handed me the check to endorse.

"I assume you want American dollars?" she asked, and without waiting for my reply counted out $786.73 in Yankee currency and coin. I pushed back two $50 bills. "I would appreciate it if you would take care of the necessary people, since I was so careless," I said, smiling.

She beamed. "Of course, Captain. You are very kind," she said. "Have a safe flight and please come back to see us."

I took a cab to Orly, instructing the driver to let me off at the TWA entrance. I by-passed the TWA ticket counter in the lobby and presented my FAA license and Pan Am ID card to the TWA operations officer. He checked his manifest. "Okay, First Officer Frank Williams, deadheading to Rome. Gotcha. Fill this out, please." He handed me the familiar pink form for nonrevenue passengers and I penned in the pertinent data. I picked up my bag and walked to the customs gate marked "CREW MEMBERS ONLY." I started to heft my bag to the counter top but the inspector, a wizened old man with a wispy mustache, recognized me and waved me through.

A young boy fell in beside me as I walked to the plane, gazing with unabashed admiration at my uniform with its burnished gold stripes and other adornments.

"You the pilot?" he asked. He was English from his accent.

2

"Nah, just a passenger like you," I replied. "I fly for Pan Am."

"You fly 707s?"

I shook my head. "Used to," I said. "Right now I'm on DC-8s." I like kids. This one reminded me of myself a few years past.

An attractive blond stewardess met me as I stepped aboard and helped me to stow my gear in the crew's luggage bin. "We've got a full load this trip Mr. Williams," she said. "You beat out two other guys for the jump seat. I'll be serving the cabin."

"Just milk for me," I said. "And don't worry about that if you get busy. Hitchhikers aren't entitled to anything more than the ride."

I ducked into the cabin. The pilot, co-pilot and flight engineer were making their pre-takeoff equipment and instrument check but they paused courteously at my entrance. "Hi, Frank Williams, Pan Am, and don't let me interrupt you," I said.

"Gary Giles," said the pilot, sticking out his hand. He nodded toward the other two men. "Bill Austin, number two, and Jim Wright. Good to have you with us." I shook hands with the other two airmen and dropped into the jump seat, leaving them to their work.

We were airborne within twenty minutes. Giles took the 707 up to 30,000 feet, checked his instruments, cleared with the Orly tower and then uncoiled himself from his seat. He appraised me with casual thoroughness and then indicated his chair. "Why don't you fly this bird for a while, Frank," he said. "I'll go back and mingle with the paying passengers."

His offer was a courtesy gesture sometimes accorded a deadheading pilot from a competing airline. I dropped my cap on the cabin floor and slid into the command seat, very much aware that I had been handed custody of 140 lives, my own included. Austin, who had taken the controls when Giles vacated his seat, surrendered them to me. "You got it, Captain," he said, grinning.

I promptly put the giant jet on automatic pilot and hoped to hell the gadget worked, because I couldn't fly a kite.

I wasn't a Pan Am pilot or any other kind of pilot. I was an impostor, one of the most wanted criminals on four continents, and at the moment I was doing my thing, putting a super hype on some nice people.

I was a millionaire twice over and half again before I was twenty-one. I stole every nickel of it and blew the bulk of the bundle on fine threads, gourmet foods, luxurious lodgings, fantastic foxes, fine wheels and other sensual goodies. I partied in every capital in Europe, basked on all the famous beaches and good-timed it in South America, the South Seas, the Orient and the more palatable portions of Africa.

It wasn't altogether a relaxing life. I didn't exactly keep my finger on the panic button, but I put a lot of mileage on my running shoes. I made a lot of exits through side doors, down fire excapes or over rooftops. I abandoned more wardrobes in the course of five years than most men acquire in a lifetime. I was slipperier than a buttered *escargot.*

Oddly enough, I never felt like a criminal. I was one, of course, and I was aware of the fact. I've been described by authorities and news reporters as one of this century's cleverest bum-check passers, flimflam artists and crooks, a con man of Academy Award caliber. I was a swindler and poseur of astonishing ability. I sometimes astonished myself with some of my impersonations and shenanigans, but I never at any time deluded myself. I was always aware that I was Frank Abagnale, Jr., that I was a check swindler and a faker, and if and when I were caught I wasn't going to win any Oscars. I was going to jail.

I was right, too. I did time in a French poky, served a stint in a Swedish slammer and cleansed myself of all my

American sins in the Petersburg, Virginia, federal jug. While in the last prison, I voluntarily subjected myself to a psychological evaluation by a University of Virginia criminologist-psychiatrist. He spent two years giving me various written and oral tests, using truth-serum injections and polygraph examinations on various occasions.

The shrink concluded that I had a very low criminal threshold. In other words, I had no business being a crook in the first place.

One of the New York cops who'd worked hardest to catch me read the report and snorted. "This head doctor's gotta be kiddin' us," he scoffed. "This phony rips off several hundred banks, hustles half the hotels in the world for everything but the sheets, screws every airline in the skies, including most of their stewardesses, passes enough bad checks to paper the walls of the Pentagon, runs his own goddamned colleges and universities, makes half the cops in twenty countries look like dumb-asses while he's stealing over $2 million, and he has a *low* criminal threshold? What the hell would he have done if he'd had a *high* criminal threshold, looted Fort Knox?"

The detective confronted me with the paper. We had become amiable adversaries. "You conned this shrink, didn't you, Frank?"

I told him I'd answered every question asked me as truthfully as possible, that I'd completed every test given me as honestly as I could. I didn't convince him. "Nah," he said. "You can fool these feds, but you can't fool me. You conned this couch turkey." He shook his head. "You'd con your own father, Frank."

I already had. My father was the mark for the first score I ever made. Dad possessed the one trait necessary in the perfect pigeon, blind trust, and I plucked him for $3,400. I was only fifteen at the time.

I was born and spent my first sixteen years in New York's Bronxville. I was the third of four children and my dad's namesake. If I wanted to lay down a baby con, I could say I was the product of a broken home, for Mom and Dad separated when I was twelve. But I'd only be bum-rapping my parents.

The person most hurt by the separation and subsequent divorce was Dad. He was really hung up on Mom. My mother, Paulette Abagnale, is a French-Algerian beauty whom dad met and married during his World War II army service in Oran. Mom was only fifteen at the time, and Dad was twenty-eight, and while the difference in ages didn't seem to matter at the time, I've always felt it had an influence on the breakup of their marriage.

Dad opened his own business in New York City after his discharge from the army, a stationery store at Fortieth and Madison Avenue called Gramercy's. He was very successful. We lived in a big, luxurious home and if we weren't fabulously wealthy, we were certainly affluent. My brothers, my sister and I never wanted for anything during our early years.

A kid is often the last to know when there's serious trouble between his parents. I know that's true in my case and I don't think my siblings were any more aware than I. We thought Mom was content to be a housewife and mother and she was, up to a point. But Dad was more than just a successful businessman. He was also very active in politics, one of the Republican wheels in the Bronx precincts. He was a member and past president of the New York Athletic Club, and he spent a lot of his time at the club with both business and political cronies.

Dad was also an avid salt-water fisherman. He was always flying off to Puerto Rico, Kingston, Belize or some other Caribbean spa on deep-sea fishing expeditions. He never took Mom along, and he should have. My mother was a women's libber before Gloria Steinem learned her Maidenform was flammable. And one day Dad came back from a marlin-chasing jaunt to find his home creel empty. Mom had packed up and moved herself, us three boys and Sis into a large apartment. We kids were somewhat mystified, but Mom quietly explained that she and Dad were no longer compatible and had elected to live apart.

Well, she had elected to live apart, anyway. Dad was shocked, surprised and hurt at Mom's action. He pleaded with her to come back home, promising he'd be a better husband and father and that he'd curtail his deep-sea outings. He even offered to forgo politics.

Mom listened, but she made no promises. And it soon became apparent to me, if not Dad, that she had no intention of reconciling. She enrolled in a Bronx dental college and started training to be a dental technician.

Dad didn't give up. He was over at our apartment at every opportunity, pleading, cajoling, entreating and flattering her. Sometimes he'd lose his temper. "Damn it, woman—can't you see I love you!" he'd roar.

The situation did have its effect on us boys, of course. Me in particular. I loved my dad. I was the closest to him, and he commenced to use me in his campaign to win back Mom. "Talk to her, son," he'd ask of me. "Tell her I love her. Tell her we'd be happier if we all lived together. Tell her you'd be happier if she came home, that all you kids would be happier."

He'd give me gifts to deliver to Mom, and coach me in speeches designed to break down my mother's resistance.

As a juvenile John Alden to my father's Myles Standish and my mother's Priscilla Mullins, I was a flop. My mother couldn't be conned. And Dad probably hurt his own case because Mom resented his using me as a pawn in their game of marital chess. She divorced Dad when I was fourteen.

Dad was crushed. I was disappointed, for I had really wanted them to get back together. I'll say this for Dad: when he loved a woman, he loved her forever. He was still trying to win Mom back when he died in 1974.

When Mom finally divorced my father, I elected to live with Dad. Mom wasn't too keen on my decision, but I felt Dad needed one of us, that he shouldn't have to live alone, and I persuaded her. Dad was grateful and pleased. I have never regretted the decision, although Dad probably did.

Life with Father was a whole different ball game. I spent a lot of time in some of New York's finest saloons. Businessmen, I learned, not only enjoy three-martini lunches, but they belt out a lot of boilermaker brunches and whack out scores of scotch and soda dinners. Politicians, I also noted quickly, had a better grasp of world affairs and a looser lid on their pork barrels when they were attached to a bourbon on the rocks. Dad did a lot of his business dealing and a goodly amount of his political maneuvering close to a bar, with me waiting nearby. My father's drinking habits alarmed me at first. I didn't think he was an alcoholic, but he was a two-fisted drinker and I worried that he had a drinking problem. Still, I never saw him drunk although he drank constantly and after a while I assumed he was immune to the juice.

I was fascinated by my dad's associates, friends and acquaintances. They ranged the gamut of the Bronx's social stratum: ward heelers, cops, union bosses, business executives, truckers, contractors, stock brokers, clerks, cabbies and promoters. The whole smear. Some were right out of the pages of Damon Runyon.

After hanging out with Dad for six months, I was street-wise and about five-eighths smart, which is not exactly the kind of education Dad had in mind for me, but it's the kind you get in sauce parlors.

Dad had a lot of political clout. I learned this when I started playing hookey from school and running with some loose-end kids from my neighborhood. They weren't gang members or anything like that. They weren't into anything really heavy. They were just guys with a screwed-up family situation, trying to get attention from someone, if only the truant officer. Maybe that's why I started hanging out with them. Perhaps I was seeking attention myself. I did want my parents together again, and I had vague notions at the time that if I acted like a juvenile delinquent, it might provide a common ground for a reconciliation.

I wasn't too good as a juvenile delinquent. Most of the time I felt plain foolish, swiping candy and slipping into movies. I was much more mature than my companions, and much bigger. At fifteen I was physically grown, six feet and 170 pounds, and I guess we got away with a lot of minor mischief because people who saw us abroad thought I was a teacher shepherding some students or a big brother looking out for the younger crowd. I sometimes felt that way myself, and I was often irritated at their childishness.

What bothered me most was their lack of style. I learned early that class is universally admired. Almost any fault, sin or crime is considered more leniently if there's a touch of class involved.

These kids couldn't even boost a car with any finesse. The first set of wheels they lifted, they came by to pick me up, and we weren't a mile from my house when a squad car pulled us over. The jerks had taken the car from a driveway while the owner was watering his lawn. We all ended up in the Juvenile Hilton.

Dad not only got me out, but he had all mention of my part in the incident erased from the records. It was a bit of ward-heeling wizardry that was to cost a lot of cops a lot of sleep in future years. Even an elephant is easier to find if you can pick up his trail at the start of the hunt.

Dad didn't chew me out. "We all make mistakes, son," he said. "I know what you were trying to do, but that's not the way to do it. Under the law, you're still a child, but you're man-sized. Maybe you ought to try thinking like a man."

I dropped my erstwhile chums, started going to school regularly again and got a part-time job as a shipping clerk in a Bronxville warehouse. Dad was pleased—so pleased he bought me an old Ford, which I proceeded to fix up into a real fox trap.

If I had to place any blame for my future nefarious actions, I'd put it on the Ford.

That Ford fractured every moral fiber in my body. It introduced me to girls, and I didn't come to my senses for six years. They were wonderful years.

There are undoubtedly other ages in a man's life when his reasoning power is eclipsed by his libido, but none presses on the prefrontal lobes like the post-puberty years when the thoughts are running and every luscious chick who passes increases the flow. At fifteen I knew about girls, of course. They were built differently than boys. But I didn't know why until I stopped at a red light one day, after renovating the Ford, and saw this girl looking at me and my car. When she saw she had my attention, she did something with her eyes, jiggled her front and twitched her behind, and suddenly I was drowning in my thoughts. She had ruptured the dam. I don't remember how she got into the car, or where we went after she got in, but I do remember she was all silk, softness, nuzzly, warm, sweet-smelling and absolutely delightful, and I knew I'd found a contact sport that I could really enjoy. She did things to me that would lure a hummingbird from a hibiscus and make a bulldog break his chain.

I am not impressed by today's tomes on women's rights in the bedroom. When Henry Ford invented the Model-T, women shed their bloomers and put sex on the road.

Women became my only vice. I reveled in them. I couldn't get enough of them. I woke up thinking of girls. I went to bed thinking of girls. All lovely, leggy, breathtaking, fantastic and enchanting. I went on girl scouting forays at sunrise. I went out at night and looked for them with a flashlight. Don Juan had only a mild case of the hots compared to me. I was obsessed with foxy women.

I was also a charming broke after my first few close encounters of the best kind. Girls are not necessarily expensive, but even the most frolicsome Fräulein expects a hamburger and a Coke now and then, just for energy purposes. I simply wasn't making enough bread to pay for my cake. I needed a way to juggle my finances.

I sought out Dad, who was not totally unaware of my discovery of girls and their attendant joys. "Dad, it was really neat of you to give me a car, and I feel like a jerk asking for more, but I've got problems with that car," I pleaded. "I need a gas credit card. I only get paid once a month, and what with buying my school lunches, going to the games, dating and stuff, I don't have the dough to buy gas sometimes. I'll try and pay the bill myself, but I promise I won't abuse your generosity if you'll let me have a gas card."

I was as glib as an Irish horse trader at the time, and at the time I was sincere. Dad mulled the request for a few moments, then nodded. "All right, Frank, I trust you," he said, taking his Mobil card from his wallet. "You take this card and use it. I won't charge anything to Mobil from now on. It'll be your card, and within reason, it'll be your responsibility to pay this bill each month when it comes in. I won't worry about your taking advantage of me."

He should have. The arrangement worked fine the first month. The Mobil bill came in and I bought a money order for the amount and sent it to the oil firm. But the payment left me strapped and once again I found myself hampered in my constant quest for girls. I began to feel frustrated. After all, the pursuit of happiness was an inalienable American privilege, wasn't it? I felt I was being deprived of a constitutional right.

Someone once said there's no such thing as an honest man. He was probably a con man. It's the favorite rationale of the pigeon dropper. I think a lot of people do fantasize about being a supercriminal, an international diamond thief or something like that, but they confine their larceny to daydreams. I also think a lot of other people are actually tempted now and then to commit a crime, especially if there's a nice bundle to be had and they think they won't

11

be connected with the caper. Such people usually reject the temptation. They have an innate perception of right and wrong, and common sense prevails.

But there's also a type of person whose competitive instincts override reason. They are challenged by a given situation in much the same manner a climber is challenged by a tall peak: because it's there. Right or wrong are not factors, nor are consequences. These people look on crime as a game, and the goal is not just the loot; it's the success of the venture that counts. Of course, if the booty is bountiful, that's nice, too.

These people are the chess players of the criminal world. They generally have a genius-level IQ and their mental knights and bishops are always on the attack. They never anticipate being checkmated. They are always astonished when a cop with average intelligence rooks them, and the cop is always astonished at their motives. Crime as a challenge? Jesus.

But it was the challenge that led me to put down my first scam. I needed money, all right. Anyone with a chronic case of the girl crazies needs all the financial assistance that's available. However, I really wasn't dwelling on my lack of funds when I stopped at a Mobil station one afternoon and spotted a large sign in front of the station's tire display racks. "PUT A SET ON YOUR MOBIL CARD—WE'LL PUT THE SET ON YOUR CAR" the sign read. It was the first inkling I'd had that the Mobil card was good for more than gas or oil. I didn't need any tires—the ones on the Ford were practically new—but as I studied the sign I was suddenly possessed by a four-ply scheme. Hell, it might even work, I thought.

I got out and approached the attendant, who was also the owner of the station. We were casual acquaintances from the many pit stops I'd made at the station. It was not a busy gas stop. "I'd make more money holding up filling stations than running one," he'd once complained.

"How much would it cost me for a set of whitewalls?"
I asked.

"For this car, $160, but you got a good set of treads,"
the man said.

He looked at me and I knew he sensed he was about
to be propositioned. "Yeah, I don't really need any tires,"
I agreed. "But I got a bad case of the shorts. Tell you what
I'll do. I'll buy a set of those tires and charge them on this
card. Only I don't take the tires. You give me $100 instead.
You've still got the tires, and when my dad pays Mobil
for them, you get your cut. You're ahead to start with,
and when you do sell the tires, the whole $160 goes into
your pocket. What do you say? You'll make out like a
dragon, man."

He studied me, and I could see the speculative greed
in his eyes. "What about your old man?" he asked cautiously.

I shrugged. 'He never looks at my car. I told him I
needed some new tires and he told me to charge them."

He was still doubtful. "Lemme see your driver's license.
This could be a stolen card," he said. I handed him my
junior driver's license, which bore the same name as the
card. "You're only fifteen? You look ten years older," the
station owner said as he handed it back.

I smiled. "I got a lot of miles on me," I said.

He nodded. "I'll have to call into Mobil and get an ap-
proval—we have to do that on any big purchase," he said.
"If I get an okay, we got a deal."

I rolled out of the station with five twenties in my wallet.

I was heady with happiness. Since I hadn't yet had my
first taste of alcohol, I couldn't compare the feeling to a
champagne high, say, but it was the most delightful sensation I'd ever experienced in the *front* seat of a car.

In fact, my cleverness overwhelmed me. If it worked
once, why wouldn't it work twice? It did. It worked so
many times in the next several weeks, I lost count. I can't

remember how many sets of tires, how many batteries, how many other automobile accessories I bought with that charge card and then sold back for a fraction of value. I hit every Mobil station in the Bronx. Sometimes I'd just con the guy on the pumps into giving me $10 and sign a ticket for $20 worth of gas and oil. I wore that Mobil card thin with the scam.

I blew it all on the broads, naturally. At first I operated on the premise that Mobil was underwriting my pleasures, so what the hell? Then the first month's bill landed in the mailbox. The envelope was stuffed fuller than a Christmas goose with charge receipts. I looked at the total due and briefly contemplated entering the priesthood, for I realized Mobil expected Dad to pay the bill. It hadn't occurred to me that Dad would be the patsy in the game.

I threw the bill into the wastebasket. A second notice mailed two weeks later also went into the trash. I thought about facing up to Dad and confessing, but I didn't have the courage. I knew he'd find out, sooner or later, but I decided someone other than me would have to tell him.

Amazingly, I didn't pull up while awaiting a summit session between my father and Mobil. I continued to work the credit-card con and spend the loot on lovely women, even though I was aware I was also diddling my dad. An inflamed sex drive has no conscience.

Eventually, a Mobil investigator sought Dad out in his store. The man was apologetic.

"Mr. Abagnale, you've had a card with us for fifteen years and we prize your account. You've got a top credit rating, you've never been late with a payment and I'm not here to harass you about your bill," said the agent as Dad listened with a puzzled expression. "We are curious, sir, and would like to know one thing. Just how in the hell can you run up a $3,400 bill for gas, oil, batteries and tires for one 1952 Ford in the space of three months? You've put fourteen sets of tires on that car in the past sixty days, bought twenty-two batteries in the past ninety days and you can't be getting over two miles to the gallon on gas. We figure you don't even have an oil pan on the damned thing. . . . Have you given any thought to trading that car in on a new one, Mr. Abagnale?"

Dad was stunned. "Why, I don't even use my Mobil card—my son does," he said when he recovered. "There must be some mistake."

The Mobil investigator placed several hundred Mobil charge receipts in front of Dad. Each bore his signature in my handwriting. "How did he do this? And why?" Dad exclaimed.

"I don't know," replied the Mobil agent. "Why don't we ask him?"

They did. I said I didn't know a thing about the swindle. I didn't convince either of them. I had expected Dad to be furious. But he was more confused than angry. "Look, son, if you'll tell us how you did this, and why, we'll forget it. There'll be no punishment and I'll pay the bills," he offered.

My dad was a great guy in my book. He never lied to me in his life. I promptly copped out. "It's the girls, Dad," I sighed. "They do funny things to me. I can't explain it."

Dad and the Mobil investigator nodded understandingly. Dad laid a sympathetic hand on my shoulder. "Don't worry about it, boy. Einstein couldn't explain it, either," he said.

If Dad forgave me, Mom didn't. She was really upset over the incident and blamed my father for my delinquencies. My mother still had legal custody of me and she decided to remove me from Dad's influences. Worse still, on the advice of one of the fathers who worked with Catholic Charities, with which my mother has always been affiliated, she popped me into a C.C. private school for problem boys in Port Chester, New York.

As a reformatory, the school wasn't much. It was more of a posh camp than a remedial institution. I lived in a neat cottage with six other boys, and except for the fact that I was restricted to campus and constantly supervised, I was subjected to no hardships.

The brothers who ran the school were a benevolent lot. They lived in much the same manner as their wards. We all ate in a common dining hall, and the food was good and plentiful. There was a movie theater, a television room, a recreation hall, a swimming pool and a gymnasium. I never did catalogue all the recreational and sports facilities that were available. We attended classes from 8 A.M. to 3 P.M., Monday through Friday, but otherwise our time was our own to do with as we liked. The brothers didn't harangue us about our misdeeds or bore us with pontifical lectures, and you really had to mess up to be punished, which usually meant being confined to your cottage for a couple of days. I never encountered anything like the school until I landed in a U.S. prison. I have often wondered since if the federal penal system isn't secretly operated by Catholic Charities.

The monastic lifestyle galled me, however. I endured it, but I looked on my stint in the school as punishment and undeserved punishment at that. After all, Dad had forgiven me and he had been the sole victim of my crimes. So what was I doing in the place? I'd ask myself. What I disliked most about the school, however, was its lack of girls. It was strictly an all-male atmosphere. Even the sight of a nun would have thrilled me.

I would have been even more depressed had I known what was happening to Dad during my stay. He never went into details, but while I was in the school he ran into some severe financial difficulties and lost his business.

He was really wiped out. He was forced to sell the house and his two big Cadillacs and everything else he had of material value. In the space of a few months, Dad went from living like a millionaire to living like a postal clerk.

That's what he was when he came to get me after I'd spent a year in the school. A postal clerk. Mom had relented and had agreed to my living with Dad again. I was shocked at the reversal of his fortunes, and more than a little guilt-ridden. But Dad would not allow me to blame myself. The $3,400 I'd ripped him off for was not a factor in his business downfall, he assured me. "Don't even think of it, kid. That was a drop in the bucket," he said cheerfully.

He did not seem to be bothered by his sudden drop in status and finances, but it bothered me. Not for myself, but for Dad. He'd been so high, a real wheeler-dealer, and now he was working for wages. I tried to pump him for the causes. "What about your friends, Dad?" I asked. "I remember you were always pulling them out of tight spots. Didn't any of them offer to help you?"

Dad just smiled wryly. "You'll learn, Frank, that when you're up there're hundreds of people who'll claim you as a friend. When you're down, you're lucky if one of them will buy you a cup of coffee. If I had it to do over again, I'd select my friends more carefully. I do have a couple of good friends. They're not wealthy, but one of them got me my job in the post office."

He refused to dwell on his misfortunes or to discuss them at length, but it bugged me, especially when I was with him in his car. It wasn't as good as my Ford, which he'd sold for me and placed the money in an account in my name. His car was a battered old Chevy. "Doesn't it bother you at all to drive this old car, Dad?" I asked him one day.

"I mean, this is really a comedown from a Cadillac. Right?"

Dad laughed. "That's the wrong way to look at it, Frank. It's not what a man has but what a man is that's important. This car is fine for me. It gets me around. I know who I am and what I am, and that's what counts, not what other people might think of me. I'm an honest man, I feel, and that's more important to me than having a big car. . . . As long as a man knows what he is and who he is, he'll do all right."

Trouble was, at the time I didn't know what I was or who I was.

Within three short years I had the answer. "Who are you?" asked a lush brunette when I plopped down on Miami Beach beside her.

"Anyone I want to be," I said. I was, too.

CHAPTER TWO

The Pilot

I left home at sixteen, looking for me.

There was no pressure on me to leave, although I wasn't happy. The situation on my dual home front hadn't changed. Dad still wanted to win Mom back and Mom didn't want to be won. Dad was still using me as a mediator in his second courtship of Mom, and she continued to resent his casting me in the role of Cupid. I disliked it myself. Mom had graduated from dental technician's school and was working for a Larchmont dentist. She seemed satisfied with her new, independent life.

I had no plans to run away. But every time Dad put on his postal clerk's uniform and drove off to work in his old car, I'd feel depressed. I couldn't forget how he used to wear Louis Roth suits and drive big expensive cars.

One June morning of 1964, I woke up and knew it was

time to go. Some remote corner of the world seemed to be whispering, "Come." So I went.

I didn't say good-bye to anyone. I didn't leave any notes behind. I had $200 in a checking account at the Westchester branch of the Chase Manhattan Bank, an account Dad had set up for me a year before and which I'd never used. I dug out my checkbook, packed my best clothes in a single suitcase and caught a train for New York City. It wasn't exactly a remote corner of the globe, but I thought it would make a good jumping-off place.

If I'd been some runaway from Kansas or Nebraska, New York, with its subway bedlam, awesome skyscrapers, chaotic streams of noisy traffic and endless treadmills of people, might have sent me scurrying back to the prairies. But the Big Apple was my turf. Or so I thought.

I wasn't off the train an hour when I met a boy my own age and conned him into taking me home with him. I told his parents that I was from upstate New York, that both my mother and father were dead, that I was trying to make it on my own and that I needed a place to stay until I got a job. They told me I could stay in their home as long as I wanted.

I had no intentions of abusing their hospitality. I was eager to make a stake and leave New York, although I had no ideas at the moment as to where I wanted to go or what I wanted to do.

I did have a definite goal. I was going to be a success in some field. I was going to make it to the top of some mountain. And once there, no one or nothing was going to dislodge me from the peak. I wasn't going to make the mistakes my dad had made. I was determined on that point.

The Big Apple quickly proved less than juicy, even for a native son. I had no problem finding a job. I'd worked for my father as a stock clerk and delivery boy and was experienced in the operation of a stationery store. I started calling on large stationery firms, presenting myself in a truthful light. I was only sixteen, I said, and I was a high school dropout, but I was well versed in the stationery business. The manager of the third firm I visited hired me at $1.50 an hour. I was naïve enough to think it an adequate salary.

I was disillusioned within the week. I realized I wasn't going to be able to live in New York on $60 a week, even if I stayed in the shabbiest hotel and ate at the Automats. Even more disheartening, I was reduced to the role of spectator in the dating game. To the girls I'd met so far, a stroll in Central Park and a hot dog from a street vendor's cart would not qualify as an enchanted evening. I wasn't too enchanted with such a dalliance myself. Hot dogs make me belch.

I analyzed the situation and arrived at this conclusion: I wasn't being paid lowly wages because I was a high school dropout but because I was only sixteen. A boy simply wasn't worth a man's wages.

So I aged ten years overnight. It had always surprised people, especially women, to learn I was still a teen-ager. I decided that since I appeared older, I might as well be older. I had excelled in graphic arts in school. I did a credible job of altering the birth date on my driver's license from 1948 to 1938. Then I went out to test the job market as a twenty-six-year-old high school dropout, with proof of my age in my wallet.

I learned the pay scale for a man without a high school diploma wasn't something that would embarrass the creators of the Minimum Wage Act. No one questioned my new age, but the best offer made me was $2.75 an hour as a truck driver's helper. Some prospective employers bluntly told me that it wasn't age that determined a worker's salary, but education. The more education he had, the more he was paid. I ruefully concluded that a high school dropout was like a three-legged wolf in the wilderness.

21

He might survive, but he'd survive on less. It did not occur to me until later that diplomas, like birth dates, are also easily faked.

I could have survived on $110 a week, but I couldn't *live* on that amount. I was too enamored of the ladies, and any horse player can tell you that the surest way to stay broke is playing the fillies. The girls I was romancing were all running fillies, and they were costing me a bundle.

I started writing checks on my $200 account whenever I was low on fun funds.

It was a reserve I hadn't wanted to tap, and I tried to be conservative. I'd cash a check for only $10, or at most $20, and at first I conducted all my check transactions in a branch of the Chase Manhattan Bank. Then I learned that stores, hotels, grocery markets and other business firms would also cash personal checks, provided the amount wasn't overly large and proper identification was presented. I found my altered driver's license was considered suitable identification, and I started dropping in at the handiest hotel or department store whenever I needed to cash a $20 or $25 check. No one asked me any questions. No one checked with the bank to see if the check was good. I'd simply present my jazzed-up driver's license with my check and the driver's license would be handed back with the cash.

It was easy. Too easy. Within a few days I knew I was overdrawn on my account and the checks I was writing were no good. However, I continued to cash a check whenever I needed money to supplement my paycheck or to finance a gourmet evening with some beautiful chick. Since my paycheck seemed always in need of a subsidy, and because New York has more beautiful chicks than a poultry farm, I was soon writing two or three bad checks daily.

I rationalized my actions. Dad would take care of the insufficient checks, I told myself. Or I'd assuage my conscience with con man's salve: if people were stupid enough to cash a check without verifying its validity, they deserved to be swindled.

I also consoled myself with the fact that I was a juvenile. Even if I were caught, it was unlikely that I'd receive any stern punishment, considering the softness of New York's juvenile laws and the leniency of the city's juvenile judges. As a first offender, I'd probably be released to my parents. I probably wouldn't even have to make restitution.

My scruples fortified by such nebulous defenses, I quit my job and began to support myself on the proceeds of my spurious checks. I didn't keep track of the number of bum checks I passed, but my standard of living improved remarkably. So did my standard of loving.

After two months of cranking out worthless checks, however, I faced myself with some unpleasant truths. I was a crook. Nothing more, nothing less. In the parlance of the streets, I had become a professional paperhanger. That didn't bother me too much, for I was a successful paperhanger, and at the moment to be a success at anything was the most important factor in the world to me.

What did bother me were the occupational hazards involved in being a check swindler. I knew my father had reported my absence to the police. Generally, the cops don't spend a lot of time looking for a missing sixteen-year-old, unless foul play is suspected. However, my case was undoubtedly an exception, for I had provided plenty of foul play with my scores of bad checks. The police, I knew, were looking for me as a thief, not a runaway. Every merchant and businessman I'd bilked was also on the alert for me, I speculated.

In short, I was hot. I knew I could elude the cops for a while yet, but I also knew I'd eventually be caught if I stayed in New York and continued to litter cash drawers with useless chits.

The alternative was to leave New York, and the prospect frightened me. That still-remote corner of the world suddenly seemed chill and friendless. In Manhattan, despite my brash show of independence, I'd always clutched a security blanket. Mom and Dad were just a phone call or a short train ride away. I knew they'd be loyal, no matter my misdeeds. The outlook appeared decidedly gloomy if I fled to Chicago, Miami, Washington or some other distant metropolis.

I was practiced in only one art, writing fraudulent checks. I didn't even contemplate any other source of income, and to me that was a matter of prime concern. Could I flimflam merchants in another city as easily as I had swindled New Yorkers? In New York I had an actual, if valueless, checking account, and a valid, if ten years off, driver's license, which together allowed me to work my nefarious trade in a lucrative manner. Both my stack of personalized checks (the name was real, only the funds were fictional) and my tinseled driver's license would be useless in any other city. I'd have to change my name, acquire bogus identification and set up a bank account under my alias before I could operate. It all seemed complex and danger-ridden to me. I was a successful crook. I wasn't yet a confident crook.

I was still wrestling with the perplexities of my situation several days later while walking along Forty-second Street when the revolving doors of the Commodore Hotel disgorged the solution to my quandary.

As I drew near the hotel entrance, an Eastern Airlines flight crew emerged: a captain, co-pilot, flight engineer and four stewardesses. They were all laughing and animated, caught up in a joie de vivre of their own. The men were all lean and handsome, and their gold-piped uniforms lent them a buccaneerish air. The girls were all trim and lovely, as graceful and colorful as butterflies abroad in a meadow. I stopped and watched as they boarded a crew bus, and I thought I had never seen such a splendid group of people.

I walkèd on, still enmeshed in the net of their glamour,

and suddenly I was seized with an idea so daring in scope, so dazzling in design, that I whelmed myself.

What if I were a pilot? Not an actual pilot, of course. I had no heart for the grueling years of study, training, flight schooling, work and other mundane toils that fit a man for a jet liner's cockpit. But what if I had the uniform and the trappings of an airline pilot? Why, I thought, I could walk into any hotel, bank or business in the country and cash a check. Airline pilots are men to be admired and respected. Men to be trusted. Men of means. And you don't expect an airline pilot to be a local resident. Or a check swindler.

I shook off the spell. The idea was too ludicrous, too ridiculous to consider. Challenging, yes, but foolish.

Then I was at Forty-second and Park Avenue and the Pan American World Airways Building loomed over me. I looked up at the soaring office building, and I didn't see a structure of steel, stone and glass. I saw a mountain to be climbed.

The executives of the famed carrier were unaware of the fact, but then and there Pan Am acquired its most costly jet jockey. And one who couldn't fly, at that. But what the hell. It's a scientific fact that the bumblebee can't fly, either. But he does, and makes a lot of honey on the side.

And that's all I intended to be. A bumblebee in Pan Am's honey hive.

I sat up all night, cogitating, and fell asleep just before dawn with a tentative plan in mind. It was one I'd have to play by ear, I felt, but isn't that the basis of all knowledge? You listen and you learn.

I awoke shortly after 1 P.M., grabbed the Yellow Pages and looked up Pan Am's number. I dialed the main switchboard number and asked to speak to someone in the purchasing department. I was connected promptly.

"This is Johnson, can I help you?"

Like Caesar at the Rubicon, I cast the die. "Yes," I said.

"My name is Robert Black and I'm a co-pilot with Pan American, based in Los Angeles." I paused for his reaction, my heart thumping.

"Yes, what can I do for you, Mr. Black?" He was courteous and matter-of-fact and I plunged ahead.

"We flew a trip in here at eight o'clock this morning, and I'm due out of here this evening at seven," I said. I plucked the flight times from thin air and hoped he wasn't familiar with Pan Am's schedules. I certainly wasn't.

"Now, I don't know how this happened," I continued, trying to sound chagrined. "I've been with the company seven years and never had anything like this happen. The thing is, someone has stolen my uniform, or at least it's missing, and the only replacement uniform I have is in my home in Los Angeles. Now, I have to fly this trip out tonight and I'm almost sure I can't do it in civilian clothes. . . . Do you know where I can pick up a uniform here, a supplier or whatever, or borrow one, just till we work this trip?"

Johnson chuckled. "Well, it's not that big a problem," he replied. "Have you got a pencil and paper?"

I said I did, and he continued. "Go down to the Well-Built Uniform Company and ask for Mr. Rosen. He'll fix you up. I'll call him and tell him you're coming down. What's your name again?"

"Robert Black," I replied, and hoped he was asking simply because he'd forgotten. His final words reassured me.

"Don't worry, Mr. Black. Rosen will take good care of you," Johnson said cheerfully. He sounded like a Boy Scout who'd just performed his good deed for the day, and he had.

Less than an hour later I walked into the Well-Built Uniform Company. Rosen was a wispy, dour little man with a phlegmatic manner, a tailor's tape dangling on his chest. "You Officer Black?" he asked in a reedy voice and, when I said I was, he crooked a finger. "Come on back here."

26

I followed him through a maze of clothing racks boasting a variety of uniforms, apparently for several different airlines, until he stopped beside a display of dark blue suits.

"What's your rank?" Rosen asked, sifting through a row of jackets.

I knew none of the airline terminology. "Co-pilot," I said, and hoped that was the right answer.

"First officer, huh?" he said, and began handing me jackets and trousers to try on for size. Finally, Rosen was satisfied. "This isn't a perfect fit, but I don't have time to make alterations. It'll get you by until you can find time to get a proper fitting." He took the jacket to a sewing machine and deftly and swiftly tacked three gold stripes on each sleeve cuff. Then he fitted me with a visored cap.

I suddenly noticed the uniform jacket and cap each lacked something. "Where's the Pan Am wings and the Pan Am emblem?" I asked.

Rosen regarded me quizzically and I tensed. I blew it, I thought. Then Rosen shrugged. "Oh, we don't carry those. We just manufacture uniforms. You're talking about hardware. Hardware comes directly from Pan Am, at least here in New York. You'll have to get the wings and the emblem from Pan Am's stores department."

"Oh, okay," I said, smiling. "In L.A. the same people who supply our uniforms supply the emblems. How much do I owe you for this uniform? I'll write you a check." I was reaching for my checkbook when it dawned on me that my checks bore the name Frank Abagnale, Jr., and almost certainly would expose my charade.

Rosen himself staved off disaster. "It's $289, but I can't take a check." I acted disappointed. "Well, gosh, Mr. Rosen, I'll have to go cash a check then and bring you the cash."

Rosen shook his head. "Can't take cash, either," he said. "I'm going to have to bill this back to your employee account number and it'll be deducted from your uniform allowance or taken out of your paycheck. That's the way we do it here." Rosen was a veritable fount of airline operations information and I was grateful.

He handed me a form in triplicate and I commenced to fill in the required information. Opposite the space for my name were five small connected boxes, and I assumed rightly that they were for an employee's payroll account number. Five boxes. Five digits. I filled in the boxes with the first five numbers that came to mind, signed the form and pushed it back to Rosen. He snapped off the bottom copy, handed it to me.

"Thank you very much, Mr. Rosen," I said, and left, carrying the lovely uniform. If Rosen answered, I didn't hear him.

I went back to my room and dialed the Pan Am switchboard again. "Excuse me, but I was referred to the stores department," I said, acting confused. "What is that, please? I'm not with the company, and I have to make a delivery there."

The switchboard girl was most helpful. "Stores is our employee commissary," she said. "It's in Hangar Fourteen at Kennedy Airport. Do you need directions?"

I said I didn't and thanked her. I took an airport bus to Kennedy and was dismayed when the driver let me off in front of Hangar 14. Whatever stores Pan Am kept in Hangar 14, they had to be valuable. The hangar was a fortress, surrounded by a tall cyclone fence topped with strands of barbed wire and its entrances guarded by armed sentries. A sign on the guard shack at each entrance warned "EMPLOYEES ONLY."

A dozen or more pilots, stewardesses and civilians entered the compound while I reconnoitered from the bus stop. I noticed the civilians stopped and displayed identification to the guards, but most of the uniformed personnel, pilots and stewardesses, merely strolled through the gate, some without even a glance at the guard. Then one turned back to say something to a sentry and I noticed he had an ID card clipped to his breast pocket below his wings.

It was a day that threatened rain. I had brought a rain-coat along, a black one similar to the ones some of the pilots had draped over their arms. I had my newly acquired pilot's uniform in a small duffle bag. I felt a little like Custer must have felt when he chanced upon Sitting Bull's Sioux.

I reacted just like Custer. I charged. I went into one of the airport toilets and changed into the uniform, stuffing my civies into the duffle bag. Then I left the terminal and walked directly toward Hangar 14's nearest entrance.

The guard was in his shack, his back toward me. As I neared the gate, I flipped the raincoat over my left shoulder, concealing the entire left side of my jacket, and swept off my hat. When the guard turned to confront me, I was combing my hair with my fingers, my hat in my left hand.

I didn't break stride. I smiled and said crisply, "Good evening." He made no effort to stop me, although he returned my greeting. A moment later I was inside Hangar 14. It was, indeed, a hangar. A gleaming 707, parked at the rear of the building, dominated the interior. But Hangar 14 was also an immense compartmented office structure containing the offices of the chief pilot and chief stewardess, the firm's meteorology offices and dozens of other cubicles that I presumed accommodated other Pan Am functions or personnel. The place was teeming with human traffic. There seemed to be dozens of pilots, scores of stewardesses and innumerable civilians milling around. I presumed the latter were clerks, ticket agents, mechanics and other nonflying personnel.

I hesitated in the lobby, suddenly apprehensive. Abruptly I felt like a sixteen-year-old and I was sure that anyone who looked at me would realize I was too young to be a pilot and would summon the nearest cop.

I didn't turn a head. Those who did glance at me displayed no curiosity or interest. There was a large placard on a facing wall listing various departments and with arrows pointing the way. Stores was down a corridor to my left, and proved to be a military-like cubicle with a myriad of box-holding shelves. A lanky youth with his name embroidered on the right side of his shirt rose from a chair in front of a large desk as I stopped at the counter.

"Can I he'p ya?" he asked in molasses tones. It was the first real southern drawl I'd ever heard. I liked it.

"Yes," I said and attempted a rueful grin. "I need a pair of wings and a hat emblem. My two-year-old took mine off my uniform last night and he won't, or can't, tell me what he did with them."

The storekeeper laughed. "We got mo' wings on kids 'n gals 'n we got on pilots, I 'spect," he said drolly. "We shore replace a lot of 'em, anyway. Here you are. Gimme yore name and employee number." He took a form from a file slot on his desk and laid it on the counter with a pair of golden wings and a Pan Am cap badge and stood, pen poised.

"Robert Black, first officer, 35099," I said, affixing the hat emblem and pinning the wings on my tunic. "I'm out of Los Angeles. You need an address there?"

He grinned. "Nah, damned computers don't need nothin' but numbers," he replied, handing me a copy of the purchase form.

I loitered leaving the building, trying to mingle unobtrusively with the crowd.

I wanted to pick up as much information as possible on airline pilots and airline operations, and this seemed a good opportunity to glean a few tidbits. Despite the number of pilots and other aircrewmen in the building, they all seemed to be strangers to one another. I was especially interested in the plastic-enclosed cards, obviously identification of some sort, that most of the pilots sported on their breasts. The stewardesses, I observed, had similar ID cards but had them clipped to their purse straps.

A couple of pilots were scanning notices tacked on a large bulletin board in the lobby. I stopped and pretended to look at some of the notices, FAA or Pan Am memos mostly, and was afforded a close-up view of one pilot's

ID card. It was slightly larger than a driver's license and similar to the one in my pocket, save for a passport-sized color photograph of the man in the upper right-hand corner and Pan American's firm name and logo across the top in the company's colors.

Obviously, I reflected as I left the building, I was going to need more than a uniform if I was to be successful in my role of Pan Am pilot. I would need an ID card and a great deal more knowledge of Pan Am's operations than I possessed at the moment. I put the uniform away in my closet and started haunting the public library and canvassing bookstores, studying all the material available on pilots, flying and airlines. One small volume I encountered proved especially valuable. It was the reminiscences of a veteran Pan American flight captain, replete with scores of photographs, and containing a wealth of airline terminology. It was not until later I learned that the pilot's phraseology was somewhat dated.

A lot of the things I felt I ought to know, however, were not in the books or magazines I read. So I got back on the pipe with Pan Am. "I'd like to speak to a pilot, please," I told the switchboard operator. "I'm a reporter for my high school newspaper, and I'd like to do a story on pilots' lives—you know, where they fly, how they're trained and that sort of stuff. Do you think a pilot would talk to me?"

Pan Am has the nicest people. "Well, I can put you through to operations, the crew lounge," said the woman. "There might be someone sitting around there that might answer some of your questions."

There was a captain who was happy to oblige. He was delighted that young people showed an interest in making a career in the airline field. I introduced myself as Bobby Black, and after some innocuous queries, I started to feed him the questions I wanted answered.

"What's the age of the youngest pilot flying for Pan Am?"

"Well, that depends," he answered. "We have some

flight engineers who're probably no older than twenty-three or twenty-four. Our youngest co-pilot is probably up in his late twenties. Your average captain is close to forty or in his forties, probably."

"I see," I said. "Well, would it be impossible for a co-pilot to be twenty-six, or even younger?"

"Oh, no," he answered quickly. "I don't know that we have that many in that age bracket, but some of the other airlines do have a lot of younger co-pilots, I've noticed. A lot depends, of course, on the type of plane he's flying and his seniority. Everything is based on seniority, that is, how long a pilot has been with a company."

I was finding a lot of nuggets for my poke. "When do you hire people; I mean, at what age can a pilot go to work for an airline, say Pan Am?"

"If I remember correctly, you can come on the payroll at twenty as a flight engineer," said the captain, who had an excellent memory.

"Then feasibly, with six or eight years' service, you could become a co-pilot?" I pressed.

"It's possible," he conceded. "In fact, I'd say it wouldn't be unusual at all for a capable man to make co-pilot in six or eight years, less even."

"Are you allowed to tell me how much pilots earn?" I asked.

"Well, again, that depends on seniority, the route he flies, the number of hours he flies each week and other factors," said the captain. "I would say the maximum salary for a co-pilot would be $32,000, a captain's salary around $50,000."

"How many pilots does Pan Am have?" I asked.

The captain chuckled. "Son, that's a tough one. I don't know the exact number. But eighteen hundred would probably be a fair estimate. You can get better figures from the personnel manager."

"No, that's okay," I said. "How many places are these pilots?"

"You're talking about bases," he replied. "We have five bases in the United States: San Francisco, Washington D.C., Chicago, Miami and New York. Those are cities where our aircrews live. They report to work in that city, San Francisco, say, fly out of that city and eventually terminate a flight in that city. It might help you to know that we are not a domestic carrier, that is, we don't fly from city to city in this country. We're strictly an international carrier, serving foreign destinations."

The information helped me a lot. "This may sound strange to you, Captain, and it's more curiosity than anything else, but would it be possible for me to be a co-pilot based in New York City, and you to be a co-pilot also based in New York, and me never to meet you?"

"Very possible, even more so with co-pilots, for you and I would never fly together in the same plane," said the talkative captain. "Unless we met at a company meeting or some social function, which is improbable, we might never encounter one another. You'd be more apt to know more captains and more flight engineers than co-pilots. You might fly with different captains or different flight engineers and run into them again if you're transferred, but you'd never fly with another co pilot. There's only one to a plane.

"There're so many pilots in the system, in fact, that no one pilot would know all the others. I've been with the company eighteen years, and I don't think I know more than sixty or seventy of the other pilots."

The captain's verbal pinballs were lighting up all the lights in my little head.

"I've heard that pilots can fly free, I mean as a passenger, not as a pilot. Is that true?" I prompted.

"Yes," said the captain. "But we're talking about two things, now. We have pass privileges. That is, me and my family can travel somewhere by air on a stand-by basis. That is, if there's room, we can occupy seats, and our only cost is the tax on the tickets. We pay that.

"Then there's deadheading. For example, if my boss told me tonight that he wanted me in L.A. tomorrow to fly a trip out of there, I might fly out there on Delta, Eastern, TWA or any other carrier connecting with Los Angeles that could get me there on time. I would either occupy an empty passenger seat or, more likely, ride in the jump seat. That's a little fold-down seat in the cockpit, generally used by deadheading pilots, VIPs or FAA check riders."

"Would you have to help fly the plane?" I quizzed.

"Oh, no," he replied. "I'd be on another company's carrier, you see. You might be offered a control seat as a courtesy, but I always decline. We fly on each other's planes to get somewhere, not to work." He laughed.

"How do you go about that, deadheading, I mean?" I was really enthused. And the captain was patient. He must have liked kids.

"You want to know it all, don't you?" he said amiably, and proceeded to answer my question.

"Well, it's done on what we call a pink slip. It works this way. Say I want to go to Miami on Delta. I go down to Delta operations, show them my Pan Am ID card and I fill out a Delta pink slip, stating my destination and giving my position with Pan Am, my employee number and my FAA pilot's license number. I get a copy of the form and that's my 'jump.' I give that copy to the stewardess when I board, and that's how I get to ride in the jump seat."

I wasn't through, and he didn't seem to mind my continuing. "What's a pilot's license look like?" I asked. "Is it a certificate that you can hang on the wall, or like a driver's license, or what?"

He laughed. "No, it's not a certificate you hang on the wall. It's kind of hard to describe, really. It's about the size of a driver's license, but there's no picture attached. It's just a white card with black printing on it."

I decided it was time to let the nice man go back to his

comfortable seat. "Gee, Captain, I sure thank you," I said. "You've been really super."

"Glad to have helped you, son," he said. "I hope you get those pilot's wings, if that's what you want."

I already had the wings. What I needed was an ID card and an FAA pilot's license. I wasn't too concerned about the ID card. The pilot's license had me stumped. The FAA was not exactly a mail-order house.

I let my fingers do the walking in my search for a suitable ID card. I looked in the Yellow Pages under IDENTIFICATION, picked a firm on Madison Avenue (any ID company with a Madison Avenue address had to have class, I thought) and went to the firm dressed in a business suit.

It was a prestigious office suite with a receptionist to screen the walk-in trade. "Can I help you?" she asked in efficient tones.

"I'd like to see one of your sales representatives, please," I replied in equally businesslike inflections.

The sales representative had the assured air and manner of a man who would disdain talking about a single ID card, so I hit him with what I thought would best get his attention and win his affection, the prospect of a big account.

"My name is Frank Williams, and I represent Carib Air of Puerto Rico," I said crisply. "As you probably know, we are expanding service to the continental United States, and we presently have two hundred people in our facilities at Kennedy. Right now we're using only a temporary ID card made of paper, and we want to go to a formal, laminated, plastic-enclosed card with a color photograph and the company logo, similar to what the other airlines use here. We want a quality card, and I understand you people deal only in quality products."

If he knew that Carib Air existed and was expanding to the United States, he knew more than I did. But he was not a man to let the facts stand in the way of a juicy sale.

"Oh, yes, Mr. Williams. Let me show you what we have along that line," he said enthusiastically, leading me to his office. He pulled down a huge, leather-bound sample catalogue from a shelf, leafed through the contents, which ranged from vellum to beautifully watermarked bond, and displayed a whole page of various identification forms.

"Now, most of the airlines we serve use this card here," he said, pointing out one that seemed a duplicate of Pan Am's ID cards. "It has employee number, base, position, description, photograph and, if you wish, a company logo. I think it would do very nicely."

I nodded in complete agreement. "Yes, I think this is the card we want," I said. It was certainly the card I wanted. He gave me a complete cost rundown, including all the variables.

"Can you give me a sample?" I asked on impulse. "I'd like to show it to our top people, since they're the ones who'll have the final say."

The salesman obliged in a matter of minutes. I studied the card. "This is fine, but it's blank," I said. "Tell you what. Why don't we fix this up, so they'll have an idea of what the finished product looks like? We can use me as the subject."

"That's an excellent suggestion," said the salesman, and led me to an ID camera that produced ID-sized mug shots within minutes.

He took several photographs, we selected one (he graciously gave me the culls) and he affixed it to the space on the card, trimming it neatly. He then filled in my phony name, adopted rank (co-pilot), fictitious employee number, height, weight, coloring, age and sex in the appropriate blanks. He then sealed it in a clear, tough plastic and handed it to me with his business card.

"I'm sure we can do a good job for you, Mr. Williams," he said, ushering me out.

He already had done a good job for me, save for one detail. The lovely ID card lacked Pan Am's distinctive logo and firm name. I was wondering how to resolve the problem when a display in the window of a hobby shop caught my eye. There, poised on gracefully curved mounts, was an array of model planes, among them several commercial airliners. And among them a beautiful Pan Am jet, the firm's famed logo on its tail, and the company legend, in the copyrighted lettering used by the airline, on the fuselage and wings.

The model came in several sizes. I bought the smallest, for $2.49, in an unassembled state, and hurried back to my room. I threw the plane parts away. Following instructions in the kit, I soaked the decal and lettering in water until they separated from their holding base. Both the logo and the company name were of microscopically thin plastic. I laid the Pan Am logo on the upper left-hand corner of the ID card and carefully arranged the firm legend across the top of the card. The clear decals, when they dried, appeared to have been printed on the card.

It was perfect. An exact duplicate of a Pan Am identification card. It would have required an examination with a spectroscope to reveal that the decals were actually on the outside of the plastic seal. I could have clipped the ID card on my breast pocket and passed muster at a Pan Am board meeting.

As a fake pilot, however, I was still grounded. I recalled the words of the captain I'd interviewed under false pretenses: "Your license is the most important thing. You've got to have it on your person at all times when operating an aircraft. I carry mine in a folder that also contains my ID. You'll be asked to show your license as often as you're asked for your ID."

I mulled the issue over for days, but could think of no solution short of working my way through commercial aviation school. I started frequenting bookstores again, thumbing through the various flying publications. I wasn't sure of what I was looking for, but I found it.

There it was, a small display ad in the back of one of

the books placed by a plaque-making firm in Milwaukee that catered to professional people. The firm offered to duplicate any pilot's license, engraved in silver and mounted on a handsome eight-by-eleven-inch hardwood plaque, for only $35. The company used the standard, precut license die used by the FAA. All a pilot had to do was supply the pertinent information, including his FAA license number and ratings, and the firm would return a silver replica of his license, suitable for display anywhere. The FAA did have a mail-order branch, it appeared.

I wanted one of the plaques, naturally. I felt there had to be a way, plaque in hand, to reduce it to the proper size on appropriate paper. And I'd have my pilot's license!

I was feverish with the idea. I didn't write the firm; I called their offices in Milwaukee. I told the salesman I wanted one of the plaques and asked if the transaction could be handled by telephone.

He expressed no curiosity as to why I was in such a hurry. "Well, you can give me all the necessary information over the telephone, but we'll have to have a check or money order before we actually make up the plaque," said the man. "In the meantime, we can start roughing it out and we'll treat it as a special order. It'll be $37.50, including postage and special handling."

I didn't quibble. I gave him my alias, Frank Williams. I gave him my spurious age and my correct weight, height, color of hair and eyes and social security number. A pilot's license or certificate number is always the same as his social security number. I gave myself the highest rating a pilot can attain, an air transport rating. I told the man I was checked out on DC-9s, 727s and 707s. I gave him my address in care of general delivery, New York City (not unusual for commercial pilots who spend a lot of time in transit), and told him I'd have a money order in the mail that same day. I had the money order in the mail within an hour, in fact. It was the only valid draft I'd given in several weeks.

The plaque arrived within a week. It was gorgeous. Not only was I certified as a pilot in sterling, but the license replica even boasted the signature of the head of the Fed eral Aviation Agency.

I took the plaque to a hole-in-the-wall print shop in Brooklyn and sought out the head printer. "Look, I'd like to get my license reduced down so I can carry it in my wallet, you know, like you would a diploma. Can it be done?" I asked.

The printer studied the plaque admiringly. "Geez, I didn't know pilots got this sort of thing when they learned to fly," he said. "It's fancier'n a college diploma."

"Well, an actual license is a certificate, but it's back at my home in L.A.," I said. "This is something my girl gave me as a gift. But I'll be based here for several months and I would like to have a wallet-sized copy of my license. Can you do it with this or will I have to send for the certificate?"

"Nah, I can do it from this," he said, and, using a special camera, he reduced it to actual size, printed it on heavy white stock, cut it out and handed it to me. The whole process took less than thirty minutes and cost me five bucks. I laminated it with two pieces of plastic myself. I'd never seen a real pilot's license, but this sure as hell looked like one.

I put on my pilot's uniform, which I had had altered to a perfect fit, tilted my cap at a rakish angle and caught a bus to La Guardia Airport.

I was ready for flight duty. Provided someone else flew the plane.

CHAPTER THREE

Fly a Crooked Sky

There is enchantment in a uniform, especially one that marks the wearer as a person of rare skills, courage or achievement.

A paratrooper's wings tell of a special breed of soldier. A submariner's dolphin denotes the unusual sailor. A policeman's blue symbolizes authority. A forest ranger's raiment evokes wilderness lore. Even a doorman's gaudy garb stirs vague thoughts of pomp and royalty.

I felt great in my Pan Am pilot's uniform as I walked into La Guardia Airport. I obviously was commanding respect and esteem. Men looked at me admiringly or enviously. Pretty women and girls smiled at me. Airport policemen nodded courteously. Pilots and stewardesses smiled, spoke to me or lifted a hand in greeting as they passed. Every man, woman and child who noticed me seemed warm and friendly.

It was heady stuff and I loved it. In fact, I became instantly addicted. During the next five years the uniform was my alter ego. I used it in the same manner a junkie shoots up on heroin. Whenever I felt lonely, depressed, rejected or doubtful of my own worth, I'd dress up in my pilot's uniform and seek out a crowd. The uniform bought me respect and dignity. Without it on, at times, I felt useless and dejected. With it on, during such times, I felt like I was wearing Fortunatus' cap and walking in seven-league boots.

I milled with the crowd in La Guardia's lobby that morning, glorying in my make-believe status. I fully intended to bluff my way aboard a flight to a distant city and start operating my check swindles there, but I delayed implementing my decision. I was having too much fun luxuriating in the attention and deference I was receiving.

I became hungry. I stepped into one of the airport's many coffee shops, dropped onto a stool at the counter and ordered a sandwich and milk. I was almost finished eating when a TWA co-pilot sat down on a stool cater-cornered from me. He looked at me and nodded. He ordered coffee and a roll, then regarded me with mild curiosity.

"What's Pan Am doing here at La Guardia?" he asked casually. Apparently, Pan Am did not fly out of La Guardia.

"Oh, I just deadheaded in from Frisco on the first flight I could catch," I replied. "I'll catch a chopper to Kennedy."

"What kind of equipment you on?" he asked, biting into his roll.

My brains turned to ice cubes. I nearly freaked out. Equipment? What did he mean, equipment? Engines? Cockpit instruments? What? I couldn't recall having heard the word before in connection with commercial airlines. I frantically searched for an answer for it was obviously a normal question for him to ask. I mentally reread the reminiscences of the veteran Pan Am captain, a little book

41

I'd really liked and which I'd virtually adopted as a manual. I couldn't recall his ever using the word "equipment."

It had to have some significance, however. The TWA airman was looking at me, awaiting my reply. "General Electric," I said hopefully. It was definitely not the right answer. His eyes went frosty and a guarded look crossed his features. "Oh," he said, the friendliness gone from his voice. He busied himself with his coffee and roll.

I gulped the rest of my milk and dropped three dollars on the counter, more than ample payment for my snack. I stood up and nodded to the TWA pilot. "So long," I said, and headed for the door.

"Fruzhumtu," he growled. I wasn't sure of his exact words, but they sounded suspiciously like something I couldn't actually do to myself.

Whatever, I knew I wasn't sufficiently prepared to attempt a deadheading venture, despite all my prior work and research. It was evident that I needed a better command of airline terminology, among other things. As I was leaving the terminal, I noticed a TWA stewardess struggling with a heavy bag. "Can I help you?" I asked, reaching for the luggage.

She relinquished it readily. "Thanks," she said with a grin. "That's our crew bus just outside there."

"Just get in?" I asked as we walked toward the bus.

She grimaced. "Yes, and I'm pooped. About half the people in our load were whiskey salesmen who'd been to a convention in Scotland, and you can imagine what that scene was like."

I could, and laughed. "What kind of equipment are you on?" I asked on impulse.

"Seven-o-sevens, and I love 'em," she said as I heaved her suitcase aboard the bus. She paused at the bus door and stuck out her hand. "Thanks much, friend. I needed your muscles."

"Glad I could help," I said, and meant it. She was slim and elegant, with pixie features and auburn hair. Really attractive. Under other circumstances I would have pressed to know her better. I didn't even ask her name. She was lovely, but she also knew everything there was to know about flying passengers from this place to that one, and a date with her might prove embarrassing.

Airline people manifestly loved to talk shop, and at the moment I obviously wasn't ready to punch in at the factory. So equipment was an airplane, I mused, walking to my own bus. I felt a little stupid, but halfway back to Manhattan I burst out laughing as a thought came to mind. The TWA first officer was probably back in the pilot's lounge by now, telling other TWA crewmen he'd just met a Pan Am jerk who flew washing machines.

I spent the next few days in the boneyard. In the past I'd found my best sources of information on airlines were airlines themselves, so I started calling the various carriers and pumping their people for information. I represented myself as a college student doing a paper on transportation, as an embryo book author or magazine writer, or as a cub reporter for one of the area's dailies.

Generally I was referred to the airline's public relations department. Airline PR people love to talk about their particular airline, I found. I quickly confirmed my suspicions that my aviation education was strictly elementary, but within a week I had zoomed through high school and was working on my bachelor's degree.

The airline flacks, a lot of whom had been members of aircrews themselves, obligingly filled me in on a wealth of juicy facts and technical tidbits: the types of jets used by both American and foreign carriers, fuel capacities and speeds, altitudes, weight limits, passenger capacities, number of crewmen, weight limits and other such goodies.

I learned, for instance, that a large number of commercial airline pilots are drawn from the military. Those without an air force or naval aviation background had come up from small, bush-league airlines or were graduates of private flying schools such as Embry-Riddle, I was told.

Embry-Riddle Aeronautical University in Daytona Beach, Florida, is the most respected, and probably the largest, commercial flight-training school in the nation, I was informed. It's the Notre Dame of the air. A kid out of high school, with no knowledge of aeronautics whatsoever, could enter ground school at Embry-Riddle and leave several years later able to fly any current jet liner.

"Those of our pilots who didn't come to us from the air force or the navy came to us from Embry-Riddle," said one airline flack pridefully.

I knew nothing about the military. I couldn't tell a private from a vice admiral. So I awarded myself a scholarship to Embry-Riddle, graduated fantasy cum laude, and then gave myself a few years of mythical experience with Eastern Airlines.

As my knowledge of airlines and airline terminology broadened, my confidence returned. I opened a checking account in the name of Frank Williams, with a post-office box address, and when my order for two hundred personalized checks arrived general delivery, I tried cashing a few checks in my guise as an airline pilot.

It was like going on safari in the Bronx Zoo. Cashiers couldn't get the money out of the tills fast enough. Most of them didn't even ask for identification. I shoved my phony ID card and my ersatz pilot's license in their faces anyway. I didn't want my handiwork to go unnoticed. The first couple of checks I wrote were good. The others had all the value of bubble-gum wrappers.

I started hanging around La Guardia regularly, not with any intentions of catching a flight, but to meet airline personnel and to eavesdrop on airline talk. Testing my vocabulary, so to speak. I shunned Kennedy, since Pan Am operated out of there. I was afraid that the first Pan Am pilot I encountered at Kennedy would recognize me as a fraud, court-martial me on the spot and strip me of my wings and buttons.

At La Guardia I made out like a possum in a persimmon tree. Some books *are* judged by their covers, it seems, and in my uniform I was an immediate best seller. I'd walk into a coffee shop, where there would usually be a dozen or more pilots or other crewmen taking a break, and invariably someone would invite me to join him or them. More often it was them, for airline people tend to gaggle like geese. It was the same in cocktail lounges around the airport. I never took a drink in the bars, since I had yet to try alcohol and wasn't sure how it would affect me, but no one questioned my abstinence.

Any pilot, I'd learned, could gracefully decline a drink by pleading the required "twelve hours between the bottle and the throttle." It apparently never occurred to anyone that I'd never seen a throttle. I was always accepted at par value. I wore the uniform of a Pan Am pilot, therefore I must be a Pan Am pilot. Barnum would have loved airline people.

I didn't do a lot of talking initially. I usually let the conversations flow around me, monitoring the words and phrases, and within a short time I was speaking airlinese like a native. La Guardia, for me, was the Berlitz of the air.

Some of my language books were absolutely gorgeous. I guess the stewardesses just weren't that used to seeing a really young pilot, one that appeared to be an age peer. "*Hel-looo!*" one would say in passing, putting a pretty move on me, and the invitation in her voice would be unmistakable. I felt I could turn down only so many invitations without seeming to be rude, and I was soon dating several of the girls. I took them to dinner, to the theater, to the ballet, to the symphony, to night clubs and to movies. Also to my place or their place.

I loved them for their minds.

The rest of them was wonderful, too. But for the first time I was more interested in a girl's knowledge of her

45

work than in her body. I didn't object, of course, if the one came with the other. A bedroom can be an excellent classroom.

I was an apt student. I mean, it takes a certain degree of academic concentration to learn all about airline travel-expense procedures, say, when someone is biting you on the shoulder and digging her fingernails into your back. It takes a dedicated pupil to say to a naked lady, "Gee, is this your flight manual? It's a little different from the ones our stewardesses use."

I picked their brains discreetly. I even spent a week in a Massachusetts mountain resort with three stewardesses, and not one of them was skeptical of my pilot's status, although there were some doubts expressed concerning my stamina.

Don't get the impression that stewardesses, as a group, are promiscuous. They aren't. The myth that all stewardesses are passionate nymphs is just that, a myth. If anything, "stews" are more circumspect and discriminating in their sexual lives than women in other fields. The ones I knew were all intelligent, sophisticated and responsible young women, good in their jobs, and I didn't make out en masse. The ones who were playmates would have hopped into bed with me had they been secretaries, nurses, bookkeepers or whatever. Stews are good people. I have very pleasant memories of the ones I met, and if some of the memories are more pleasant than others, they're not necessarily sexually oriented.

I didn't score at all with one I recall vividly. She was a Delta flight attendant whom I'd met during my initial studies of airline jargon. She had a car at the airport and offered to drive me back to Manhattan one afternoon.

"Would you drop me at the Plaza?" I requested as we walked through the lobby of the terminal. "I need to cash a check and I'm known there." I wasn't known there, but I intended to be.

The stewardess stopped and gestured at the dozens of

airline ticket counters that lined every side of the huge lobby. There must be more than a hundred airlines that have ticket facilities at La Guardia. "Cash your check at one of those counters. Any one of them will take your check."

"They will?" I said, somewhat surprised but managing to conceal the fact. "It's a personal check and we don't operate out of here, you know."

She shrugged. "It doesn't matter," she said. "You're a Pan Am pilot in uniform, and any airline here will take your personal check as a courtesy. They do that at Kennedy, don't they?"

"I don't know. I've never had occasion to cash a check at a ticket counter before," I said truthfully.

American's counter was the nearest. I walked over and confronted a ticket clerk who wasn't busy. "Can you cash a $100 personal check for me?" I asked, checkbook in hand.

"Sure, be glad to," he said, smiling, and took the bouncing beauty with barely a glance at it. He didn't even ask me for identification.

I had occasion to cash checks at airline counters frequently thereafter. I worked La Guardia like a fox on a turkey ranch. The air facility was so immense that the risk of my being caught was minimal. I'd cash a check at the Eastern counter, for instance, then go to another section of the terminal and tap some other airline's till. I was cautious. I never went back to the same counter twice. I worked a condensed version of the scam at Newark, and hit Teterboro a few elastic licks. I was producing rubber faster than a Ceylon planter.

Every gambler has a road game. Mine was hitting the hotels and motels where airline crews put up in transit. I even bought a round-trip airline ticket to Boston, an honest ticket paid for with dishonest money, and papered Logan Airport and its surrounding crew hostelries with scenic chits before scurrying back to New York.

Flushed with success, emboldened by the ease with

which I passed myself off as a pilot, I decided I was finally ready for "Operation Deadhead."

I'd been living in a walk-up flat on the West Side. I'd rented the small apartment under the name Frank Williams and I'd paid my rent punctually and in cash. The landlady, whom I saw only to tender the rent money, thought I worked in a stationery store. None of the other tenants knew me and I'd never appeared around the building in my pilot's uniform. I had no telephone and I'd never received mail at the address.

When I packed and left the flat, there was no trail to follow. The best bell-mouthed hound in the Blue Ridge Mountains couldn't have picked up my spoor.

I took a bus to La Guardia and went to Eastern's operations office. There were three young men working behind the enclosure's counter. "Yes, sir, can I help you?" one of them asked.

"I need to deadhead to Miami on your next flight, if you've got room," I said, producing my sham Pan Am ID.

"We've got one going out in fifteen minutes, Mr. Williams," he said. "Would you like to make that one, or wait until our afternoon flight? The jump seat's open on either one."

I didn't want to tarry. "I'll take this flight," I said. "It'll give me more time on the beach."

He slid a pink form toward me. I'd never seen one before, but it was familiar because of my interview with the helpful Pan Am captain. The information elicited was minimal: name, company, employee number and position. I filled it out, handed it back to him and he popped off the top copy and handed it to me. I knew that was my boarding pass.

Then he picked up the telephone and asked for the FAA tower, and my stomach was suddenly full of yellow butterflies.

"This is Eastern," he said. "We've got a jump on Flight 602 to Miami. Frank Williams, co-pilot, Pan Am. . . . Okay, thanks." He hung up the telephone and nodded toward a door outside the glass window. "You can go through there, Mr. Williams. The aircraft is boarding at the gate to your left."

It was a 727. Most of the passengers had already boarded. I handed my pink slip to the stewardess at the door to the aircraft and turned toward the cockpit like I'd been doing this for years. I felt cocky and debonair as I stowed my bag in the compartment indicated by the stewardess and squeezed through the small hatch into the cabin.

"Hi, I'm Frank Williams," I said to the three men seated inside. They were busy with what I later learned was a check-off list, and ignored me except for nods of acceptance.

I looked around the instrument-crammed cabin and the butterflies started flying again. I didn't see a jump seat, whatever a jump seat looked like. There were only three seats in the cockpit and all of them were occupied.

Then the flight engineer looked up and grinned. "Oh, sorry," he said, reaching behind me and closing the cabin door. "Have a seat."

As the door closed, a tiny seat attached to the floor clicked down. I eased down into the small perch, feeling the need for a cigarette. And I didn't smoke.

No one said anything else to me until we were airborne. Then the captain, a ruddy-faced man with tints of silver in his brown hair, introduced himself, the co-pilot and the flight engineer. "How long you been with Pan Am?" asked the captain, and I was aware from his tone that he was just making conversation.

"This is my eighth year," I said, and wished immediately I'd said six.

None of the three evinced any surprise, however. It apparently was a tenure compatible with my rank. "What kind of equipment are you on?" queried the co-pilot.

"Seven-o-sevens," I said. "I was on DC-8s until a couple of months ago."

Although I felt like I was sitting on a bed of hot coals

all the way to Miami, it was really ridiculously easy. I was asked where I had received my training and I said Embry-Riddle. I said Pan Am had hired me right out of school. After that, the conversation was desultory and indifferent and mostly among the three Eastern officers. Nothing else was directed toward me that might threaten my assumed status. At one point the co-pilot, who was handling traffic, handed me a pair of earphones and asked if I wanted to listen in, but I declined, saying I preferred a rock station. That brought a laugh. I did monitor their talk diligently, storing up the slang phrases that passed among them and noting how they used the airline jargon. They were all three married and a lot of their conversation centered around their families.

The stewardess who served the cabin was a cute little brunette. When I went to the toilet I stopped en route back to the cockpit and engaged her in a conversation. I learned she was laying over in Miami and before I returned to the cabin I had made a date with her for that night. She was staying with a girl friend who lived there.

I thanked the flying officers before deplaning. They casually wished me luck and the captain said the jump seat was generally available "anytime you need it."

I'd never been to Miami before. I was impressed and excited by the colorful tropical vegetation and the palms around the terminal, the warm sun and the bright, clean air. The lack of tall buildings, the seeming openness of the landscape, the gaudy and casual attire of the people milling around the airport terminal made me feel like I'd been set down in a strange and wonderful land. I was inside the terminal before I realized I didn't have the slightest idea where Pan Am housed its people in Miami. Well, there was an easy way to find out.

I walked up to the Pan Am ticket counter and the girl behind the counter, who was busy with passengers, excused herself and stepped over to face me. "Can I help you?" " she asked, looking at me curiously.

"Yes," I said. "This is my first layover in Miami. I'm

here on a replacement status. I normally don't fly trips in here, and I came in such a hurry that no one told me where the hell we stay here. Where do we lay over here?"

"Oh, yes, sir, we stay at the Skyway Motel if it's going to be less than twenty-four hours," she responded, suddenly all aid and assistance.

"It will be," I said.

"Well, it's only a short distance," she said. "You can wait on the crew bus or you can just take a cab over there. Are you going to take a cab?"

"I think so," I replied. I knew I was going to take a cab. I wasn't about to get on a bus full of real Pan Am flight people.

"Wait a minute, then," she said and stepped over to her station. She opened a drawer and took out a claim-check-sized card and handed it to me. "Just give that to any of the cab drivers out front. Have a good stay."

Damned if it wasn't a ticket for a free cab ride, good with any Miami cab firm. Airline people lived in the proverbial land of milk and honey, I thought as I walked out of the terminal. I liked milk and I knew I was in the right hive when I checked in at the motel. I registered under my phony name and put down General Delivery, New York, as my address. The registration clerk took the card, glanced at it, then stamped "AIRLINE CREW" in red ink across its face.

"I'll be checking out in the morning," I said.

She nodded. "All right. You can sign this now if you want, and you won't have to stop by here in the morning."

"I'll just sign it in the morning," I replied. "I might run up some charges tonight." She shrugged and filed the card.

I didn't see any Pan Am crewmen around the motel. If there were any around the pool, where a lively crowd was assembled, I drew no attention from them. In my room, I changed into casual attire and called the Eastern stewardess at the number she'd given me.

She picked me up in her friend's car and we had a ball

51

in the Miami Beach night spots. I didn't put any moves on her, but I wasn't being gallant. I was so turned on by the success of my first adventure as a bogus birdman that I forgot about it. By the time I remembered, she'd dropped me at the Skyway and gone home.

I checked out at 5:30 the next morning. There was only a sleepy-faced night clerk on duty when I entered the lobby. He took my key and gave me my room bill to sign.

"Can I get a check cashed?" I asked as I signed the tab.

"Sure, do you have your ID card?" he said.

I handed it to him and wrote out a check for $100, payable to the hotel. He copied the fictitious employee number from my fake ID card onto the back of the check and handed me back my ID and five $20 bills. I took a cab to the airport and an hour later deadheaded to Dallas on a Braniff flight. The Braniff flight officers were not inquisitive at all, but I had a few tense moments en route. I wasn't aware that Pan Am didn't fly out of Dallas. I was aware that deadheading pilots were always supposed to be on business.

"What the hell are you going to Dallas for?" the co-pilot asked in casually curious tones. I was searching for a reply when he gave me the answer. "You in on a charter or something?"

"Yeah, freight," I said, knowing Pan Am had worldwide freight service, and the subject was dropped.

I stayed overnight at a motel used by flight crews of several airlines, stung the inn with a $100 bum check when I left in the morning and deadheaded to San Francisco immediately. It was a procedural pattern I followed, with variations, for the next two years. Modus operandi, the cops call it.

Mine was a ready-made scam, one for which the airlines, motels and hotels set themselves up. The hotels and motels around metropolitan or international airports considered it just good business, of course, when they entered into agreements with as many airlines as possible to house transit flight crews. It assured the hostelries of at least a minimum rate of occupancy, and no doubt most of the operators felt the presence of the pilots and stewardesses would attract other travelers seeking lodging. The airlines considered it a desirable arrangement because the carriers were guaranteed room space for their flight crews, even during conventions and other festive affairs when rooms were at a premium. I know from numerous conversations on the subject that the flight crews liked the plan whereby the airlines were billed directly for lodging and allotted meals. It simplified their expense-account bookkeeping.

The deadheading arrangement between airlines everywhere in the world was also a system based on good business practices. It was more than a courtesy. It afforded a maximum of mobility for pilots and co-pilots needed in emergency or essential situations.

However, supervision, auditing or other watchdog procedures concerning the agreements and arrangements were patently, at least during that period, lax, sloppy or nonexistent. Airport security, understandably, was minimal at the time. Terrorist raids on terminals and plane hijackings were yet to become the vogue. Airports, small cities that they are in themselves, had a low crime ratio, with theft the common problem.

No one, apparently, save under extreme circumstances, ever went behind the pink "jump" forms and checked out the requesting pilot's *bona fides*. The deadheading form consisted of an original and two copies. I was given the original as a boarding pass and I gave that to the stewardess in charge of boarding. I knew the operations clerk always called the FAA tower to inform the tower operators that such-and-such flight would have a jump passenger aboard, but I didn't know that a copy of the pink pass was given the FAA. Presumably, the third copy was kept in the operations files of the particular airline. An airline official who made a statement to police concerning my escapades offered what seemed to him a logical explanation:

"You simply don't expect a man in a pilot's uniform, with proper credentials and obvious knowledge of jump procedures, to be an impostor, dammit!"

But I have always suspected that the majority of the jump forms I filled out ended up in the trash, original and both copies.

There were other factors, too, that weighed the odds in my favor. I was not at first a big operator. I limited the checks I cashed at motels, hotels and airline counters to $100, and not infrequently I was told there wasn't enough cash on hand to handle a check for more than $50 or $75. It always took several days for one of my worthless checks to traverse the clearing-house routes to New York, and by the time the check was returned stamped "insufficient funds," I was a long time gone. The fact that I had a legitimate (on the face of it, at least) account had a bearing on my success also. The bank didn't return my checks with the notation "worthless," "fraudulent" or "forgery." They merely sent them back marked "insufficient funds to cover."

Airlines and hostelries do a volume business by check. Most of the checks returned to them because of insufficient funds aren't attempts to defraud. It's usually a bad case of the shorts on the part of the people who tendered the checks. In most instances, such persons are located and their checks are made good. In many cases involving checks I passed, the checks were first placed for collection before any attempt to locate me was made through Pan Am. In many other instances, I'm sure, the victimized business simply wrote off the loss and didn't pursue the matter.

Those who did usually turned the matter over to local police, which further aided and abetted me. Very few police departments, if any, have a hot-check division or bunco squad that is adequately staffed, not even metropolitan forces.

And no detective on any police force is burdened with

a case load heavier than the officer assigned to the check-fraud detail. Fraudulent check swindles are the most common of crimes, and the professional paperhanger is the wiliest of criminals, the hardest to nab. That's true today and it was true then, and it's no reflection on the abilities or determination of the officers involved. Their success ratio is admirable when you consider the number of complaints they handle daily. Such policemen usually work on priorities. Say a team of detectives is working on a bum-check operation involving phony payroll checks that's bilking local merchants of $10,000 weekly, obviously the handiwork of a ring. They also have a complaint from a jeweler who lost a $3,000 ring to a hot-check artist. And one from a banker whose bank cashed a $7,500 counterfeit cashier's check. Plus a few dozen cases involving resident forgers. Now they're handed a complaint from a motel manager who says he lost $100 to a con artist posing as an airline pilot. The offense occurred two weeks past.

So what do the detectives do? They make the routine gestures, that's what. They ascertain the man's New York address is a phony. They learn Pan Am has no such pilot on its payroll. Maybe they go so far as to determine the impostor bilked the one airline out of a free ride to Chicago, Detroit, Philadelphia, Los Angeles or some other distant point. They put a message to whichever city is appropriate on the police teletype and pigeonhole the complaint for possible future reference, that's what they do. They've done as much as they could.

And like the bumblebee, I kept flying and making honey on the side.

So it's not too amazing that I could operate so freely and brazenly when you consider the last two factors in my hypothesis. The National Crime Information Center (NCIC) did not exist as a police tool during the period. Had I had to contend with the computerized police link, with its vast and awesome reservoir of criminal facts and figures, my career would probably have been shortened by years. And lastly, I was pioneering a scam that was so implausible, so seemingly impossible and so brass-balled blatant that it worked.

In the last months of my adventures, I ran into a Continental captain with whom I had deadheaded a couple of times. It was a tense moment for me, but he dispelled it with the warmth of his greeting. Then he laughed and said, "You know, Frank, I was talking to a Delta stewardess a couple of months ago and she said you were a phony. I told her that was bullshit, that you'd handled the controls of my bird. What'd you do to that girl, boy, kick her out of bed?"

My adventures. The first few years that's exactly what they were for me, adventures. Adventures in crime, of course, but adventures nonetheless.

I kept a notebook, a surreptitious journal in which I jotted down phrases, technical data, miscellaneous information, names, dates, places, telephone numbers, thoughts and a collection of other data I thought was necessary or might prove helpful.

It was a combination log, textbook, little black book, diary and airline bible, and the longer I operated, the thicker it became with entries. One of the first notations in the notebook is "glide scopes." The term was mentioned on my second deadhead flight and I jotted it down as a reminder to learn what it meant. Glide scopes are runway approach lights used as landing guides. The journal is crammed with all sorts of trivia that was invaluable to me in my sham role. If you're impersonating a pilot it helps to know things like the fuel consumption of a 707 in flight (2,000 gallons an hour), that planes flying west maintain altitudes at even-numbered levels (20,000 feet, 24,000 feet, etc.) while east-bound planes fly at odd-numbered altitudes (19,000 feet, 27,000 feet, etc.), or that all airports are identified by code (LAX, Los Angeles; JFK or LGA, New York, etc.).

Little things mean a lot to a big phony. The names of

every flight crew I met, the type of equipment they flew, their route, their airline and their base went into the book as some of the more useful data.

Like I'd be deadheading on a National flight.

"Where you guys out of?"

"Oh, we're Miami-based."

A sneak look into my notebook, then: "Hey, how's Red doing? One of you's gotta know Red O'Day. How is that Irishman?"

All three knew Red O'Day. "Hey, you know Red, huh?"

"Yeah, I've deadheaded a couple of times with Red. He's a great guy."

Such exchanges reinforced my image as a pilot and usually averted the mild cross-examinations to which I'd been subjected at first.

Just by watching and listening I became adept in other things that enhanced my pose. After the second flight, whenever I was offered a pair of earphones with which to listen in on airline traffic, I always accepted, although a lot of pilots preferred a squawk box, in which case no earphones were needed.

I had to improvise a lot. Whenever I'd deadhead into a city not used by Pan Am, such as Dallas, and didn't know which motels or hotels were used by airline crews, I'd simply walk up to the nearest airline ticket counter. "Listen, I'm here to work a charter that's coming in tomorrow. Where do the airlines stay around here?" I'd ask.

I was always supplied with the name or names of a nearby inn or inns. I'd pick one, go there and register, and I was never challenged when I asked that Pan Am be billed for my lodging. All they asked was Pan Am's address in New York.

At intervals I'd hole up in a city for two or three weeks for logistics purposes. I'd open an account in, say, a San Diego bank, or a Houston bank, giving the address of an apartment I'd rented for the occasion (I always rented a pad that could be had on a month-to-month basis), and when my little box of personalized checks arrived, I would pack up and take to the airways again.

I knew I was a hunted man, but I was never sure how closely I was being pursued or who was in the posse those first two years. Any traveling con man occasionally gets the jitters, certain he's about to be collared, and I was no exception. Whenever I got a case of the whibbies, I'd go to earth like a fox.

Or with a fox. Some of the girls I dated came on pretty strong, making it apparent they thought I was marriage material. I had a standing invitation from several to visit them in their homes for a few days and get to know their parents. When I felt the need to hide out, I'd drop in on the nearest one and stay for a few days or a week, resting and relaxing. I hit it off well with the parents in every instance. None of them ever found out they were aiding and abetting a juvenile delinquent.

When I felt the situation was cool again, I'd take off, promising the particular girl that I'd return soon and we'd talk about our future. I never went back, of course. I was afraid of marriage.

Besides, my mother would not have permitted it. I was only seventeen.

CHAPTER FOUR

If I'm a Kid Doctor, Where's My Jar of Lollipops?

National Flight 106, New Orleans to Miami. A routine deadheading deception. I was now polished in my pettifoggery as a pilot without portfolio. I had grown confident, even cocky, in my pre-empting of cockpit jump seats. After two hundred duplicitous flights, I occupied a jump seat with the same assumption of a Wall Street broker in his seat on the stock exchange.

I even felt a little nostalgic as I stepped into the flight cabin of the DC-8. My first fraudulent flight had been on a National carrier to Miami. Now, two years later, I was returning to Miami, and again on a National jet. I thought it appropriate.

"Hi, Frank Williams. Nice of you to give me a lift," I said with acquired poise, and shook hands all around. Captain Tom Wright, aircraft commander, forties, slightly rumpled look of competence. First Officer Gary Evans, early thirties, dapper, with amused features. Flight Engineer Bob Hart, late twenties, skinny, serious demeanor, new uniform, a rookie. Nice guys. The kind I liked to soft-con.

A stewardess brought me a cup of coffee as we taxied toward the runway. I sipped the brew and watched the plane traffic on the strip ahead. It was late Saturday night, moonless, and the aircraft, distinguishable only by their interior lights and flickering exhausts, dipped and soared like lightning bugs. I never ceased to be fascinated by air traffic, night or day.

Wright was apparently not one to use the squawk box. All three officers had headsets, and none of the three had offered me a set for monitoring. If you weren't offered, you didn't ask. The cockpit of a passenger plane is like the captain's bridge on a ship. Protocol is rigidly observed, if that's the tone set by the skipper. Tom Wright operated his jet by the book, it seemed. I didn't feel slighted. The conversation between the three and the tower was clipped and cursory, rather uninteresting, in fact, as most such one-sided exchanges are.

Suddenly it was real interesting, so interesting that I started to pucker at both ends.

Wright and Evans exchanged arch-browed, quizzical looks, and Hart was suddenly regarding me with solemn-eyed intensity. Then Wright twisted around to face me. "Do you have your Pan Am identification card?" he asked.

"Uh, yeah," I said and handed it to him, stomach quaking as Wright studied the artistic fake. "This is National 106 back to tower . . . uh, yes, I have an ID card here . . . Pan Am . . . looks fine. . . . Employee number? Uh, three-five-zero-niner-niner. . . . Uh-huh. . . . Uh, yeah. M-mm, just a moment."

He turned again to me. "Do you have your FAA license?"

"Yes, of course," I said, attempting to act puzzled and keep my bladder under control. It was bulging like a Dutch dike at high tide.

Wright examined the forgery closely. He was the first real pilot to inspect the illicit license. He scrutinized it with the intensity of an art expert judging the authenticity of a Gauguin. Then: "Uh, yeah. FAA license, number zero-seven-five-three-six-six-eight-zero-five. . . . Yes . . . multiengine . . . check-out ATR. . . . Looks fine to me . . . I see nothing wrong with it. . . . Uh, yes, six foot, brown hair, brown eyes. . . . Okay, you got it."

He twisted and handed back my ID card and the purported license, his face reflecting a mixture of chagrin and apology. "I don't know what that was all about," he said with a shrug, and did not ask me if I had any ideas on the subject.

I did, but I didn't volunteer any of them. I tried to convince myself that nothing was amiss, that the tower operator in New Orleans was just overly officious, or doing something he thought he should be doing. Maybe, I told myself, there was an FAA regulation requiring such an inquiry and the tower operator was the first to observe the rule in my experiences, but that didn't wash. It had clearly been an unusual incident for Tom Wright.

The three officers seemed to have dismissed the matter. They asked the usual questions and I gave the usual answers. I took part when the conversation was industry-oriented, listened politely when the three talked of their families. I was nervous all the way to Miami, my insides as tightly coiled as a rattler in a prickly pear patch.

Wright had no sooner touched down in Miami than the sword of Damocles was once more suspended over my head. The ominous one-sided conversation commenced while we were taxiing to the dock.

"Yeah, we can do that. No problem, no problem," Wright said curtly in answer to some query from the tower. "Take over, I'll be right back," he said to Evans, getting out of his seat and leaving the flight cabin.

I knew then with certainty that I was in trouble. No captain ever vacated his seat while taxiing save under extreme circumstances. I managed to peer around the cab-in-door combing. Wright was engaged in a whispered conversation with the chief stewardess. There was no doubt in my mind that I was the subject of the conversation.

Wright said nothing when he returned to his seat. I assumed a casual mien, as if nothing was amiss. I sensed that any overt nervousness on my part could prove disastrous, and the situation was already castastrophic.

I was not surprised at all when the jetway door opened and two uniformed Dade County sheriff's officers stepped aboard. One took up a position blocking the exit of the passengers. The other poked his head in the flight cabin.

"Frank Williams?" he asked, his eyes darting from man to man.

"I'm Frank Williams," I said, getting out of the jump seat.

"Mr. Williams, would you please come with us?" he said, his tone courteous, his features pleasant.

"Certainly," I said. "But what's this all about, anyway?"

It was a question that also intrigued the three flight officers and the stewardesses. All of them were looking on with inquisitive expressions. None of them asked any questions, however, and the officers did not satisfy their curiosity. "Just follow me, please," he instructed me, and led the way out the exit door. His partner fell in behind me. It was a matter of conjecture on the part of the flight crew as to whether or not I had been arrested. No references had been made to arrest or custody. I was not placed in handcuffs. Neither officer touched me or gave the impression I was being restrained.

I had no illusions. I'd been busted.

The officers escorted me through the terminal and to their patrol car, parked at the front curb. One of the deputies opened the right rear door. "Will you get in, please, Mr. Williams. We have instructions to take you downtown."

The officers said nothing to me during the ride to the

sheriff's offices. I remained silent myself, assuming an air of puzzled indignation. The deputies were clearly uncomfortable and I had a hunch this was an affair in which they weren't really sure of their role.

I was taken to a small room in the detective division and seated in front of a desk. One of the deputies seated himself in the desk chair while the other stood in front of the closed door. Neither man made an effort to search me, and both were overly polite.

The one behind the desk cleared his throat nervously. "Mr. Williams, there seems to be some question as to whether you work for Pan Am or not," he said, more in explanation than accusation.

"What!" I exclaimed. "Why that's crazy! Here's my ID and here's my FAA license. Now you tell me who I work for." I slapped the phony documents down on the desk, acting as if I'd been accused of selling nuclear secrets to the Russians. He examined the ID card and the pilot's license with obvious embarrassment and passed them to the second officer, who looked at them and handed them back with a nervous smile. They both gave the impression they'd just arrested the President for jaywalking.

"Well, sir, if you'll just bear with us, I'm sure we can get this straightened out," the one behind the desk observed. "This really isn't our deal, sir. The people who asked us to do this will be along shortly."

"Okay," I agreed. "But who are these people?" He didn't have to tell me. I knew. And he didn't tell me.

An uncomfortable hour passed, more uncomfortable for the officers than for me. One of them left for a short time, returning with coffee, milk and sandwiches, which they shared with me. There was little conversation at first. I acted miffed and they acted like I should have been acting—like they wanted to be somewhere else. Oddly enough, I grew relaxed and confident as time passed, dropped my pose of righteous indignation and tried to ease their obvious discomfiture. I told a couple of airline jokes and they started to relax and ask me questions about my experiences as a pilot and the types of planes I flew.

The queries were casual and general, but of the kind designed to establish if I was a bona-fide airline pilot. One of the officers, it developed, was a private pilot himself, and at the end of thirty minutes he looked at his partner and said, "You know, Bill, I think someone's made a helluva mistake here."

It was near midnight when the "someone" arrived. He was in his late twenties, wearing an Ivy League suit and a serious expression. He extended a credentials folder in which nestled a gold shield. "Mr. Williams? FBI. Will you come with me, please?"

I thought we were going to the FBI offices, but instead he led me to an adjoining office and shut the door. He flashed a friendly smile. "Mr. Williams, I was called over here by the Dade County authorities, who, it seems, were contacted by some federal agency in New Orleans. Unfortunately, the officer who took the call didn't take down the caller's name or the agency he represented. He thought it was our agency. It wasn't. We really don't know what the problem is, but apparently there's some question as to whether you work for Pan Am.

"Frankly, Mr. Williams, we're in a bit of a quandary. We've been proceeding on the assumption the complaint is legitimate, and we're trying to clarify the matter one way or the other. The problem is, the employee records are in New York and the Pan Am offices are closed over the weekend." He paused and grimaced. Like the deputies, he wasn't certain he was on firm ground.

"I work for Pan Am, as you will learn when the offices open Monday morning," I said, affecting a calmly indignant attitude. "In the meantime, what do you do? Put me in jail? If you intend to do that, I have a right to call a lawyer. And I intend . . ."

He cut me off with a raised hand, palm outward. "Look,

Mr. Williams, I know what the situation is, if you're for real, and I have no reason to believe you are not. Listen, do you have any local superiors we can contact?"

I shook my head. "No, I'm based in L.A. I just dead-headed in here to see a girl, and I was going to deadhead back to the Coast Monday. I know a lot of pilots here, but they're with other airlines. I know several stewardesses, too, but again they're with other carriers."

"May I see your credentials, please?"

I handed over the ID card and FAA license. He inspected the two documents and returned them with a nod. "Tell you what, Mr. Williams," he offered. "Why don't you give me the names of a couple of pilots you know here, and the names of some of the stewardesses, too, who can verify your status. I don't know what this is about, but it's obviously a federal situation and I'd like to resolve it."

I fished out my book of facts and names and gave him the names and telephone numbers of several pilots and stewardesses, hoping all the while some of them were home and remembered me fondly. And as an actual pilot.

I really was a "hot" pilot at the moment, I thought wryly while awaiting the FBI agent's return, but so far I'd been incredibly lucky concerning the situation. Obviously, the FAA tower operator in New Orleans had questioned my status and had made an effort to pursue his doubts. What had aroused his suspicions? I didn't have the answer and I wasn't going to seek one. The sheriff's office had committed a faux pas in bobbling the source of the inquiry, and the FBI agent was apparently compounding the error by ignoring the FAA as a source of information. That puzzled me, too, but I wasn't going to raise the question. If a check with the FAA did occur to him, I would really be in the grease.

I spent an anxious forty-five minutes in the room alone and then the agent popped through the door. He was smiling. "Mr. Williams, you're free to go. I have confirmation from several persons as to your status, and I apologize for the inconvenience and embarrassment I know we've caused you. I'm really sorry, sir."

A Dade County sheriff's sergeant was behind him. "I want to add our apologies, too, Mr. Williams. It wasn't our fault. Just a damned mix-up. It was an FAA complaint from New Orleans. They asked us to pick you up when you got off the plane and, well, we didn't know where to go from there, so I contacted the local FBI and, well, I'm just sorry as hell about it, sir."

I didn't want the FBI agent to pick up on the FAA bit. The sergeant had obviously corrected his department's error. I spread my hands in a peace gesture and smiled. "Hey, don't worry about it. I understand, and I'm glad you guys are doing your job. I wouldn't want anyone flying around masquerading as a pilot, either."

"We appreciate your being so nice about it, Mr. Williams," said the sergeant. "Oh, your bag is over there by my desk."

Obviously it hadn't been searched. There was more than $7,000 in currency stashed in the bottom, among my underwear. "I gotta go, gentlemen," I said, shaking hands with each of them. "I've got a girl waiting, and if she doesn't believe this wild tale, I may be calling one of you."

The FBI agent grinned and handed me his card. "Call me," he said. "Especially if she has a beautiful friend."

I split like a jack rabbit. Outside, I hailed a cab and had the driver take me to the bus station. "The company's on an economy kick," I said as I paid him off. A smile replaced the quizzical expression on his face.

I went into the bus station rest room and changed out of my uniform, grabbed another cab and went straight to the airport. The earliest flight leaving Miami, departing within thirty minutes, was a Delta hop to Atlanta. I bought a one-way ticket on the flight under the name Tom Lombardi and paid cash for it. But I didn't totally relax until we were at cruising altitude and flying west. Once, during the short flight, I thought about the young FBI agent and hoped his boss didn't find out how the kid had goofed. The agent didn't seem the type who'd enjoy a tour of duty in Tucumcari, New Mexico, or Nogales, Arizona.

There was a girl in Atlanta, an Eastern stewardess. In any city, there was always a girl. I told this one I was on a six-month holiday, accumulated leave and sick time. "I thought I'd spend a couple months in Atlanta," I said.

"Make that one month, Frank," she said. "I'm being transferred to New Orleans in thirty days. But you can put up here until then."

It was a very pleasant and relaxing month, at the end of which I rented a truck and moved her to New Orleans. She wanted me to stay with her there for the remainder of my "vacation," but I didn't feel comfortable in New Orleans. My instincts told me to get the hell away from the Crescent City, so I went back to Atlanta, where, for reasons I didn't attempt to fathom, I felt hidden and secure.

The singles complex was a still-rare innovation in apartment construction at the time. One of the most elegant in the nation was River Bend, located on the outskirts of Atlanta. It was a sprawling, spa-like cluster of apartment units boasting a golf course, an Olympic-sized pool, saunas, tennis courts, a gymnasium, game rooms and its own club. One of its advertisements in the Atlanta *Journal* caught my eye and I went out to scout the premises.

I don't smoke. I've never had an urge to try tobacco. I didn't drink at the time, and still don't save on rare occasions. I didn't have any quarrel with alcohol or its users. My abstinence was part of the role I was playing. When I first began masquerading as a pilot I had the impression that pilots didn't drink to any great degree, so I abstained on the premise that it would reinforce my image as a flyer. When I learned that some pilots, like other people, get soused to the follicle pits under permissible circumstances, I'd lost all interest in drinking.

My one sensuous fault was women. I had a Cyprian lust for them. The River Bend ad had touted it as a "scintillating" place to live, and the builder was obviously a firm advocate of truth in advertising. River Bend sparkled with scintillators, most of them young, leggy, lovely, shapely and clad in revealing clothing. I instantly decided that I wanted to be one of the bulls in this Georgia peach orchard.

River Bend was both expensive and selective. I was given a lengthy application to fill out when I told the manager I wanted to lease a one-bedroom unit for one year. The form demanded more information than a prospective mother-in-law. I elected to stay Frank W. Williams since all the phony identification with which I had supplied myself was in that name. I paused at the space for occupation. I wanted to put down "airline pilot," for I knew that the uniform would attract girls like a buck rub lures a doe. But if I did that I'd have to specify Pan Am as my employer, and that made me wary. Maybe, just maybe, someone in the manager's office might check with Pan Am.

On impulse, nothing more, I put down "medical doctor" as my occupation. I left the spaces for relatives and references blank and, hopeful it would distract attention from the questions I'd ignored, I said I'd like to pay six months' rent in advance. I put twenty-four $100 bills on top of the application.

The assistant manager who accepted the application, a woman, was inquisitive. "You're a doctor?" she asked, as if doctors were as rare as whooping cranes. "What type of doctor are you?"

I thought I'd better be the kind of doctor that would never be needed around River Bend. "I'm a pediatrician," I lied. "However, I'm not practicing right now. My practice is in California, and I've taken a leave of absence for one year to audit some research projects at Emory and to make some investments."

"That's very interesting," she said, and then looked at

the pile of $100 bills. She gathered them up briskly and dropped them into a steel cash box in the top drawer of her desk. "It'll be nice having you with us, Dr. Williams."

I moved in the same day. The one-bedroom pad wasn't overly large, but it was elegantly furnished, and there was ample room for the action I had in mind.

Life at River Bend was fascinating, delightful and satisfying, if sometimes frenetic. There was a party in someone's pad almost every night, and side action all over the place. I was generally invited to be a part of the scene, whatever it was. The other tenants accepted me quickly, and save for casual inquiries, easily handled, made no effort to pry into my personal life or affairs. They called me "Doc," and of course there were those few who don't differentiate between doctors. This guy had a complaint about his foot. That one had mysterious pains in his stomach. There was a brunette who had an "odd, tight feeling" around her upper chest.

"I'm a pediatrician, a baby doctor. You want a podiatrist, a foot doctor," I told the first man.

"I'm not licensed to practice in Georgia. I suggest you talk to your own doctor," I told the other one.

I examined the brunette. Her brassiere was too small.

No sea offers calm sailing all the time, however, and one Saturday afternoon I encountered a squall that quickly built into a tragicomic hurricane.

I answered a knock on my door to face a tall, distinguished-looking man in his middle fifties, casually attired but still managing to appear impeccably groomed. He had a smile on his pleasant features and a drink in his hand.

"Dr. Williams?" he said, and assuming he was correct, proceeded to the point. "I'm Dr. Willis Granger, chief resident pediatrician of Smithers Pediatric Institute and General Hospital in Marietta."

I was too stunned to reply and he went on with a grin, "I'm your new neighbor. Just moved in yesterday, right below you. The assistant manager, Mrs. Prell, told me you were a pediatrician. I couldn't help but come up and introduce myself to a colleague. I'm not interrupting anything, am I?"

"Uh, no—no, not at all, Dr. Granger. Come in," I said, hoping he'd refuse. He didn't. He walked in and settled on my sofa.

"Where'd you go to school, here?" he asked. It was a normal question for doctors meeting, I suppose.

I knew only one college that had a school of medicine. "Columbia University in New York," I said, and prayed he wasn't an alumnus.

He nodded. "A great school. Where'd you serve your internship?"

Internship. That was done in a hospital, I knew. I'd never been in a hospital. I'd passed a lot of them, but the name of only one stuck in my mind. I hoped it was the kind of hospital that had interns. "Harbor Childrens Hospital in Los Angeles," I said and waited.

"Hey, terrific," he said, and much to my relief dropped the personal line of probing.

"You know, Smithers is a new facility. I've just been appointed to head up the pediatrics staff. It'll be a seven-story hospital when it's finished, but we've got only six floors open at the moment, and not too much traffic as yet. Why don't you come up and have lunch with me some afternoon and let me show you around the place. You'll like it, I think."

"That sounds great, I'd love it," I replied, and soon afterward he left. I was suddenly glum and depressed in the wake of his visit, and my first impulse was to pack and get the hell out of River Bend, if not Atlanta. Granger living right below me posed a definite threat to my existence at River Bend.

If I stayed, it would be only a matter of time before he'd know I was a phony, and I doubted he'd let it go at that. He'd probably call in the authorities.

I was tired of running. I'd been on the run for two years, and at the moment I wasn't recalling the excitement, glamour and fun of it all; I just wanted a place to call home, a place where I could be at peace for a while, a place where I had some friends. River Bend had been that place for two months, and I didn't want to leave. I was happy at River Bend.

A stubborn anger replaced my depression. To hell with Granger. I wouldn't let him force me back to the paperhanger's circuit. I'd just avoid him. If he came to visit, I'd be busy. When he was in, I'd be out.

It wasn't that easy. Granger was a likable man and a gregarious one. He started showing up at the parties to which I was invited. If he wasn't invited, he'd invite himself. And he was soon one of the most popular men in the complex. I couldn't avoid him. When he'd see me abroad, he'd hail me and stop me for a chat. And when he knew I was at home, he'd call on me.

Granger had a saving grace. He wasn't one to talk shop. He preferred to talk about the many lovely women he'd met at River Bend, and the fun he was having with them. "You know, I was never really a bachelor, Frank," he confided. "I got married young, a marriage neither of us should have entered into, and we stayed with it too long. Why, I don't know. But I'm having a ball, now. I feel like a thirty-year-old man again." Or he'd talk politics, world affairs, cars, sports, ethics and anything else. He was a learned and articulate man, informed on an amazing range of subjects.

I started to relax around Granger. In fact, I found him enjoyable company and even started seeking him out. Wary that the subject of pediatrics would recur sooner or later, however, I started spending a lot of time in the Atlanta library, reading books by pediatricians, medical journals with articles on children's medicine and any other available printed matter that dealt with the subject. I quickly acquired a broad general knowledge of pediatrics, enough knowledge, I felt, to cope with any casual conversations concerning pediatrics.

I felt well-enough informed, after several weeks of study, in fact, to accept Granger's invitation to have lunch with him at the hospital.

He met me in the lobby and promptly introduced me to the receptionist. "This is Dr. Williams, a friend of mine from Los Angeles and, until he returns to California, my neighbor." I'm not sure why I was introduced to the receptionist, unless Granger thought he was being helpful. She was a lovely young woman.

A similar introduction was made frequently during an exacting tour of the hospital. We visited every department. I met the hospital administrator, the chief radiologist, the head of physical therapy, the head nurse, interns, other doctors and dozens of nurses. We had lunch in the hospital cafeteria, and from the number of doctors and nurses who joined us at the dorm-type table where we sat, it was obvious Dr. Granger was a popular and well-liked man.

I returned to the hospital frequently thereafter, chiefly because of Brenda Strong, a nurse I had met there and started dating, but also because the hospital had a large medical library with up-to-the-minute books, journals and medical magazines dealing with every facet of pediatrics.

I could browse around in the library as long as I wanted, which was sometimes hours, without arousing any suspicions. In fact, I learned my frequent use of the library earned me respect beyond professional recognition from the hospital's staff doctors. "Most of the doctors think you're pretty sharp, keeping up in your field even though you're on a leave of absence," Brenda told me.

"I think you're pretty sharp, too."

She was thirty, a ripe, luscious brunette with a zest for making it. I sometimes wondered what she'd think if she knew her lover was an eighteen-year-old fraud. However, I never thought of myself as a teen-ager anymore, save on rare occasions. When I looked in a mirror, I saw a mature man of twenty-five or thirty and that's how I felt about myself, too. I'd been just an adventurous boy when I altered my chronological age, but my mental clock, during the past two years, had set itself ahead to correspond.

Still, I'd always had mature tastes in women. There were several tantalizing candy-stripers among the volunteer staff of the hospital, all in their late teens, but I was never attracted to any one of them. I preferred sophisticated, experienced women in their twenties or older. Like Brenda.

After several visits to the hospital, my initial trepidations dissipated, I began to enjoy my spurious role as a medico. I experienced the same vicarious pleasures, the same ego boosts, I'd known as a bogus pilot.

I'd walk down the corridor on one of the hospital floors and a pretty nurse would smile and say, "Good morning, Dr. Williams."

Or I'd encounter a group of staff interns and they'd nod respectfully and chant in unison, "Good afternoon, Dr. Williams."

Or I'd encounter one of the senior staff physicians and he'd shake hands and say, "Good to see you again, Dr. Williams."

And all day long I'd go around feeling like Hippocrates in my hypocrite's mantle. I even started sporting a tiny gold caduceus in my lapel.

No one tried to put me in a corner. I had no problems at all until one afternoon, following lunch with Granger and Brenda, I was leaving the hospital when John Colter, the administrator, hailed me.

"Dr. Williams! May I see you just a moment, sir." Without waiting for an answer, he headed straight for his office nearby.

"Oh, shit," I said, and didn't realize I'd said it aloud until a passing orderly gave me a grin. I had an impulse to bolt, but suppressed the urge. Colter's voice had not reflected any irritation or doubt. The request, while brusque, seemed devoid of suspicion. I followed him into his office.

"Doctor, have a seat, please," said Colter, motioning to a comfortable lounge chair as he settled behind his desk. I relaxed immediately. He was still addressing me as "doctor," and his manner now was almost ingratiating.

Colter, in fact, seemed embarrassed. He cleared his throat. "Dr. Williams, I'm about to ask you for a very big favor, a favor I have no right to ask," Colter said with a wry grimace. "I know that what I'm about to propose will be imposing on you, but I'm in a box, and I think you're the man who can solve my problem. Will you help me?"

I looked at him, perplexed. "Well, I'll be happy to, if I can, sir," I replied cautiously.

Colter nodded and his tone became brisk. "Here's my problem, Doctor. On my midnight-to-eight shift, I have a resident who supervises seven interns and about forty nurses. He had a death in the family this afternoon, a sister in California. He's left to go out there, and will be gone about ten days. Doctor, I've got nobody to cover that shift. Nobody. If you've been keeping up with the situation here, and I know from your activities that you have, you know we've got a severe shortage of doctors in Atlanta at the moment. I can't find a doctor to replace Jessup, and I can't do it myself. I'm not a medical doctor, as you know.

"I can't use an intern. The law requires a general practitioner or a specialist in one of the medical fields be the supervising resident of a hospital like this. Do you follow me?"

I nodded. I was following him, but in the same manner a jackal follows a tiger. Way back.

Colter plunged on. "Now, Dr. Granger tells me you're pretty well unencumbered here, that you spend a lot of time around your apartment, just taking it easy and playing with the girls." He held up a hand and smiled. "No offense, Doctor. I envy you."

His voice became pleading. "Dr. Williams, could you come up here and just sit around for ten days from midnight to eight? You won't have to do anything, I assure you. Just be here, so I can meet the state's requirements. I need you, Doctor. We'll pay you well, Doctor. Hell, as a bonus, I'll even put Nurse Strong on the shift for the ten days. I tell you, Doctor, I'm in a bind. If you refuse me, I don't know what the hell I can do."

The request astonished me, and I promptly objected. "Mr. Colter, I'd like to help you, but there's no way I could agree," I protested.

"Oh, why not?" Colter asked.

"Well, in the first place, I don't have a license to practice medicine in Georgia," I began, but Colter silenced me with an emphatic shake of his head.

"Well, you wouldn't really be doing anything," said Colter. "I'm not asking that you actually treat patients. I'm just asking that you act in a stand-in capacity. As for a license, you don't really need one. You have a California license, and California standards are as high as, if not higher than, Georgia standards, and recognized by our medical association. All I have to do, Doctor, is to bring you before a panel of five doctors, licensed by this state and members of this hospital's staff, for an interview conference, and they have the authority to ask the state for a temporary medical certificate that will allow you to practice in Georgia. Doctor, I'd like to have that conference in the morning. What do you say?"

Reason told me to refuse. There were too many hazards to my posture involved. Any one of the questions that might be asked me on the morrow could strip me of my pretense and expose me for the "doctor" I was in reality. A snake-oil specialist.

But I was challenged. "Well, if there's not that much difficulty involved, and if it won't take a lot of my time, I'll be happy to help you out," I agreed. "Now, specifically, what will be my duties? Mine has been an office practice only, you know. Save for calling on patients that I've had to admit for one reason or another, I know nothing of hospital routines."

Colter laughed. He was obviously relieved and happy. "Hot dog! Your duty? Just be here, Doctor. Walk around. Show yourself. Play poker with the interns. Play grab-ass with the nurses. Hell, Frank—I'm gonna call you Frank because you're a friend of mine, now—do anything you want to do. Just be here!"

I did have misgivings when I walked into the conference room the next morning to face the five doctors. I knew all of them from my frequent visits to the hospital, and Granger headed up the panel. He flashed me a conspiratorial grin as I walked in.

The interview was a farce, much to my delight. I was asked only basic questions. Where'd I go to medical school? Where'd I intern? My age? Where did I practice? How long had I been a practicing pediatrician? Not one of the doctors posed a question that would have tested any medical knowledge I might have possessed. I walked out of the conference with a letter appointing me temporary resident supervisor on the staff of the hospital, and the next day Granger brought me another letter from the state medical board authorizing me to use my California medical certificate to practice in Georgia for a period of one year.

One of my favorite television programs is "M*A*S*H," the seriocomic story of a fictional Army medical unit on the Korean War front. I never see a "M*A*S*H" segment without recalling my "medical career" at Smithers. I imagine there are several doctors in Georgia today who also can't view the program without memories of a certain resident supervisor.

My first shift set the tone for all my subsequent "duty tours." I was aware from the moment I accepted Colter's plea that there was only one way I could carry out my monumental bluff. If I was going to fake out seven interns, forty nurses and literally dozens of support personnel, I was going to have to give the impression that I was something of a buffoon of the medical profession.

I decided I'd have to project the image of a happy-go-lucky, easygoing, always-joking rascal who couldn't care less whether the rules learned in medical school were kept or not. I put my act on the road the minute I arrived for duty the first night and was met by Brenda in the R.S.'s office. Colter had not been jesting, it seemed. She was smiling.

"Here you are, Doctor, your smock and your stethoscope," she said, handing them to me. "Hey, you don't have to work this dog shift," I said, shrugging into the white garment. "When Colter said he'd assign you to this shift, I thought he was kidding. I'll talk to him tomorrow."

She flashed an impish look. "He didn't assign me," she said. "I asked the head nurse to put me on this shift for the duration—your duration."

I promptly donned the earpieces of the stethoscope and reached inside her blouse to apply the disk to her left breast. "I always knew your heart was in the right place, Nurse Strong," I said. "What's the first order of business tonight?"

"Not that," she said, pulling my hand away. "I suggest you make a floor check before you start thinking about a bed check."

The pediatrics ward took in the entire sixth floor of the hospital. It included the nursery, with about a dozen newborn babies, and three wings for children convalescing from illness, injury or surgery, or children admitted for diagnosis or treatment. There were about twenty children, ranging in age from two to twelve, in my charge. Fortunately, they weren't technically under my care, since each was in the care of his or her own pediatrician who prescribed all treatment and medication.

Mine was strictly a supervisor's or observer's role, although I was expected to be the medical doctor available for any emergencies. I hoped there wouldn't be any emergencies, but I had a plan for such a contingency. I spent the first night cultivating the interns, who were actually the guardians of the patients. All of them wanted to be pediatricians, and the sixth floor was an excellent proving ground. They seemed to me, after several hours of watching them, to be as competent and capable as some of the staff doctors, but I wasn't really in a position to pass judgment. It would have been akin to an illiterate certifying Einstein's theory of relativity.

But I sensed before morning that the interns, to a man, liked me as a supervisor and weren't likely to cause a flap.

The first shift was lazy, pleasant and uneventful until about 7 A.M., when the nurse in charge of the sixth-floor station contacted me. "Doctor, don't forget before you go off duty that you need to write charts for me," she said.

"Uh, yeah, okay, get them ready for me," I said. I went up to the station and looked over the stack of charts she had ready for me. There was one for each patient, noting medication given, times, the names of the nurses and interns involved and instructions from the attending physician. "That's your space," said the nurse, pointing to a blank area on the chart opposite the heading SUPERVISING RESIDENT'S COMMENTS.

I noticed the other doctors involved had written in Latin. Or Greek. Or maybe it was just their normal handwriting. I sure couldn't read it.

I sure as hell didn't want anyone reading what I wrote, either. So I scribbled some hieroglyphics all over each chart and signed my name in the same indecipherable manner in each instance.

"There you go, Miss Murphy," I said, handing back the charts. "You'll note I gave you an A."

She laughed. I got a lot of laughs during the following shifts with my wisecracking manner, seeming irreverence for serious subjects and zany actions. For example, an obstetrician came in early one morning with one of his patients, a woman in the last throes of labor. "You want to scrub up and look in on this? I think it's going to be triplets," he asked.

"No, but I'll see you have plenty of boiling water and lots of clean rags," I quipped. Even he thought it was hilarious.

But I knew I was treading on thin ice, and about 2:30 A.M. at the end of my first week, the ice started cracking. *"Dr. Williams! To Emergency, please. Dr. Williams! To Emergency, please."*

I had so far avoided the emergency ward, and it was my understanding with Colter that I wouldn't have to handle emergency cases. There was supposed to be a staff doctor manning the emergency ward. I presumed there was. I hate the sight of blood. I can't stand the sight of blood. Even a little blood makes me ill. I once passed near the emergency ward and saw them bringing in an accident victim. He was all bloody and moaning, and I hurried to the nearest toilet and vomited.

Now here I was being summoned to the emergency room. I knew I couldn't say I hadn't heard the announcement—two nurses were talking to me when the loudspeaker blared the message—but I dawdled as much as possible en route.

I used the toilet first. Then I used the stairs instead of the elevator. I knew my delay might be harmful to whomever needed a doctor, but it would be just as harmful if I rushed to the emergency ward. I wouldn't know what to do once I got there. Especially if the patient was bleeding.

This one wasn't, fortunately. It was a kid of about thirteen, white-faced, propped up on his elbows on the table and looking at the three interns grouped around him. The interns looked at me as I stopped inside the door.

"Well, what do we have here?" I asked.

"A simple fracture of the tibia, about five inches below the patella, it looks like," said the senior intern, Dr. Hollis

Carter. "We were just getting ready to take some X rays. Unless we find something more severe, I'd say put him in a walking cast and send him home."

I looked at Carl Farnsworth and Sam Bice, the other two interns. "Dr. Farnsworth?" He nodded. "I concur, Doctor. It may not even be broken."

"How about you, Dr. Bice?"

"I think that's all we've got here, if that much," he said.

"Well, gentlemen, you don't seem to have much need of me. Carry on," I said and left. I learned later the kid had a broken shin bone, but at the time he could have needed eyeglasses for all I knew.

I had other emergency-ward calls in ensuing nights, and each time I let the interns handle the situation. I would go in, question one of them as to the nature of the illness or injury and then ask him how he would treat the patient. On being told, I'd confer with one or both of the other interns who were usually present. If he or they concurred, I'd nod authoritatively and say, "All right, Doctor. Have at it."

I didn't know how well my attitude set with the interns concerning such incidents, but I soon found out. They loved it. "They think you're great, Frank," said Brenda.

"Young Dr. Carter especially thinks you're terrific. I heard him telling some friends of his visiting from Macon how you let him get real practice, that you just come in, get his comments on the situation and let him proceed. He says you make him feel like a practicing doctor."

I smiled. "I'm just lazy," I replied.

But I realized after the first shift that I needed some help. I located a pocket dictionary of medical terms, and thereafter when I'd hear the interns or nurses mention a word or phrase, the meaning of which I didn't know, I'd slip upstairs to the unfinished seventh floor, go into one of the empty linen closets and look up the word or words. Sometimes I'd spend fifteen or twenty minutes in the closet just leafing through the dictionary.

On what I thought would be my last night in the guise of resident supervisor, Colter sought me out. "Frank, I know I've got no right to ask this, but I have to. Dr. Jessup isn't coming back. He's decided to stay and practice in California. Now, I'm pretty sure I can find a replacement within a couple of weeks, so could I presume on you to stay that long?" He waited, a pleading look on his face.

He caught me at the right time. I was in love with my role as doctor. I was enjoying it almost as much as my pretense of airline pilot. And it was much more relaxing. I hadn't written a bad check since assuming the pose of pediatrician. In fact, since taking the temporary position at Smithers, I hadn't even thought about passing any worthless paper. The hospital was paying me a $125-a-day "consultant's" fee, payable weekly.

I clapped Colter on the back. "Sure, John," I agreed. "Why not? I've got nothing else I'd rather do at the moment."

I was confident I could carry the scam for another two weeks, and I did, but then the two weeks became a month and the month became two months, and Colter still hadn't found a replacement for Jessup. Some of the confidence began to wane, and at times I was nagged by the thought that Colter, or some doctor on the staff, even Granger, maybe, might start checking into my medical credentials, especially if a sticky situation developed on my shift.

I maintained my cocky, to-hell-with-rules-and-regulations demeanor with the interns, nurses and others under my nominal command, and the midnight-to-eight shift staff continued to support me loyally. The nurses thought I was a darling kook and appreciated the fact that I never tried to corner them in an unoccupied room. The interns were proud to be on my shift. We'd developed a real camaraderie, and the young doctors respected me. They thought I was wacky, but competent. "You don't treat us like the other staff doctors, Dr. Williams," Carter confided. "When they walk in while we're treating a patient, they say 'Move aside,' and just take over. You don't. You let us go ahead and handle the case. You let us be real doctors."

I sure as hell did. I didn't know a damned thing about medicine. Those young doctors didn't know it until years later, but they were the sole reason I was able to keep up my medical masquerade. When things got tough—at least tough for me, and a headache was too stout for my medical knowledge— I'd leave it to the interns and flee to my linen closet on the seventh floor.

Fortunately, during my tenure at Smithers, I was never faced with a life-or-death situation, but there were ticklish positions where only my antic's mien saved me. Early one morning, for instance, an obstetrics team nurse sought me out. "Dr. Williams, we just delivered a baby, and Dr. Martin was called across the hall to do a Caesarian section while we were still tying the cord. He asks if you'd be kind enough to make a routine examination of the child."

I couldn't very well refuse. I was chatting with two nurses on my shift at the time the request was made. "I'll help you, Dr. Williams," volunteered the one, Jana Stern, a dedicated RN who was attending medical school herself and hoped to be a pediatrician specializing in newborns.

She led the way to the nursery and I reluctantly followed. I had sometimes paused outside the plate-glass window of the nursery to look at the tiny, wrinkled newborns in their incubators or box-like bassinets, but I'd never gone inside. They reminded me of so many mewling kittens, and I've always been slightly leery of cats, even little ones.

I started to shove open the door of the nursery and Nurse Stern grabbed my arm. "Doctor!" she gasped.

"What's wrong?" I asked, looking around desperately for one of my trusty interns.

"You can't go in like that!" she scolded me. "You have to scrub up and put on a smock and mask. You know that!" She handed me a green jacket and a sterile mask.

I grimaced. "Help me on with these damned things," I growled. "Why do we need a mask? I'm only gonna look at the kid, not stick him up." I realized why I needed a mask. I was trying to cover. And I did. She clucked. "Honest, Doctor, you're too much at times," she said in exasperated tones.

It was a baby boy, still glistening redly from his rough passage through the narrow channel of life. He regarded me with a lugubrious expression. "Okay, kid, take a deep breath and milk it back," I commanded in mock military tone, starting to apply my stethoscope to the baby's chest.

Nurse Stern grabbed my arm again, laughing. "Doctor! You can't use that stethoscope on a newborn! You use a pediatrics stethoscope." She busted out and returned with a smaller version of the one I held. I hadn't known they came in sizes. "Will you quit fooling around, please? We've got a lot of work to do."

I stepped back and waved at the baby. "Tell you what, Dr. Stern. You examine the boy. I'd like to check your style."

She rose to the bait. "Well, I can do it," she said, as if I'd insulted her, but still visibly pleased. She applied the stethoscope, then draped it around her neck and proceeded to manipulate the baby's arms, legs and hips, peered into his eyes, ears, mouth and anus and ran her hands over his head and body. She stepped back and stared at me challengingly. "Well?"

I leaned down and kissed her on the forehead. "Thank you, Doctor, you've saved my only son," I said with mock tearfulness.

The baby had lost his doleful look. No one is really certain if newborn infants have thoughts or are aware of what is going on around them. No one but me, that is. That kid knew I was a phony. I could see it in his face.

I examined several newborns after that. I never knew what I was doing, of course, but, thanks to Nurse Stern, I knew how to do it.

But I still spent a lot of time in my seventh-floor linen closet.

There were times, too, I'm sure, when my tomfool demeanor irked people. Like the night, in the eleventh month of my impersonation, when a nurse rushed up to the nursing station where I was writing my undecipherable comments on charts. "Dr. Williams! We've got a blue baby in 608! Come quickly." She was a new nurse, barely a month out of school. And I'd nipped her with one of my practical jokes. Her first night on duty I'd told her to "bring me a bucket of steam to the nursery. I want to sterilize the place." She'd eagerly rushed off to the boiler room, where a helpful intern had steered her.

Oddly enough, in the eleven months I'd posed as a doctor, I'd never heard the term "blue baby." I thought she was getting back at me.

"I'll be right along," I said, "but first I've got to check the green baby in 609." When I made no move, she rushed off, shouting for one of the interns. I stepped around the corner and consulted my medical dictionary. I learned a blue baby was one suffering from cyanosis, or lack of oxygen in the blood, usually due to a congenital heart defect. I took off for Room 608, and was relieved to find one of my interns had bailed me out again. He was adjusting a portable oxygen tent around the infant. "I've called his doctor. He's on his way. I'll handle it until he gets here, if it's all right with you, sir."

It was all right with me. The incident shook me. I realized I was playing a role that had reached its limits. I'd been lucky so far, but I suddenly knew some child could die as a result of my impersonation. I determined to seek out Colter and resign, and I determined not to be swayed by any entreaties.

He sought me out instead.

"Well, Frank, you can go back to being a playboy," he said cheerfully. "We've got a new resident supervisor. Got him from New York. He'll be here tomorrow."

I was relieved. I dropped around the next day to pick up my final paycheck and wasn't at all disappointed when I didn't meet my replacement. I was leaving the hospital when I encountered Jason, the elderly janitor on the midnight-to-eight shift.

"You're coming to work a little early, aren't you, Jason?" I asked.

"Workin' a double shift today, Doctor," said Jason.

"If you haven't heard, Jason, I won't be around anymore," I said. "They finally found a replacement."

"Yes, sir, I heard," said Jason. He looked at me quizzically. "Doctor, can I ask you somethin'?"

"Sure, Jason. Anything." I liked him. He was a nice old man.

He drew a deep breath. "Doctor, you never knowed it, but I always spent my relaxin' time up there on the seventh floor. And, Doctor, for nearly a year now I been seein' you go in a linen closet up there. You never go in with anythin', and you never come out with anythin'. I know you don't drink, and, Doctor, there ain't nothin' in that closet, nothin'! I done searched it a dozen times. Doctor, my curiosity's about to drive me to drink. Just what did you do in that linen closet, Doctor? I won't tell nobody, I swear!"

I laughed and hugged him. "Jason, I was contemplating my navel in that closet. That's all. I swear it."

But I know he never believed me. He's probably still inspecting that closet.

CHAPTER FIVE

A Law Degree Is Just An Illegal Technicality

A week after I severed my connection with the hospital, my lease at Balmorhea came up for renewal and I decided to leave Atlanta. There was no compulsion for me to go; at least I felt none, but I thought it unwise to stay. The fox who keeps to one den is the easiest caught by the terriers, and I felt I had nested too long in one place. I knew I was still being hunted and I didn't want to make it easy for the hounds.

I later learned that my decision to leave Atlanta was an astute one. About the same time, in Washington, D.C., FBI Inspector Sean O'Riley was ordered to drop all his other cases and concentrate solely on nabbing me. O'Riley was a tall, dour man with the countenance of an Irish bishop and the tenacity of an Airedale, an outstanding agent dedicated to his job, but an eminently fair man in all respects.

I came to admire O'Riley, even while making every effort to thwart his task and to embarrass him professionally. If O'Riley has any personal feelings concerning me, I am certain animosity is not among such emotions. O'Riley is not a mean man.

Of course, I had no knowledge of O'Riley's existence, even, at the time I vacated Atlanta. Save for the young special agent in Miami, and the Dade County officers I'd encountered there, the officers on my case were all phantoms to me.

I decided to hole up for a month or so in the capital city of another southern state. As usual, I was prompted in my choice by the fact that I knew an airline stewardess there. I was yet to find a more delightful influence on my actions than a lovely woman.

Her name was Diane and I had known her intermittently for about a year. I had never flown with her, having met her in the Atlanta airport terminal, and she knew me under the alias Robert F. Conrad, a Pan Am first officer, an allonym I used on occasion. I was forced to maintain the nom de plume with her, for we developed a close and pleasing relationship, during the course of which, initially, she had delved into my personal background, including my educational history. Most pilots have a college degree, but not all of them majored in the aeronautical sciences. I told Diane that I had taken a law degree but had never practiced, since a career as an airline pilot had loomed as not only more exciting but also much more lucrative than law. She readily accepted the premise that a man might shun the courtroom for the cockpit.

She also remembered my concocted law degree. A few days after my arrival in her city she took me to a party staged by one of her friends and there introduced me to a pleasant fellow named Jason Wilcox.

"You two ought to get along. Jason is one of our assistant state's attorneys," Diane told me. She turned to Wilcox. "And Bob here is a lawyer who never hung out his shingle. He became a pilot instead."

Wilcox was immediately interested. "Hey, where'd you go to law school?"

"Harvard," I said. If I was going to have a law degree, I thought I might as well have one from a prestigious source.

"But you never practiced?" he asked.

"No," I said. "I got my Commercial Pilot's License the same week I took my master's in law, and Pan Am offered me a job as a flight engineer. Since a pilot makes $30,000 to $40,000, and since I loved flying, I took the job. Maybe someday I'll go back to law, but right now I fly only eighty hours a month. Not many practicing lawyers have it that good."

"No, you're right there," Wilcox agreed. "Where do you fly to? Rome? Paris? All over the world, I guess."

I shook my head. "I'm not flying at the moment," I said. "I've been furloughed. The company made a personnel cutback last month and I didn't have seniority. It may be six months or a year before they call me back. Right now I'm just loafing, drawing unemployment. I like it."

Wilcox studied me with bemused eyes. "How'd you do at Harvard?" he asked. I felt he was leading up to something.

"Pretty well, I guess," I replied. "I graduated with a 3.8 average. Why?"

"Well, the attorney general is looking for lawyers for his staff," Wilcox replied. "In fact, he's really in a bind. Why don't you take the bar here and join us? I'll recommend you. The job doesn't pay an airline pilot's salary, of course, but it pays better than unemployment. And you'll get in some law practice, which sure as hell couldn't hurt you."

I almost rejected his proposal outright. But the more I thought about it, the more it intrigued me. The challenge again. I shrugged. "What would it entail for me to take the bar examination in this state?" I asked.

"Not much, really," said Wilcox. "Just take a transcript from Harvard over to the state bar examiner's office and apply to take the bar. They won't refuse you. Of course, you'd have to bone up on our civil and criminal statutes, but I've got all the books you'd need. Since you're from another state, you'll be allowed three cracks at the bar here. You shouldn't have any trouble."

A transcript from Harvard. That might prove difficult, I mused, since the university and I were strangers. But then I'd never had any pilot's training, either. And I had a valid-appearing FAA pilot's license in my pocket stating I was qualified to fly passenger jets, didn't I? My bumblebee instincts began buzzing.

I wrote to the registrar of the Harvard Law School and asked for a fall schedule and a law school catalogue, and within a few days the requested material was deposited in my mailbox. The catalogue listed all the courses necessary for a doctor of law from Harvard, and it also boasted some lovely logos and letterheads. But I still didn't have the foggiest notion of what a college transcript looked like.

Diane was an Ohio University graduate, who had majored in business administration. I casually engaged her in a conversation revolving around her student years.

She had been heavily involved in campus activities, it developed, something of a playgirl in college. "You must not have done much studying," I said jestingly.

"Oh, yes, I did," she maintained. "I had a 3.8 average. In fact, I was on the dean's list my senior year. You can have fun and still make good grades, you know."

"Aw, come on! I don't believe you had that kind of average. I'd have to see your transcript to believe that," I protested.

She grinned. "Well, smart-ass, I just happen to have one," she said, and returned from her bedroom a few minutes later with the document.

The transcript consisted of four legal-sized sheets of lined paper and was, in fact, a certified photocopy of her four years of college work, attested to and notarized by the registrar. The first page was headed by the name of the university in large, bold letters, beneath which appeared the state seal of Ohio. Then came her name, the year she had graduated, the degree she had received and the college (College of Business Administration) awarding the degree. The remainder of the pages was filled, line by line, with the courses she had taken, the dates, the hours of credit she had accumulated and her grades. A grade average was given at the end of each year and a final entry noted her over-all average, 3.8. In the bottom right-hand corner of the last page was the Ohio University seal, with a notary's seal superimposed and bearing the signature of the school registrar.

I committed the structure of the transcript to memory, absorbing it as a sponge absorbs water, before handing it back. "Okay, you're not only sexy, you're also brainy," I said in mock apology.

I went shopping the next day at a graphic arts supply house, a stationery store and an office-supply firm, picking up some legal-sized bond paper, some layout material, some press-on letters in several different type faces, some artist's pens and pencils, an X-Acto knife, some glue and a right-angle ruler, some gold seals and a notary's press.

I started by simply cutting out the Harvard Law School logo and pasting it at the top of a piece of bond paper. I then affixed the school seal, also filched from the catalogue, beneath the school heading. Next I filled in my name, year of graduation, degree and then, using the right angle and a fine artist's pen, I carefully lined several pages of the legal-sized bond. Afterward, using block press-on letters, I carefully entered every course required for a law degree from Harvard, my electives and my fictitious grades. Since Wilcox might see the transcript, I gave myself a three-year over-all grade average of 3.8.

The finished, pasted-up product looked like leavings from a layout artist's desk, but when I ran the pages through a do-it-yourself copying machine, it came out beautifully. It had all the appearances of something coughed out by a duplicating computer. I finished the six-page counterfeit by attaching a gold seal to the bottom of the last page and impressing over it, in a deliberately blurred manner, the notary stamp, which I filled in by hand, using a heavy pen, and signing with a flourish the name of the Harvard Law School registrar, noting below the forgery that the registrar was also a notary.

Whether or not it resembled an actual Harvard transcript, I didn't know. The acid test would come when I presented the phony document to the state bar examiner's office. Wilcox had been practicing law for fifteen years, and had been an assistant state's attorney for nine years. He also had a wide acquaintance among the state's lawyers. He said I was the first Harvard graduate he'd ever met.

I spent three weeks poring over the volumes in Wilcox's office library, finding law a much easier, if somewhat duller, subject than I had assumed, and then with bated breath presented myself at the state bar examiner's office. A law student acting as a clerk in the office leafed through my fake transcript, nodded approvingly, made a copy of the phony instrument and handed my original counterfeit back to me, along with an application to take the bar examination. While I was filling out the form, he thumbed through a calendar and called someone on the telephone.

"You can take the exam next Wednesday, if you think you're ready," he stated, and then grinned encouragingly. "It should be no hill at all for a Harvard stepper."

His colloquialism might have been true in regard to an actual Ivy League law graduate. For me it was a mountain, eight hours of surmises, I hopes, maybes, confident conjecture and semieducated guesses.

I flunked.

To my astonishment, however, the notification that I had failed was attached to the test I had taken, which reflected the answers I had correctly given and the questions I had missed. Someone in the SBE's office obviously liked me.

I went back to Wilcox's office and camped in his library, concentrating on the sections of the test I had missed. Whenever possible Wilcox himself tutored me. After six weeks I felt I was ready to attempt the test a second time.

I blew it again. But again my test papers were returned to me, showing where I had succeeded and where I had failed. I was gaining. In fact, I was delighted at the number of legal questions I had answered correctly and I was determined to pass the examination on my final try.

I took the third examination seven weeks later and passed! Within two weeks I received a handsome certificate attesting to the fact that I had been admitted to the state bar and was licensed to practice law. I cracked up. I hadn't even finished high school and had yet to step on a college campus, but I was a certified lawyer! However, I regarded my actual lack of academic qualifications merely a technicality, and in my four months of legal cramming I'd learned the law is full of technicalities. Technicalities are what screw up justice.

Wilcox fulfilled his promise. He arranged a job interview for me with the state attorney general, who, on Wilcox's recommendation, hired me as an assistant. My salary was $12,800 annually.

I was assigned to the corporate law division, one of the AG's civil departments. The division's attorneys handled all the small claims made against the state, trespass-to-try-title suits, land-condemnation cases and various other real estate actions.

That is, most of them did. The senior assistant to whom

I was assigned as an aide was Phillip Rigby, the haughty scion of an old and established local family. Rigby considered himself a southern aristocrat and I impinged on two of his strongest prejudices. I was a Yankee, but even worse, I was a Catholic Yankee! He relegated me to the role of "gopher"—go for coffee, go for this book or that book, go for anything he could think of for me to fetch. I was the highest-paid errand boy in the state. Rigby was a rednecked coprolite. Mine was an opinion shared by many of the other younger assistants, most of whom were natives themselves but surprisingly liberal in their views.

I was popular with the young bachelors in the division. I still had over $20,000 in my boodle and I spent it freely on the friends I made on the AG's staff, treating them to dinners in fine restaurants, riverboat outings and evenings in posh night clubs.

I deliberately gave the impression that I was from a wealthy New York family without making any such direct claim. I lived in a swank apartment overlooking a lake, drove a leased Jaguar and accumulated a wardrobe worthy of a British duke. I wore a different suit to work each day of the week, partly because it pleased me but mostly because my extensive wardrobe seemed to irritate Rigby. He had three suits to my knowledge, one of which I was sure was a hand-me-down from his Confederate colonel grandfather. Rigby was also penurious.

If my grooming was resented by Rigby, it was approved by others. One day in court, during a short delay in the case at hand, the judge leaned forward on his bench and addressed me:

"Mr. Conrad, you may not contribute much in the way of legal expertise to the proceedings before this court, but you certainly add style, sir. You are the best-dressed gopher in Dixie, Counselor, and the court commends you." It was a genuine tribute and I was pleased, but Rigby nearly had an apoplectic seizure.

Actually, I was satisfied with my errand-boy role. I had

no real desire to actually try a case. There was too much danger that my basic lack of knowledge of the law would be exposed. And the work Rigby and I did was dull and uninteresting the majority of the time, a boresome task that I was content to let him handle. Occasionally he did throw me a bone, allowing me to present some minor land issue or make the opening argument in a given case, and I did enjoy those incidents and on the whole handled them without detriment to the law profession, I thought. Rigby was a highly competent lawyer, and I learned a lot sitting behind him, much more than I had gleaned from the law-books or the examinations.

Basically, my position was a haven, a lair not likely to be discovered by the hounds. When you're looking for a criminal, you don't often think to look for him on the attorney general's staff of prosecutors, especially if you're seeking a teen-age high school dropout.

Several weeks after I joined the AG's staff, Diane was transferred to Dallas. I was only momentarily saddened at losing her. I was soon dating Gloria, the daughter of a high state official. Gloria was a lively, personable, vibrant girl, and if our relationship had a fault, it was that she was not exactly a bosom companion. But I was learning that a woman can also be delightful with her clothes on.

Gloria was a member of a staunch Methodist family and I often squired her to church, with the understanding that I was not a candidate for conversion. It was a gesture of interdenominational respect on my part that was appreciated by her parents, and actually I enjoyed it. In fact, I formed a close friendship with the young pastor of the church and he persuaded me to become involved in the church's youth programs. I participated actively in building several children's playgrounds in blighted areas of the city and served on several committees governing other urban youth projects. It was an odd pastime for a con man, but I had no real sense of hypocrisy. For the first time in my life I was giving unselfishly of myself, with no thought of any return, and it made me feel good.

A sinner toiling in the vineyards of the Church, however, no matter how worthy his labors, shouldn't put in too much overtime. I accepted one too many committee appointments and the grapes began to sour.

There was a real Harvard graduate on this particular panel. Not just a Harvard graduate, but a Harvard *Law* graduate, and he was delighted to meet me. He was practically delirious with joy. I have since learned something about Harvard men. They're like badgers. They like to stick together in their own barrows. A lone badger is going to find another badger. A Harvard man in a strange area is going to find another Harvard man. And they're going to talk about Harvard.

This one pounced on me immediately, with all the enthusiasm of Stanley encountering Livingstone in darkest Africa. When had I graduated? Who had my instructors been? Who were the girls I knew? To what club had I belonged? What pubs had I frequented? Who had my friends been?

I successfully fended him off that first night, with either inane answers or by ignoring him and concentrating on the committee business at hand. But thereafter he sought me out at every opportunity. He'd call me to have lunch. He'd drop by my office when he chanced to be in the area. He called me to invite me to parties or outings, to play golf or to take in some cultural event. And always he managed to steer the conversation around to Harvard. What buildings had I had classes in? Didn't I know Professor So-and-So? Had I been acquainted with any of the old families of Cambridge? Harvard men around other Harvard men seem to be rather limited in their conversational topics.

I couldn't avoid him, and of course I couldn't answer many of his questions. His suspicions aroused, he began to build a *res gestae* case against me as a bogus Harvard man if not a phony lawyer. It became *res judicata* for me when I learned he was making numerous inquiries into my background on several fronts, seriously questioning my honesty and integrity.

Like the proverbial Arab, I folded my tent and silently stole away. Not, however, without drawing a final paycheck. I did say good-bye to Gloria, although she wasn't aware it was a final farewell. I merely told her I'd had a death in the family and had to return to New York for a couple of weeks.

I turned in my leased Jaguar and purchased a bright orange Barracuda. It wasn't the most inconspicuous set of wheels for a wanted fugitive to drive, but I liked it and I wanted it, so I bought it. I justified the action by telling myself that since the car, if not the driver, was cool, it would probably prove a wise investment. Largely it was an astute move, for in the past I had simply rented cars and then abandoned them at airports when I was through with them, and O'Riley, unknown to me, was making good use of this practice to compile a pattern of my movements.

I had posed as a doctor for nearly a year. I had played the role of lawyer for nine months. While I was hardly leading a straight life during those twenty months, I hadn't passed any bad checks or done anything else to attract the attention of the authorities. Provided Rigby or the AG himself didn't press the issue of my sudden departure from my post as assistant attorney general, I felt justified in assuming I was not the object of any pressing manhunt. And I wasn't, save for O'Riley's dogged efforts, and despite his persistence he was as yet following a cold trail.

I attempted to keep it that way, since I was still in no bind for funds. My flight from my "Harvard colleague's" inquisition turned into something of a vacation. I meandered around the western states for several weeks, touring Colorado, New Mexico, Arizona, Wyoming, Nevada, Idaho and Montana, dallying wherever the scenery intrigued me. Since the scenery usually included some very lovely and susceptible women, I stayed perpetually intrigued.

Although the image of myself as a criminal gradually blurred and dimmed, I entertained no thoughts of rehabilitation. In fact, looking to the future, I stopped long enough in a large Rocky Mountain metropolis to equip myself with dual identities as a fictitious airline pilot.

Using the same procedures that had enabled me to assume the alias of Frank Williams, a first officer for Pan Am, I created Frank Adams, an alleged co-pilot for Trans World Airways, complete with uniform, sham ID and counterfeit FAA pilot's license. I also assembled a set of duplicitous credentials that would allow me, in my posture as Frank Williams, to be a pilot for either Pan Am or TWA.

Shortly afterward I was in Utah, a state notable for not only its spectacular geography and Mormon history but also for its proliferation of college campuses. Having purloined a couple of college degrees, I thought it only fair that I at least acquaint myself with a university campus and so I visited several Utah colleges, strolling around the grounds and taking in the academic sights, especially the coeds. There were so many lovely girls on one campus that I was tempted to enroll as a student.

Instead I became a teacher.

While I was lolling around my motel room one afternoon, reading the local newspaper, my attention was drawn to an expected shortage of summer instructors at one university. The news item quoted the faculty dean, one Dr. Amos Grimes, as being most concerned about finding summer replacements for the school's two sociology professors. "It appears we will have to look out of state for qualified people willing to teach for only three months," said Dr. Grimes in the story.

A vision of myself ensconced in a classroom with a dozen or so nubile beauties took hold of my imagination, and I couldn't resist. I rang up Dr. Grimes.

"Dr. Grimes, Frank Adams here," I said briskly. "I have a Ph.D. in sociology from Columbia University in New York. I'm visiting here, Doctor, and I see by the newspaper that you're looking for sociology instructors."

"Yes, we're definitely interested in finding some people," Dr. Grimes replied cautiously. "Of course, you understand it would be only a temporary position, just for the summer. I assume you do have some teaching experience?"

"Oh, yes," I said airily. "But it's been several years. Let me explain my position, Dr. Grimes. I am a pilot for Trans World Airways, and just recently I was furloughed for six months for medical purposes, an inflammation of the inner ear that bars me at the moment from flying status. I've been looking around for something to do in the interim, and when I saw the story it occurred to me that it might be pleasant to get back into a classroom again.

"I was a professor of sociology at City College of New York for two years before I joined TWA."

"Well, it certainly sounds like you're a likely candidate for one of our positions, Dr. Adams," said Dr. Grimes, now enthusiastic. "Why don't you come by my office tomorrow morning and we'll talk about it."

"I'd be delighted to do that, Dr. Grimes," I replied. "Since I'm a complete stranger in Utah, could you tell me what documents I will need to apply for a faculty position with your college?"

"Oh, just a transcript from Columbia will do, really," said Dr. Grimes. "Of course, if you can obtain a couple of letters of recommendation from CCNY, it would be desirable."

"No problem," I said. "I'll have to send for both my transcript and the letters of recommendation, of course. I came here unprepared on either score, since I didn't even contemplate a temporary teaching position until I saw the story."

"I understand, Dr. Adams," replied Dr. Grimes. "I'll see you in the morning."

I wrote Columbia University that afternoon, requesting a complete catalogue and any pertinent brochures on the school. I also dashed off a letter to the registrar of CCNY, stating I was a Utah graduate student seeking a teaching position in New York, preferably in sociology. I arranged to rent a box at the local post office before mailing off the missives.

My meeting with Dean Grimes was a very pleasant one. He seemed immediately impressed with me, and we spent most of the time, including a leisurely luncheon interlude in the faculty club, discussing my "career" as a pilot. Dr. Grimes, like many men with sedentary jobs, had a romantic view of airline pilots and was eager to have his exciting perspective validated. I had more than enough anecdotes to satisfy his vicarious appetite.

"I have no doubt at all that we can use you this summer, Dr. Adams," he said on my departure. "I'm personally looking forward to your being here on campus."

The materials I had requested from Columbia and CCNY arrived within the week, and I drove to Salt Lake City to purchase the supplies necessary for my current counterfeiting venture. My finished "transcript" was a beauty, giving me a 3.7 grade average and listing my doctoral thesis as a dissertation on "The Sociological Impact of Aviation on the Rural Populations of North America." As I had anticipated, the reply from the registrar of CCNY was on official college stationery. I clipped off the letterhead and, using clear white plastic tape and high-quality bond paper, created a fine facsimile of the college's stationery. I trimmed it to regulation typewriter-paper size and then sat down and wrote myself two letters of recommendation, one from the registrar and one from the head of the sociology department.

I was cautious with both letters. They merely noted that

I had been a sociology instructor at CCNY during the years 1961–62, that the faculty rating committee had given me very satisfactory marks and that I had resigned voluntarily to enter the field of commercial aviation as a pilot. I then took the letters to a Salt Lake City job printer and had him run off a dozen copies of each, telling him I was applying at several universities for a teaching position and thus needed extra copies on fine-grade bond. Apparently mine was not an unusual request, for he did the job perfunctorily.

Dr. Grimes barely glanced at the documents when I presented them to him. He introduced me to Dr. Wilbur Vanderhoff, assistant head of the sociology department, who also gave the instruments only a cursory examination before sending them on to faculty personnel for filing. I was hired within the hour to teach two six-week semesters during the summer at a salary of $1,600 per semester. I was assigned to teach a ninety-minute freshman course in the morning, three days a week, and a ninety-minute sophomore course in the afternoon, twice weekly. Dr. Vanderhoff provided me with the two textbooks to be used in the classes, as well as student attendance ledgers. "Any other supplies you might need, you can probably find in the bookstore. They have standard requisition forms on hand," said Dr. Vanderhoff. He grinned. "I'm glad to see you're young and strong. Our summer sociology classes are usually large ones, and you'll earn your salary."

I had three weeks before the first summer semester started. On the pretense of refreshing myself, I audited several of Dr. Vanderhoff's classes, just to get an idea of how a college course was conducted. At night I studied the two textbooks, which I found both interesting and informative.

Vanderhoff was right. Both my classes were large ones. There were seventy-eight students in my freshman class and sixty-three students in my sophomore course, the majority in both instances being female students.

That summer was one of the most enjoyable of my life.

I thoroughly enjoyed my role as a teacher. So did my students, I'm certain. My courses were taught by the book, as required, and I had no difficulty there. I just read one chapter ahead of the students and selected what portions of the text I wanted to emphasize. But almost daily I deviated from the textbook in both classes, lecturing on crime, the problems of young adults from broken homes and the effects on society as a whole. My departures from textbook contents—which were largely drawn from my own experiences, unknown to the students—always sparked lively discussions and debates.

Weekends I relaxed by immersing myself in one or the other of Utah's scenic wonderlands, usually accompanied by an equally wondrous companion.

The summer was gone as swiftly as the desert spring, and I knew real regret when it ended. Dr. Vanderhoff and Dr. Grimes were delighted with my work. "Keep in touch with us, Frank," said Dr. Grimes. "If ever we have a permanent opening for a sociology professor, we'd like a chance to lure you down from the skies," said Dr. Grimes.

At least fifty of my students sought me out to tell me how much they had enjoyed my classes and to wish me good-bye and good luck.

I was reluctant to leave that Utah Utopia, but I could find no valid reason for staying. If I lingered, my past was certain to catch up, and I did not want these people's image of me to be tarnished.

I headed west to California. There was a storm building in the Sierras when I crossed the mountains, but it was nothing compared to the whirlwind of crime I was soon to create myself.

CHAPTER SIX

Paperhanger in a Rolls-Royce

The former police chief of Houston once said of me: "Frank Abagnale could write a check on toilet paper, drawn on the Confederate States Treasury, sign it 'U.R. Hooked' and cash it at any bank in town, using a Hong Kong driver's license for identification."

There are several bank employees in Eureka, California, who would endorse that statement. In fact, if it were put in the form of a resolution, there are scores of tellers and bank officials around the country who would second the motion.

I was not really that crude. But some of the moves I put on bank personnel were very, very embarrassing, not to mention costly.

Eureka, for me, was my commencement as an expert forger. I was already an advanced student of paperhanging when I arrived, of course, but I took my master's degree in check swindling in California.

I didn't purposely pick Eureka as a milestone in my capricious career. It was meant merely as a pit stop en route to San Francisco, but the inevitable girl appeared and I stayed to play house for a few days and to ruminate on my future. I was possessed by an urge to flee the country, vaguely fearful that a posse of FBI agents, sheriffs and detectives was hard on my heels. There was no tangible reason for such trepidation. I hadn't bilked anyone with a bouncing check in nearly two years, and "Co-pilot Frank Williams" had been in the closet for the same length of time. I should have been feeling reasonably safe, but I wasn't. I was nervous, fretful and doubtful, and I saw a cop in every man who gave me more than a casual look.

The girl and Eureka, between them, allayed my misgivings somewhat after a couple of days, the girl with her warm and willing ways and Eureka with its potential for elevating me from petty larceny to grand theft. Eureka, in California's northern redwood forests, perched on the edge of the Pacific, is a delightful little city. It has the picturesque allure of a Basque fishing village, and in fact a large and colorful fishing fleet operates out of Eureka's harbor.

The most fascinating facet of Eureka, to me, was its banks. It had more money houses for a city its size than any comparable city I'd ever visited. And I needed money, a lot of it, if I were going to be an expatriate paperhanger.

I still had several stacks of worthless personal checks, and I was sure I could scatter a dozen or more of them around town with ease, netting $1,000 or more. But it occurred to me that the personal-check dodge wasn't really that great. It was the easiest of bum-check capers, but it generated too much heat from too many points, and the penalty for passing a worthless $100 check was the same as that for dropping $5,000 in phony parchment.

I felt I needed a sweeter type of check, one that would

yield more honey for the same amount of nectar. Like a payroll check, say. Like a Pan Am payroll check, naturally. No one would ever be able to say I wasn't a loyal thief.

I went shopping. I obtained a book of blank counter checks from a stationery store. Such checks, still in wide use at the time, were ideal for my purposes, since it was left to the payer to fill in all the pertinent details, including the respondent bank's name. I then rented an IBM electric typewriter with several different typeface spheres, including script, and some extra ribbon cartridges in various carbon densities. I located a hobby shop that handled models of Pan Am's jets and bought several kits in the smaller sizes. I made a final stop at an art store and purchased a quantity of press-on magnetic-tape numerals and letters.

Thus provisioned, I retired to my motel room and set to work. I took one of the blank counter checks and across the top affixed a PAN AMERICAN WORLD AIRWAYS decal from one of the kits. Below the legend I typed in the airline's New York address. In the upper left-hand corner of the check I applied the Pan Am logo, and in the opposite right-hand corner I typed in the words "EXPENSE CHECK," on the premise that a firm's expense checks would differ in appearance from its regular payroll checks. It was a precautionary action on my part, since some Eureka bank tellers might have had occasion to handle regular Pan Am vouchers.

I made myself, "Frank Williams," the payee, of course, in the amount of $568.70, a sum that seemed reasonable to me. In the lower left-hand corner I typed in "CHASE MANHATTAN BANK" and the bank's address, going over the bank legend with progressively blacker ribbons until the words appeared to have been printed on the counterfeit check.

Below the bank legend, across the bottom left-hand corner of the check, I laid down a series of numbers with magnetic tape. The numbers purportedly represented the

Federal Reserve District of which Chase Manhattan was a member, the bank's FRD identification number and Pan Am's account number. Such numbers are very important to anyone cashing a check and tenfold as important to a hot-check swindler. A good paperhanger is essentially operating a numbers game and if he doesn't know the right ones he's going to end up with an entirely different set stenciled across the front and back of a state-issued shirt.

The fabricating of the check was exacting, arduous work, requiring more than two hours, and I was not at all happy with the finished product. I looked at it and decided it was not a check I would cash were I a teller and someone presented the check for payment.

But a thrift-shop dress is usually taken for high fashion when it's revealed under a mink coat. So I devised a mink cover for the rabbit-fur check. I took one of the windowed envelopes, hoaxed it up with a Pan Am decal and Pan Am's New York address, stuck a blank piece of stationery inside and mailed it to myself at my motel. The missive was delivered the following morning, and the local post office had unwittingly assisted me in my scheme. The clerk who had canceled the stamp had done such a botched job with the postmark that it was impossible to tell where the letter had been mailed from. I was delighted with the man's sloppiness.

I donned my Pan Am pilot's uniform, placed the check in the envelope and stuck it in the inside pocket of my jacket. I drove to the nearest bank, walked in jauntily and presented myself at a teller's booth attended by a young woman. "Hi," I said, smiling. "My name is Frank Williams and I'm vacationing here for a few days before reporting to Los Angeles. Would you please cash this check for me? I think I have sufficient identification."

I took the envelope from my inside pocket, extracted the check and laid it on the counter, along with my phony Pan Am ID card and my illicit FAA pilot's license. I purposely dropped the envelope, with its distinctive Pan Am logo and return address, on the counter.

The girl looked at my bogus identification documents and glanced at the check, but she seemed more interested in me. Commercial airline pilots in uniform were obviously a rarity in Eureka. She pushed the check back to me for endorsement, and while she counted out the money she asked chatty questions about my work and the places I'd been, questions I answered in a manner designed to bolster her apparent romantic image of airline pilots.

I was careful to take the envelope with me when I left. I had made certain that she noticed the wrapper, and it had patently enhanced her faith in the check. The transaction also verified a suspicion I had long entertained: it's not how good a check looks but how good the person behind the check looks that influences tellers and cashiers.

I went back to my motel room and labored late into the night concocting several more of the sham checks, all in the amount of $500 or more, and the following day I successfully passed all of them in different downtown or suburban banks. Based on my knowledge of the check-routing procedures used by banks, I calculated I could spend two more days in Eureka making and dropping the bum expense checks and then have three days lead time for travel before the first one was returned as a counterfeit.

But an identity crisis, which I experienced periodically, forced me to revise my timetable.

I never immersed myself so deeply in an assumed identity that I forgot I was really Frank Abagnale, Jr. In fact, in casual encounters with people, where I felt no compulsion to play-act and nothing was to be gained by affecting a guise, I invariably presented myself as Frank Abagnale, a foot-loose fellow from the Bronx.

It was no different in Eureka. Away from my motel, where I was registered as Frank Williams, or the girl, who had succumbed to a man she believed to be a Pan Am pilot, and out of the pilot's garb, I was simply Frank

Abagnale, Jr. To a degree, my actual identity became a refuge from the pressures and tensions of posing.

In Eureka I met a fisherman off a fishing boat in a seafood restaurant. He stopped at my table to tell me he had personally caught the very fish I was eating, and then sat down to converse with me. He was a car buff, it developed, and I told him about my old Ford and what I had done to dress up the car. "Hey, that's what I'm trying to fix up now, a 1950 Ford convertible," he said. "You don't have any pictures of your heap, do you?"

I shook my head. "I do, but they're all back in my room at home," I said.

"Gimme your address in New York and I'll send you some pictures of my wheels when I'm finished with it," he said. "Heck, I might even drive to New York and look you up."

It was very unlikely that he'd either write me or come to New York to see me, and just as unlikely that I'd be there to receive either his letter or him, so I searched my pockets for a piece of paper on which to jot down my name and New York address.

I came up with one of the blank counter checks. I borrowed a pencil from a waiter and was writing my name and New York address on the back of the check when the fisherman was called to the telephone, a pay phone on the wall near the door. He talked for a few minutes and then waved at me. "Hey, listen, Frank, I gotta go back to the boat," he shouted. "Come by tomorrow, willya?" He bolted out the door before I could reply. I gave the pencil back to the waiter and asked for my tab. "You need a pencil with heavier lead," I said, indicating what I had written on the back of the counter check. The words were barely discernible.

I put the check back in my pocket instead of tearing it up, an action that was to prove both foolish and fortunate. Back in my room, I dropped it on top of the open book of counter checks, changed clothes and called the girl. We spent a pleasant evening at a fine restaurant in the tall redwoods somewhere outside of Eureka.

It was such a pleasant evening that I was still recalling it early the next morning when I sat down to create three more phony Pan Am checks. There were only three banks left in and around Eureka that didn't have one of my artistic frauds, and I didn't want to slight any of the three. I was caught up in my new scheme. All my fears of a posse pounding down my backtrail were forgotten. I had also completely forgotten the young fisherman of the past afternoon.

Finished with the first check, I slipped it into the now well-used envelope. Less than two hours later I completed the other two and was ready for my farewell foray in Eureka, one that went off without a hitch. By mid-afternoon I was back in my motel room, adding nearly $1,500 to the currency-cushioned lining of my two-suiter.

That night I told the girl I would be leaving the following day. "I'll probably be flying out of Frisco or L.A., I don't know which," I lied. "Either way I'll be back often. I'll just rent a light plane and come up. We'll look at those redwoods from the top for a change."

She believed me. "That's a deal," she said, and suggested we go down to the wharves and eat seafood. She seemed more hungry than unhappy, which was agreeable with me. But halfway through the meal I looked out the window, saw a fishing boat coming in to the dock and remembered the young fisherman. I also remembered I had jotted down my real name and my New York address—my father's address, at least—on the back of one of the counter checks. I had a puckered feeling in the nether regions at the thought, as if someone had goosed me. What the hell had I done with that check? I couldn't recall offhand, and trying to remember and carry on an ardent conversation with my companion made my last night with the girl something less than memorable.

Back in my room, I searched for the blank check, but

to no avail. I had a lot of blank checks, but they were all still in the binder. I had to conclude that I'd made that particular blank check up as a sham Pan Am expense check and had passed it at one of the three banks. But I couldn't have, I told myself. I had to endorse each check on its back, and surely I'd have noticed the writing. But would I have? I recalled how light the pencil had been. My writing had been barely legible, even in the bright light of afternoon. I could easily have overlooked the scrawled words when I endorsed the check, especially in view of the operating procedure I'd developed in Eureka. I had found that palming off one of the fake vouchers went much smoother and quicker when I kept the teller's attention on me rather than the check. And to get a woman's attention, you have to pay attention to her.

I sat down on the bed and forced a total recall of the events that had resulted in the situation, and soon satisfied myself as to what had happened. I had dropped the loose check on top of the open book of counter checks. I had picked it up first the next morning, my encounter with the fisherman unremembered, when I made up the three counterfeit expense checks. And I had placed it in the phonied-up envelope immediately after finishing it, so therefore it had been the first of the three cashed. And I now recalled the teller who'd cashed the check for me. I'd given her lots of attention. Too much, it seemed.

And a certain bank in Eureka had a counterfeit Pan Am expense check endorsed by a counterfeit co-pilot, but also bearing on the back the signature of Frank Abagnale, Jr., and the address of his father in the Bronx. Once the check was exposed as a fraud, it wouldn't take a Sherlock Holmes to make the connection. And the case.

I suddenly felt hotter than a blast furnace. I started thinking again of leaving the country, jumping the border into Mexico. Or even more southerly climes. But this time I contemplated the idea reluctantly. In Eureka I'd devised what I considered a grand new theft scheme, one that paid off better than doctored dice in a crap game. And heady with the success of the system, I'd set aside my fears of being closely pursued and had convinced myself that I was as cool as an arctic ice floe. I had intended to work my counterfeit check scam from coast to coast and border to border. It chafed me to have to abandon my plans because I'd stupidly blown my cover.

But did I have to give up the game? Had I blown my cover at this point? If I hadn't noticed the scribbling on the back of the check, maybe no one else had, either.

There was also a good possibility the check was still in the bank. I'd cashed it early in the afternoon, and it was possible it wouldn't be routed to New York until the morrow. If it hadn't left the bank, perhaps I could purchase it back. I could tell them Pan Am had issued the check in error and I shouldn't have cashed it, or some such concocted tale. I was sure I could come up with a good story if the check was still on hand. I fell asleep mulling feasible excuses to offer.

I packed, stowed my gear in my car and paid my motel bill before calling the bank the next morning. I asked for the head teller and was connected with a woman who identified herself as "Stella Waring" in brisk tones.

"Mrs. Waring, a Pan Am pilot cashed a check in your bank yesterday," I said. "Can you tell me . . . " She cut me off before I could say more.

"Yes, a bogus check," she said, abruptly indignant and without asking my identity or my reason for calling. "We've notified the FBI. They're supposed to be sending an agent for the check."

I wasn't challenged. I acted on impulse, an incitement to protect my real identity. "Yes," I said. "This is the FBI. I wanted to alert you that our agent will be there in about fifteen minutes. Do you have the check, or is there someone else he should contact?"

"Just have him see me, sir, I'll have the check," Mrs.

Waring replied. "Of course, we'd like a Xerox of the check for our records. That is all right, isn't it?"

"Of course," I assured her. "I will instruct Mr. Davis to provide you with a copy."

I was at the bank within five minutes, dressed in a blue business suit, but I discreetly cased the interior before entering. The teller who had cashed the check was nowhere in sight.

Had she been, I would not have entered. I didn't know whether she was on a coffee break or what, and I was uneasy about her appearing while I was in the bank, but I was driven to take the risk. I strode into the lobby and the receptionist directed me to Mrs. Waring's desk at one side of the floor. She was a trim, handsome woman in her thirties, with the dress and air of the complete businesswoman. She looked up as I stopped in front of her desk.

"Mrs. Waring, I'm Bill Davis of the FBI. I believe my boss called you earlier?" I said.

She nodded with a grimace. "Oh, yes, Mr. Davis," she said. "I have the check right here." She did not ask for credentials or seem suspicious of my status at all. She merely produced the check from a drawer and handed it to me. I examined it with a professional air, an attitude easily assumed since I was the manufacturer. On the back, barely perceivable, was my real name and my father's address.

"It looks pretty junky," I observed dryly. "I'm surprised anyone would cash it."

Mrs. Waring smiled sour agreement. "Yes, we have some girls here that, well, they see a handsome pilot or some other man that presents a romantic figure, and they tend to lose their cool. They're more interested in the man than in what he's handing them," she said in disapproving tones. "The girl who took this check, Miss Caster, was so upset she didn't even come in this morning."

I relaxed at the information and began to enjoy my pose

as a G-man. "Well, we will have to talk to her, but we can do that later," I said. "Have you made a copy of this yet?"

"No, but there's a Xerox machine right there in the corner, it'll only take me a minute," she said.

"I'll do it," I said, and walked quickly to the machine before she could object. I copied only the front of the check, a factor she didn't notice when I laid it on her desk.

"Let me sign this and date it," I said, picking up a pen. "This copy is your receipt. You understand we need this original as evidence. It will be in the custody of the U.S. Attorney. I think this is all we need at the moment, Mrs. Waring. We certainly appreciate your cooperation." I pocketed the damning original and left.

I learned later that I exited the bank barely five minutes before the actual FBI agent—Eureka's only G-man, in fact—arrived. I also learned later that Mrs. Waring herself was more than a little upset when she learned she had been duped, but then FBI agents do have a certain romantic aura of their own and a woman doesn't have to be young to be impressed by a glamorous figure.

Posing as an FBI agent was not the smartest move I made at that point in my criminal career. Federal agents are generally highly efficient officers, but they are even more efficient and determined when someone impersonates an FBI agent. I had circumvented, temporarily, the disclosure that Frank Williams, pilot poseur, was in reality Frank Abagnale, Jr., but unknowingly I furnished O'Riley a fresh trail to follow and thereafter it was hound and hare to the end.

However, I was still in a learning stage as a forger, albeit an advanced student, and I tended to take risks an experienced check thief would shudder to chance. I was an independent actor, writing, producing and directing my own scripts. I did not know any professional criminals, I didn't seek out criminal expertise and I shunned any place that smacked of being a criminal haunt.

The people who assisted me in my dubious capers were all honest, legitimate, respectable folk whom I duped or conned into lending me help. In reality, my total autonomy was the biggest factor in my success. The usual criminal sources of information for the police were useless to them in their search for me. The underworld grapevine simply had no intelligence on me. While my true identity was established midway in my course, the leads garnered by police were all after-the-fact leads. I was always several days gone by the time my misdeeds were exposed as such, and officers were never able to pick up my trail until I struck again, usually in some far-off city.

Once I embarked on counterfeiting checks, I realized I had reached a point of no return. I had chosen paperhanging as a profession, my means of surviving, and having chosen a nefarious occupation, I set out to perfect my working skills. In the ensuing weeks and months, I studied check transactions and banking procedures as diligently as any investor studies the markets available to him, and I did my homework in unobtrusive ways. I dated tellers and picked their brains while stroking their bodies. I went to libraries and perused banking magazines, journals and trade books. I read financial publications and created opportunities to converse with bank officials. All my wrongful techniques, in short, were polished with rightful wax.

Of course, as someone once observed, there is no right way to do something wrong, but the most successful check swindlers have three factors in their favor, and any one of the three, or the scantiest combination of the three, can pay off like three bars on a slot machine.

The first is personality, and I look on personal grooming as part of one's personality. Top con artists, whether they're pushing hot paper or hawking phony oil leases, are well dressed and exude an air of confidence and authority. They're usually, too, as charming, courteous and

113

seemingly sincere as a politician seeking reelection, although they can, at times, effect the cool arrogance of a tycoon.

The second is observation. Observation is a skill that can be developed, but I was born blessed (or cursed) with the ability to pick up on details and items the average man overlooks. Observation, as I will illustrate later, is the only necessity for successful innovative larceny. A newsman who did a story on me noted, "A good con man reads sign like an Indian, and Frank Abagnale would have made the best Pawnee scout on the frontier look like a half-blind tenderfoot."

The third factor is research, the big difference between the hard-nosed criminal and the super con man. A hood planning a bank holdup might case the treasury for rudimentary facts, but in the end he depends on his gun. A con artist's only weapon is his brain. A con man who decides to hit the same bank with a fictitious check or a sophisticated check swindle researches every facet of the caper. In my heyday as a hawker of hot paper, I knew as much about checks as any teller employed in any bank in the world and more than the majority. I'm not even sure a great many bankers possessed the knowledge I had of checks.

Here are some examples of the things I knew about checks and most tellers didn't, little things that enabled me to fleece them like sheep. All legitimate checks, for instance, will have at least one perforated (or scalloped) edge. The edge will be at the top if taken from a personal checkbook, on two or three sides if taken from a business check ledger. Some knowledgeable firms even scallop all four sides of their checks. An ingenious check counterfeiter can duplicate such vouchers, of course, but only if he invests $40,000 or more in a perforating press, and if he did that he'd hardly be ingenious. It's not something one can tote around in a suitcase.

There are worthless checks that have a perforated edge,

of course, but the checks aren't bogus. The account is. In every instance where I passed a personal check, I was actually passing an insufficient check. Whenever I went off on a personal-check-passing tangent, I would first open up a legitimate checking account, using a phony name, in order to get fifty to one hundred personalized checks. And, as mentioned previously, the first one or two I wrote were usually good. After that I was flying kites.

I said earlier that the good check swindler is really operating a numbers game, and he is. All checks, whether personal or business, have a series of numbers in the lower left-hand corners, just above the bottoms. Take a personal check that has the numbers 1130 0119 546 085 across the bottom left-hand corner. During my reign as a rip-off champion, not one out of a hundred tellers or private cashiers paid any attention to such numerals, and I'm convinced that only a handful of the people handling checks knew what the series of numbers signified. I'll decode it:

The number 11 denotes that the check was printed within the Eleventh Federal Reserve District. There are twelve and only twelve Federal Reserve Districts in the United States. The Eleventh includes Texas, where this check was printed. The 3 after the 11 tells one that the check was printed in Houston specifically, for the Third District Office of the FRD is located in that city. The 0 indicates that immediate credit is available on the check. In the middle series of numbers, the 0 identifies the clearing house (Houston) and the 119 is the bank's identification number within the district. The 546 085 is the account number assigned the customer by the bank.

How does that knowledge benefit a check counterfeiter? With a bundle in his swag and a running head start, that's how. Say such a man presents a payroll check to a teller or cashier for payment. It is a fine-looking check, issued by a large and reputable Houston firm, payable at a Houston bank, or so it states on the face of the chit. The series of numbers in the lower left-hand corner, however, starts

115

with the number 12, but the teller or cashier doesn't notice that, or if she/he does, she/he, is ignorant of the meaning of the numbers.

A computer isn't. When the check lands in the clearing-house bank, usually the same night, a computer will kick it out, because, while the face of the check says it's payable in Houston, the numbers say it's payable in San Francisco and bank computers read only numbers. The check, therefore, is sorted into a batch of checks going to the Twelfth District, San Francisco in this instance, for collection. In San Francisco another computer will reject the check because the bank identification number doesn't jibe, and at that point the check lands in the hands of a clearing-house bank clerk. In most instances, the clerk will note only the face of the check, see that it is payable at a Houston bank and hand-mail it back, attributing its arrival in San Francisco to computer error. In any event, five to seven days have passed before the person who cashed the check is aware he or she has been swindled, and the paperhanger has long since hooked 'em.

I got rich off the ignorance of bank personnel concerning their own numerical codes and the lack of knowledge of checks on the part of people who cashed checks. In San Francisco, where I tarried for several weeks after fleeing Eureka, I manufactured several dozen of the phony Pan Am expense checks and passed them in San Francisco banks, at the airport and in banks or hotels in surrounding communities, coding the checks so they were routed to such distant points as Boston, Philadelphia, Cleveland and Richmond.

No forty-niner ever struck it richer in them thar California hills than I did. My fabricated envelope was still an invaluable aid in cashing the fake vouchers, but I used it so much in the Bay Area that it started to come apart at the seams. I needed a new one.

And why not a real one? I reasoned. San Francisco was one of Pan Am's bases, and I was a Pan Am pilot, wasn't

I? Hell no, I wasn't, but who out at Pan Am operations would know that? I went to the airport and boldly sauntered into the Pan Am operations complex. "Say, where can I get some writing paper and envelopes? I'm a stranger here," I asked the first person I encountered, a radio operator.

"The stockroom, around the corner there," he said, pointing. "Help yourself."

I did, since the stockroom was unattended. I grabbed a batch of envelopes, a stack of stationery with Pan Am's letterhead, stuffed them in my briefcase and was leaving when another stack of forms caught my eye. "CHECK AUTHORIZATION," said the bold letters across the head of the top form. I picked up a sheaf and examined the top document. The forms were requests for advance expense checks or compensation for expenses incurred, authorizing the company cashier to issue a check to the named bearer when signed by Pan Am's San Francisco manager. I put a packet of the forms in my briefcase, too. No one spoke to me as I left. I don't think anyone I encountered paid the slightest heed to me.

The check authorization form was a lovely little helper. I'd fold it around one of my bastard brainchildren before slipping the check into an authentic Pan Am envelope. I always made certain that the authorization form, properly if not legally filled out, and the envelope were prominently in evidence when I cashed one of my check creations.

One day I returned from foraging among Berkeley's money houses to find there was no room in either my suitcase or my duffel bag for clothes. They were both full of loose bills. I was stealing faster than I could spend. I took $25,000, went to a San Jose bank, rented a safe-deposit box under the name of John Calcagne, paid three years' rent in advance and stowed the cash in the box. The next day I went to a bank in Oakland and repeated the procedure, using the name Peter Morelli.

Then I went back to San Francisco and fell in love.

117

Her name was Rosalie and she was a stewardess for American Airlines. She lived in an old house with five roommates, all stews for American, too, and I met her when I encountered the six of them on a bus returning from the airport. They had been to the airport on legitimate business. I had been there perpetrating a little light larceny. We started dating that same night.

Rosalie was one of the loveliest women I'd ever met, and I still think so. She had frosted blond hair and, as I learned quickly, something of a frosted nature. At twenty-four she was still a virgin, and she informed me on our second date that she intended to stay chaste until her wedding day. I told her I admired her attitude, and I did, but it still didn't stop me from trying to undress her anytime we were alone.

As a companion, Rosalie was delightful. We shared an enjoyment of music, good books, the ocean, skiing, the theater, travel and a score of other pleasures and pursuits. Rosalie was devoutly religious, and like me a Catholic, but she did not insist that I attend mass with her.

"Why don't you preach to me about my sins?" I asked her in a bantering tone one day after picking her up at church.

She laughed. "I don't know that you have any, Frank," she replied. "You sure don't have any bad habits that I'm aware of. I like you like you are."

I found myself getting closer to Rosalie each time I was with her. She had so many good qualities. She seemed the epitome of the kind of woman most young bachelors dream of finding for a wife: she was loyal, clean-cut, intelligent, even-tempered, considerate, lovely and she didn't smoke or drink. She was all apple pie, American flag, mom and sis and spring rolled up in a Girl Scout sash.

"Rosalie, I love you," I said to her one night.

She nodded. "I love you, too, Frank," she said quietly.

"Why don't we go visit my parents and tell them about us?"

Her parents lived in Downey, south of Los Angeles. It was a long drive, and en route we stopped and rented a cabin near Pismo Beach. We had a wonderful evening, and when we resumed our journey the next morning, Rosalie was no longer a virgin. I really felt bad about it, for I thought I should have been more considerate of her virtue, which I knew full well she valued highly. I apologized repeatedly as we drove down the coast in her car, which she had insisted we use.

Rosalie snuggled up to me and smiled. "Stop apologizing, Frank," she said. "I wanted to do it. Anyway, we'll just add that one to our wedding night."

Her parents were nice people. They welcomed me warmly, and when Rosalie told them we were going to be married, they were enthusiastic and congratulated us warmly. For two days all I heard was wedding plans although I hadn't actually asked Rosalie to marry me. But it seemed taken for granted that I had, and her parents obviously approved of me.

But how could I marry her? She thought I was Frank Williams, a Pan Am co-pilot with a bright future. I knew I couldn't maintain the pose if we were married. It would be only a matter of time before she learned I was really Frank Abagnale, a teen-aged swindler with a phony front and a dirty past. I couldn't do that to Rosalie, I told myself.

Or could I? I had $80,000 or $90,000 in cash, ample funds to finance the beginning of a marriage. Maybe Rosalie would believe me if I told her I didn't want to fly anymore, that I'd always wanted to own and operate a stationery store. I didn't, really, but it was the one honest trade in which I was versed. I dismissed the idea. I would still be "Frank Williams," and Frank Williams would still be a hunted outlaw.

What started as a pleasant visit turned into an ordeal

119

for me. I felt I really loved Rosalie, and I felt I really wanted to marry her, but I didn't see how under the circumstances.

However, Rosalie thought she was going to marry me. And her parents thought she was going to marry me. They happily charged ahead, setting the date for a month hence, making up a list of whom to invite, planning the reception and doing all the things parents and a daughter do when the girl's about to become a bride. I took part in many of the discussions, outwardly happy and eager for the day, but inwardly I was tortured with guilt, burning with shame and totally miserable. I had told Rosalie and her parents that my parents were on a European vacation, and they agreed they should wait until my parents returned, which I said should be within ten days, before finalizing any plans.

"I'm sure your mother will want to have a hand in this, Frank," said Rosalie's mother.

"I'm sure she would," I lied, although I was sure my mother would like to get her hands on me.

I didn't know what to do. I was staying in Rosalie's home, in the guest room, and at night I'd lie in my bed and I could hear the murmur of her parents' voices in their room across the hall, and I knew they were talking about their daughter's marriage to such a fine young man. It made me feel rotten.

One afternoon Rosalie and I went bike riding and we ended up in a park, sitting under a giant shade tree, and Rosalie, as usual, was chattering about our future—where we'd live, how many kids we'd have and so on. I looked at her as she talked and suddenly I felt she'd understand, that she loved me enough to not only understand but to forgive. One of the traits I loved most in her was her compassion.

I put my hand gently over her mouth. "Rosalie," I said, and I was surprised at my calmness and composure. "I need to tell you something, and I want you to try and understand. If I didn't love you so much, I wouldn't tell you this at all, for I've never told anyone what I'm going to tell you. And I'm telling you, Rosalie, because I love you and I do want us to get married.

"Rosalie, I am not a pilot for Pan American. I'm not twenty-eight, Rosalie. I'm nineteen. My name is not Frank Williams. My name is Frank Abagnale. I'm a crook, Rosalie, an impostor and a check swindler, and I'm wanted by the police all over the country."

She looked at me, shocked. "Are you serious?" she finally said. "But I met you at the airport. You have a pilot's license. I've seen it! You have a Pan Am ID card. You were in uniform, Frank! Why are you saying these things, Frank? What is the matter with you?"

She laughed nervously. "You're kidding me, Frank!"

I shook my head. "No, Rosalie, I'm not. Everything I've said is true," I said, and I laid it all out for her, from the Bronx to Downey. I talked for an hour, watching her face as I talked and seeing her eyes mirror in turn horror, disbelief, agony, despair and pity before her emotions were hidden behind a curtain of tears.

She buried her hands in her hair and wept uncontrollably for what seemed an eternity. Then she took my handkerchief, wiped her eyes and face and stood up. "Let's go back home, Frank," she said quietly.

"You go on, Rosalie," I said. "I'll be there shortly, but I need to be alone for a while. And Rosalie, don't say anything to anyone until I get there. When your parents learn about this, I want them to hear it from me. Promise me that, Rosalie."

She nodded. "I promise, Frank. I'll see you later."

She pedaled off, a lovely woman reduced to a forlorn figure at the moment. I got on my bike and rode around, thinking. Rosalie hadn't said a lot, really. She certainly hadn't told me everything would be all right, that she forgave me and we'd be married anyway. I really didn't know what she was thinking, or what her reaction would be when I reappeared at her home. Should I even go back? All I had at her house were some sports clothes, a couple of suits, underwear and shaving kit. I'd left my uniform in my motel room in San Francisco, and I had my fake ID and phony pilot's license in my pocket. I had never told Rosalie where I lived. I'd always called her or gone to her home. When she asked me once, I told her I lived with a couple of kooky pilots in Alameda and they were so weird they wouldn't have a telephone or television in the apartment.

That had seemed to satisfy her. She wasn't at all an inquisitive person, tending to take people as they presented themselves. That's one reason I enjoyed her company and had dated her more than usual. I felt safe around her.

But I didn't feel safe at the moment and I was beginning to doubt the wisdom of my impromptu confession. I forced myself to brush aside my misgivings. Whatever else she might do, in light of what she now knew, Rosalie wouldn't betray me, I told myself.

I contemplated phoning her to get a reading on what her feelings were now, but decided to face her and press for a decision. I approached her home from a side street and just before reaching the corner I stopped, laid the bike down and walked along a hedge bordering a neighbor's yard until I had a view of her house through the foliage.

Parked in front of Rosalie's home was an L.A. black-and-white, and a second vehicle, which, while not marked, was plainly a cop car, was parked in the driveway. A uniformed policeman was in the squad car scanning the street.

My lovely Rosalie had finked on me.

I went back to the bike and pedaled off in the opposite direction. When I reached the downtown district, I parked the bike and caught a cab to the Los Angeles airport. Within thirty minutes I was in the air, returning to San

Francisco. I was plagued with a feeling I couldn't identify the entire trip, and the nebulous emotion stayed with me as I packed, paid my motel bill and returned to the airport. I bought a ticket to Las Vegas, using the name James Franklin, and I left the Barracuda in the airport parking lot, the keys in the ignition. It was the first of many cars I purchased and abandoned.

I was still possessed by the odd feeling during the flight to Las Vegas. It wasn't anger. It wasn't sadness. It wasn't guilt. I couldn't put my finger on it until I stepped off the plane in Nevada. Then I identified the emotion.

It was relief. I was happy to have Rosalie out of my life! The knowledge astonished me, for not six hours past I'd been desperately seeking a way to make her my wife. Astonished or not, I was still relieved.

It was my first trip to Las Vegas and the city was everything and more than I'd imagined. There was a frantic, electric aura about the whole city, and the people, visitors and residents alike, seemed to be rushing around in a state of frenetic expectation. New York was a city of leisurely calm in comparison. "Gambling fever," explained a cabbie when I mentioned the dynamic atmosphere.

"Everybody's got it. Everybody's out to make a killing, especially the johns. They fly in on jets or driving big wheels and leave on their thumbs. The only winners in this town are the houses. Everybody else is a loser. Take my advice—if you're gonna play, play the dolls. A lot of them are hungry."

I took a suite at a motel and paid two weeks' rent in advance. The registration clerk wasn't impressed at all by the wad of $100 bills from which I peeled the hotel charge. A big roll in Vegas is like pocket change in Peoria, I soon learned.

I intended Las Vegas to be just an R & R stop. I followed the cabbie's advice and played the chicks. He was right about the girls. Most of them were hungry. Actually hungry. Famished, in fact. After a week with some of the more ravenous ones, I felt like Moses feeding the multitudes.

However, as the Good Book sayeth: He that giveth unto the poor shall not lack.

I am feeding a famished gamin poolside. She has been living on casino free lunches for three days while trying to contact a brother in Phoenix to ask for bus fare home. "I blew everything," she said ruefully while devouring a huge steak with all the trimmings. "All the money I brought with me, all the money in my checking account, all I could raise on my jewelry. I even cashed in my return airline ticket. It's a good thing my room was paid in advance or I'd be sleeping on lobby couches."

She grinned cheerfully. "Serves me right. I've never gambled before, and I didn't intend to gamble when I came here. But the damned place gets to you."

She looked at me quizzically. "I hope you're just being nice, buying me dinner. I know there're ways a girl can get things in this burg, but that ain't my style, man."

I laughed. "Relax. I like your style. Are you going back to a job in Phoenix?"

She nodded. "I am if I can get hold of Bud. But I may not have a job if I'm not back by Monday."

"What do you do?" I asked. She looked the secretary type.

"I'm a check designer for a firm that designs and prints checks," she said. "A commercial artist, really. It's a small firm, but we do work for a couple of big banks and a lot of business firms."

I was astonished. "Well, I'll be darned," I ventured. "That's interesting. What do you do when you design and print a check?"

"Oh, it depends on whether we're making up plain checks or fancy ones; you know, the kind with pictures, landscapes and different colors. It's a simple operation for just plain checks. I just lay it out on a big paste-up board however the customer wants it, and then we photograph it with an I-Tek camera, reducing it to size, and the camera produces an engraving. We just put the engraving on a little offset press and print up the check in blocks or sheets. Anybody could do it, really, with a little training."

Her name was Pixie. I leaned over and kissed her on the forehead. "Pixie, how'd you like to go home tonight, by air?" I asked.

"You're kidding me?" she accused, her eyes wary.

"No, I'm not," I assured her. "I'm an airline pilot for Pan Am. We don't fly out of here, but I have deadhead privileges. I can get you a seat to Phoenix on any airline that serves Vegas from there. All it'll cost is a little white lie. I'll say you're my sister. No other strings attached, okay?"

"Hey, all right!" she said delightedly and gave me a big bear hug.

While she packed, I bought her a ticket, paying for it in cash. I took her to the airport and pressed a $100 bill in her hand as she boarded the plane. "No arguments," I said. "That's a loan. I'll be around to collect one of these days."

I did get to Phoenix, but I made no effort to contact her. If I had, it wouldn't have been to collect but to pay off, for Pixie let me into the mint.

The next day I sought out a stationery printing supply firm. "I'm thinking of starting a little stationery store and job printing shop," I told a salesman.

"I've been advised that an I-Tek camera and a small offset press would probably meet my initial needs, and that good used equipment might prove just as feasible from an economic standpoint."

The salesman nodded. "That's true," he agreed. "Trouble is, used I-Tek cameras are hard to come by. We don't have one. We do have a fine little offset press that's seen

125

very limited service, and I'll make you a good deal on the press if you take it along with a new I-Tek. Let you have both for $8,000."

I was somewhat surprised by the price, but after he showed me the machines and demonstrated the operating procedure of both, I felt $8,000 was a paltry sum to invest in such gems. An I-Tek camera is simply a photoelectric engraver. It photographically produces an engraving of the original copy to be reproduced. The lightweight, flexible plate is then wrapped around the cylinder of an offset press, and the plate prints directly on the blanket of the press, which in turn offsets the image onto whatever paper stock is used. As Pixie said, anybody could do it with a little training, and I acquired my training on the spot.

The I-Tek camera and the small press, while not overly heavy, were large and bulky, not objects to be carted around the country as part of one's luggage. But I planned only a limited ownership of the machines.

I located a warehouse storage firm and rented a well-lighted cubicle for a month, paying in advance. I then obtained a cashier's check for $8,000 and bought the I-Tek camera and the press and had them delivered to the storage room. The same day I made a round of stationery stores and purchased all the supplies I needed—a drawing board, pens and pencils, rulers, a paper cutter, press-on letters and numerals, a quantity of safety paper in both blue and green card stock of the type used for the real expense checks and other items.

The next day I closeted myself in my makeshift workshop and, using the various materials, created a 16-by-24-inch facsimile of the sham Pan Am expense check I'd been reproducing by hand. Finished, I positioned my artwork under the camera, set the reduction scale for a 3½-by-7½-inch engraving and pushed the button. Within minutes I was fitting the plate around the drum of the press and printing sample copies of my invention.

I was astonished and delighted. The camera reduction had taken away any infractions and discrepancies in lines and lettering as far as the naked eye could discern. Using the paper cutter, I sliced one from the card stock and examined it. Save for the four smooth edges, I might have been holding a genuine check!

I ran off five hundred of the counterfeit checks before shutting down the little press and abandoning both it and the I-Tek camera. I went back to my hotel room, donned my pilot's uniform, stuck a packet of the checks in my coat and went out to buck the tiger.

The tiger, for me, was a pussy cat. I ironed out Vegas like a bed sheet. That afternoon and night, and the following day, I hit nearly a hundred casinos, bars, hotels, motels, night clubs and other gambling spots, and in Vegas almost any place you walk into offers some kind of action. There're slot machines In the grocery stores. No cashier showed the slightest hesitation about cashing one of my phony checks. "Would you cash this and give me $50 in chips?" I'd ask, and promptly I'd be handed $50 in markers and the balance in cash. For appearance's sake, I'd usually stay in a casino for twenty or thirty minutes, playing the tables, before hitting the next place, and much to my amusement I whacked out the casinos that way too.

I came out $300 ahead playing the slots. I won $1,600 playing blackjack. Without the slightest inkling of the game, I picked up $900 playing roulette, and I won $2,100 at the dice tables. In all, I murdered Vegas for $39,000! I left Nevada driving a rented Cadillac, although I had to put up a $1,000 deposit when I told the lessor I'd probably be using the car several weeks.

I had it for nearly three months, as a matter of fact. I made a leisurely, meandering tour of the Northwest and Midwest, maintaining the pose of an airline pilot on vacation and alternating in the role of Frank Williams and Frank Adams. Since I didn't want to leave the hounds a trail that could be too easily followed, I didn't exactly scatter my counterfeits like confetti but I did stop to make a score now and then. I picked up $5,000 in Salt Lake City, $2,000 in Billings, $4,000 in Cheyenne and I bilked Kansas City banks for $18,000 before ending up in Chicago, where I simply parked the Cadillac and walked away.

I decided to hole up in Chicago for a while and give some serious thought to the future, or at least where I wanted to spend a great deal of the future. I was again entertaining the idea of fleeing the country. I wasn't too concerned about my immediate security, but I knew that if I continued to operate in the U.S. it would be only a matter of time before I was nabbed. The principal problem I faced in trying to leave the country, of course, was obtaining a passport. I couldn't apply for one in my own name since blabbing to Rosalie, and by now the authorities must have linked Frank Williams and Frank Adams to Frank Abagnale, Jr. I mulled the situation as I went about settling in Chicago, but as things turned out I didn't have too much time for mulling.

I leased a nice apartment on Lakeshore Drive, using the name Frank Williams. I did so primarily because I was out of personalized checks and I always liked to have a supply in my possession. A lot of motels, I had learned, would not cash a company check but would accept a personal check in the amount of the bill or in cash amounts up to $100. I had forsaken personal checks as a means of swindling, but I still used them as a means of paying room rent when necessary. I didn't like to lay out hard cash when I could slide one of my soft checks.

Accordingly, I dropped into a bank a week after alighting in Chicago and opened a checking account for $500. I identified myself as a Pan Am pilot, and gave as my address for the checks that of a mail service firm in New York to which I'd recently subscribed as another means of covering my trail. "But I want my checks and my month-ly statements mailed to this address," I instructed the bank officer who handled the transaction, giving him my Lakeshore Drive address.

"You see, the reason I want an account here is because I'm in and out of Chicago all the time on company business and it's much more convenient to have an account in a local bank."

The bank officer agreed. "You'll receive your regular checks in about a week, Mr. Williams. In the meantime, here're some temporary checks you can use," he said.

Observation. A great asset for a con man, I've said. I had observed a very lovely teller when I entered the bank. Her image remained in my mind after I left the bank, and when she persisted in my thoughts over the next few days I determined to meet her. I returned to the bank several days later on the pretext of making a deposit and was filling out a deposit slip I had taken from a counter in the middle of the lobby when an even higher power of observation took command of my mind.

In the lower left-hand corner of the deposit slip was a rectangular box for the depositor's account number. I never filled in the box, for I knew it wasn't required. When a teller put a deposit slip in the small machine in his or her cage, in order to furnish you with a stamped receipt, the machine was programed to read the account number first. If the number was there, the amount of the deposit was automatically credited to the account holder. But if the number wasn't there, the account could still be credited using the name and address, so the number wasn't necessary.

There was a fellow beside me filling out a deposit slip. I noticed he neglected to give his account number. I dawdled in the bank for nearly an hour and watched those who came in to deposit cash, checks or credit-card vouchers. Not one in twenty, if that many, used the space provided for his or her account number.

I forgot about the girl. I surreptitiously pocketed a sheaf of the deposit slips, returned to my apartment and, using press-on numerals matching the type face on the bank forms, filled in the blank on each slip with my own account number.

The following morning, I returned to the bank and just as stealthily put the sheaf of deposit slips back in a slot atop a stack of others. I didn't know if my ploy would succeed or not, but it was worth a risk. Four days later I returned to the bank and made a $250 deposit. "By the way, what's my balance, please?" I asked the teller. "I forgot to enter some checks I wrote this week."

The teller obligingly called bookkeeping. "Your balance, including this deposit, is $42,876.45, Mr. Williams," she said.

Just before the bank closed, I returned and drew out $40,000 in a cashier's check, explaining I was buying a home. I didn't buy a home, of course, but I sure did feather my nest. The next morning I cashed the check at another bank and that afternoon flew to Honolulu, where a pretty Hawaiian girl greeted me with a kiss and put a lei around my neck.

I was a cad when it came to reciprocating. During the next two weeks I fashioned a $38,000 lei of fraudulent checks, spent three days hanging it around the necks of banks and hotels on the islands of Oahu, Hawaii, Maui and Kauai, and then jetted to New York.

It was the first time I'd been back in New York since hitting the paperhanger's trail, and I was tempted to call Mom and Dad and maybe even see them. I decided against any such action, however, as much from shame as anything else. I might return home a financial success beyond either Mom's or Dad's comprehension, but mine was not the kind of success either of them would appreciate or condone.

I stayed in New York just long enough to devise a new scam. I opened a checking account in one of the Chase

Manhattan branches, and when I received my personalized checks, in the name of Frank Adams, with the address of an East Side flat I'd rented, I flew to Philadelphia and scouted the city's banks. I selected one with an all-glass front, enabling prospective depositors to see all the action inside and providing the bank officers, whose desks lined the glass wall, with a good view of the cash inflow.

I wanted them to have a very pleasant view of me, so I arrived the next morning in a Rolls-Royce driven by a chauffeur I had hired for the occasion.

As the chauffeur opened the door for me, I saw one of the bank officers had indeed noticed my arrival. When I entered the bank, I walked directly to him. I had dressed befitting a man with a chauffeured Rolls-Royce—custom-tailored three-piece suit in pearl gray, a $100 homburg and alligator Ballys—and the look in his eyes told me the young banker recognized my grooming as another indication of wealth and power.

"Good morning," I said briskly, taking a seat in front of his desk. "My name is Frank Adams, Adams Construction Company of New York. We'll be doing three construction projects here during the year and I want to transfer some funds here from my New York bank. I want to open a checking account with you people."

"Yes, sir!" he replied enthusiastically, reaching for some forms. "Will you be transferring all your funds here, Mr. Adams?"

"As far as my personal funds are concerned, yes," I said. "I'm not sure about the company funds as yet, and won't be until I look closer at the projects, but in any event we'll want to place a substantial amount here."

"Well, for your personal account, Mr. Adams, all you have to do is write me a check for the remaining balance in your New York bank and that will close that account out."

"Is that all?" I said, feigning surprise. "I didn't realize it was that simple." I took my checkbook from my inside pocket and, holding it so he couldn't see it, ran my finger down an imaginary column of figures, murmuring. Then I looked up at him. "May I use your adding machine, please? I wrote some checks yesterday and didn't balance my checkbook and I'm not much on adding figures in my head."

"Certainly," he said and turned the machine for my use. I ran a few figures and then nodded.

"Well, I make my balance $17,876.28, and I'm sure that's correct," I said. "But let's just open an account for $17,000. I'll be going back to New York on occasion and I'd like to maintain a small balance there."

I wrote him a check for $17,000 and gave him the necessary information for setting up an account. I gave my address as the hotel where I had registered. "I'll be staying there until I can find a suitable apartment or house to lease," I said.

The young banker nodded. "You realize, of course, Mr. Adams, you can't write any checks on your account until your check has cleared in New York," he said. "That shouldn't take over four or five days, however, and in the meantime if you run short of funds, come to me and I'll take care of it. Here are some temporary checks for such an event."

I shook my head. "That's kind of you, but I anticipated the delay," I said. "I have ample funds for my needs."

I shook hands with him and left. That night I flew to Miami and the following afternoon I appeared in front of another glass-fronted bank, again in a Rolls-Royce but at the wheel myself, and casually but again expensively attired. I glanced at my watch as I entered the lobby. The Philadelphia bank would be open for another thirty minutes. A strikingly handsome and chicly dressed woman who had noted my arrival greeted me as I stepped into the lobby.

"May I help you, sir?" she asked, smiling. On closer

inspection she was much older than I had first thought, but she was still an alluring woman.

"I hope so," I said, returning the smile. "But I think I'd better speak to the bank manager."

Her eyes lit impishly. "I am the bank manager," she said, laughing. "Now, what's your problem? You certainly don't appear to need a loan."

I threw up my hands in mock defeat. "No, no, nothing like that," I said. "My name's Frank Adams and I'm from Philadelphia and I've been looking around Miami for years for a suitable vacation home. Well, today I found a fantastic deal, a floating house near Biscayne Bay, but the man wants cash and he wants a $15,000 deposit by five o'clock today. He won't take a personal check and I don't have a bank account here.

"I'm wondering, could I write you a check on my bank in Philadelphia and you issue me a cashier's check, payable to cash, for $15,000? I realize you'll have to call my bank to verify that I have the money, but I'll pay for the call. I really want this house. It would mean I could spend half my time down here." I paused, a pleading look on my face.

She pursed her lips prettily. "What's the name of your bank in Philadelphia, and your account number?" she asked. I gave her the name of the bank, the telephone number and my account number. She walked to a desk and, picking up the telephone, called Philadelphia.

"Bookkeeping, please," she said when she was connected. Then: "Yes, I have a check here, drawn on account number 505-602, Mr. Frank Adams, in the amount of $15,000. I would like to verify the check, please."

I held my breath, suddenly aware of the burly bank guard standing in one corner of the lobby. It had been my experience that clerks in bank bookkeeping departments, when asked to verify a check, merely looked at the balance.

They rarely went behind the request to check on the

status of the account. I hoped that would be the case here. If not, well, I could only hope the bank guard was a lousy shot.

I heard her say, "All right, thank you," and then she replaced the receiver and looked at me with a speculative expression. "Tell you what, Frank Adams," she said with another of her brilliant smiles. "I'll take your check if you'll come to a party I'm having tonight. I'm short of handsome and charming men. How about it?"

"You got a deal," I said, grinning, and wrote her a check on the Philadelphia bank for $15,000, receiving in return a $15,000 cashier's check, payable to cash.

I went to the party. It was a fantastic bash. But then she was a fantastic lady—in more ways than several.

I cashed the check the next morning, returned the Rolls-Royce and caught a plane for San Diego. I reflected on the woman and her party several times during the flight and nearly laughed out loud when I was struck with one thought.

I wondered what her reaction would be when she learned she'd treated me to two parties on the same day, and the one had been a real cash ball.

CHAPTER SEVEN

How to Tour Europe on a Felony a Day

I developed a scam for every occasion and sometimes I waived the occasion. I modified the American banking system to suit myself and siphoned money out of bank vaults like a coon drains an egg. When I jumped the border into Mexico in late 1967, I had illicit cash assets of nearly $500,000 and several dozen bank officials had crimson derrières.

It was practically all done with numbers, a statistical shell game with the pea always in my pocket.

Look at one of your own personal checks. There's a check number in the upper right-hand corner, right? That's probably the only one you notice, and you notice it only if you keep an accurate check register. Most people don't even know their own account number, and while a great number of bank employees may be able to decipher the bank code numbers across the bottom of a check, very few scan a check that closely.

In the 1960s bank security was very lax, at least as far as I was concerned. It was my experience, when presenting a personal check, drawn on a Miami bank, say, to another Miami bank, about the only security precaution taken by the teller was a glance at the number in the upper right-hand corner. The higher that number, the more readily acceptable the check. It was as if the teller was telling herself or himself, "Ah-hah, check number 2876—boy, this guy has been with his bank a long time. This check's gotta be okay."

So I'm in an East Coast city, Boston, for example. I open an account in the Bean State Bank for $200, using the name Jason Parker and a boardinghouse address. Within a few days, I receive 200 personalized checks, numbered 1–200 consecutively in the upper right-hand corner, my name and address in the left-hand corner and, of course, that string of odd little numbers across the left-hand bottom edge. The series of numbers commenced with the numbers 01, since Boston is located within the First Federal Reserve District.

The most successful cattle rustlers in the Old West were experts at brand blotting and brand changing. I was an expert in check number blotting and changing, using press-on numbers and press-on magnetic-tape numbers.

When I finished with check number 1, it was check number 3100, and the series of numbers above the left-hand bottom edge started with the number 12. Otherwise, the check looks the same.

Now I walk into the Old Settlers Farm and Home Savings Association, which is just a mile from the Bean State Bank. "I want to open a savings account," I tell the clerk who greets me. "My wife tells me we're keeping too much money in a checking account."

"All right, sir, how much do you wish to deposit?" he

or she asks. Let's say it's a he. Bank dummies are divided equally among the sexes.

"Oh, $6,500, I guess," I reply, writing out a check to the OSFHSA. The teller takes the check and glances at the number in the upper right-hand corner. He also notices it's drawn on the Bean State Bank. He smiles. "All right, Mr. Parker. Now, there is a three-day waiting period before you can make any withdrawals. We have to allow time for your check to clear, and since it's an in-town check the three-day waiting period applies."

"I understand," I reply. I do, too. I've already ascertained that's the waiting period enforced by savings and loan institutions for in-town checks.

I wait six days and on the morning of the sixth day I return to Old Settlers. But I deliberately seek out a different teller. I hand him my passbook. "I need to withdraw $5,500," I say. If the teller had questioned the amount of the withdrawal, I would have said that I was buying a house or given some other plausible reason. But few savings and loan bank tellers pry into a customer's personal affairs.

This one didn't. He checked the account file. The account was six days old. The in-town check had obviously cleared. He returned my passbook with a cashier's check for $5,500.

I cashed it at the Bean State Bank and left town . . . before my check for $6,500 returned from Los Angeles, where the clearing-house bank computer had routed it.

I invested in another I-Tek camera and printing press and did the same thing with my phony Pan Am expense checks. I made up different batches for passing in different areas of the country, although all the checks were purportedly payable by Chase Manhattan Bank, New York.

New York is in the Second Federal Reserve District. Bona fide checks on banks in New York all have a series of numerals beginning with the number 02. But all the phony checks I passed on the East Coast, or in north-eastern or southeastern states, were routed first to San Francisco or Los Angeles. All the phony checks I passed in the Southwest, Northwest or along the West Coast were first routed to Philadelphia, Boston or some other point across the continent.

My numbers game was the perfect system for floats and stalls. I always had a week's running time before the hounds picked up the spoor. I learned later that I was the first check swindler to use the routing numbers racket. It drove bankers up the wall. They didn't know what the hell was going on. They do now, and they owe me.

I worked my schemes overtime, all over the nation, until I decided I was just too hot to cool down. I had to leave the country. And I decided I could worry about a passport in Mexico as fretfully as I could in Richmond or Seattle, since all I needed to visit Mexico was a visa. I obtained one from the Mexican Consulate in San Antonio, using the name Frank Williams and presenting myself as a Pan Am pilot, and deadheaded to Mexico City on an Aero-Mexico jet.

I did not take the entire proceeds of my crime spree with me. Like a dog with access to a butcher-shop bone box and forty acres of soft ground, I buried my loot all over the United States, stashing stacks of cash in bank safe-deposit boxes from coast to coast and from the Rio Grande to the Canadian border.

I did take some $50,000 with me into Mexico, concealed in thin sheafs in the lining of my suitcases and the linings of my jackets. A good customs officer could have turned up the cash speedily, but I didn't have to go through customs. I was wearing my Pan Am uniform and was waived along with the AeroMexico crew.

I stayed in Mexico City a week. Then I met a Pan Am stewardess, enjoying a five-day holiday in Mexico, and accepted her invitation to go to Acapulco for a weekend. We were airborne when she suddenly groaned and said a naughty word. "What's the matter?" I asked, surprised to hear such language from such lovely lips.

"I meant to cash my paycheck at the airport," she said. "I've got exactly three pesos in my purse. Oh, well, I guess the hotel will cash it."

"I'll cash it, if it's not too much," I said. "I'm sending my own check off tonight for deposit, and I can just run it through my bank. How much is it?"

I really didn't care how much cash was involved. A real Pan Am check! I wanted it. I got it for $288.15, and stowed it carefully away. I never did cash it, although it netted me a fortune.

I liked Acapulco. It teemed with beautiful people, most of them rich, famous or on the make for something or other, sometimes all three. We stayed at a hotel frequented by airline crews, but I never felt in jeopardy. Acapulco is not a place one goes to talk shop.

I stayed on after the stewardess returned to her base in Miami. And the hotel manager became friendly with me, so friendly that I decided to sound him out on my dilemma.

He joined me at dinner one night and since he seemed in an especially affable mood, I decided to make a try then and there. "Pete, I'm in a helluva jam," I ventured.

"The hell you are!" he exclaimed in concerned tones.

"Yeah," I replied. "My supervisor in New York just called me. He wants me to go to London on the noon plane from Mexico City tomorrow and pick up a flight that's being held there because the pilot is sick."

Pete grinned. "That's a jam? I should have your troubles."

I shook my head. "The thing is, Pete, I don't have my passport with me. I left it in New York and I'm supposed to have it with me all the time. I can't make it back to New York in time to get my passport and get to London on schedule. And if the super learns I'm here without a passport, he'll fire me. What the hell am I gonna do, Pete?"

He whistled. "Yeah, you are in a jam, aren't you?" His features took on a musing look, and then he nodded. "I don't know that this will work, but have you ever heard of a woman named Kitty Corbett?"

I hadn't and said so. "Well, she's a writer on Mexican affairs, an old dame. She's been down here twenty or thirty years and is real respected. They say she has clout from the Presidential Palace in Mexico City to Washington, D.C., the White House even, I understand. I believe it, too." He grinned. "The thing is, that's her at the table by the window. Now, I know she plays mamma to every down-and-out American who puts a con on her, and she loves to do favors for anybody who seeks her out wanting something. Makes her feel like the queen mother, I guess. Anyway, let's go over and buy her a drink, put some sweet lines on her and cry a little. Maybe she can come up with an answer."

Kitty Corbett was a gracious old woman. And sharp. After a few minutes, she smiled at Pete. "Okay, innkeeper, what's up? You never sit down with me unless you want something. What is it this time?"

Pete threw up his hands and laughed. "I don't want a thing, honest! But Frank here has a problem. Tell her, Frank."

I told her virtually the same story I'd put on Pete, except I went a little heavier on the melodrama. She looked at me when I finished. "You need a passport real bad, I'd say," she commented.

"Trouble is, you've got one. It's just in the wrong place. You can't have two passports, you know. That's illegal."

"I know," I said, grimacing. "That worries me, too. But I can't lose this job. It might be years before another airline picked me up, if at all. I was on Pan Am's waiting list for three years." I paused, then exclaimed, "Flying jet liners is all I ever wanted to do!"

Kitty Corbett nodded sympathetically, lost in thought.

Then she pursed her mouth. "Pete, get me a telephone over here."

Pete signaled and a waiter brought a telephone to the table and plugged it into a nearby wall jack. Kitty Corbett picked it up, jiggled the hook and then began talking to the operator in Spanish. It required several minutes, but she was put through to whomever she was calling.

"Sonja? Kitty Corbett here," she said. "Listen, I've got a favor to ask . . ." She went on and detailed my predicament and then listened as the party on the other end replied.

"I know all that, Sonja," she said. "And I've got it figured out. Just issue him a temporary passport, just as you would if his had been lost or stolen. Hell, when he gets back to New York he can tear up the temporary passport, or tear up the old one and get a new one."

She listened again for a minute, then held her hand over the receiver and looked at me. "You don't happen to have your birth certificate with you, do you?"

"Yes, I do," I said. "I carry it in my wallet. It's a little worn, but still legible."

Kitty Corbett nodded and turned again to the phone. "Yes, Sonja, he has a birth certificate. . . . You think you can handle it? Great! You're a love and I owe you. See you next week."

She hung up and smiled. "Well, Frank, if you can get to the American Consulate in Mexico City by ten o'clock tomorrow, Sonja Gundersen, the assistant consul, will issue you a temporary passport. You've lost yours, understand? And if you tell anyone about this, I'll kill you."

I kissed her and ordered a bottle of the best champagne. I even had a glass myself. Then I called the airport and found there was a flight leaving in an hour. I made a reservation and turned to Pete. "Listen, I'm going to leave a lot of my stuff here. I don't have time to pack. Have someone pack what I leave and store it in your office, and

I'll pick it up in a couple of weeks, maybe sooner. I'm going to try and come back through here."

I stuffed one suitcase with my uniform and one suit, and my money. Pete had a cab waiting when I went down to the lobby. I really liked the guy, and I wished there were some way to thank him.

I thought of a way. I laid one of my phony Pan Am checks on him. On the hotel he managed, anyway.

I cashed another one at the airport before boarding the flight to Mexico City. In Mexico City, I stowed my bag in a locker after changing into my Pan Am pilot's garb and walked into Miss Gundersen's office at 9:45 A.M.

Sonja Gundersen was a crisp, starched blonde and she didn't waste any time. "Your birth certificate, please."

I took it from my wallet and handed it to her. She scanned it and looked at me. "I thought Kitty said your name was Frank Williams. This says your name is Frank W. Abagnale, Jr."

I smiled. "It is. Frank William Abagnale, Jr. You know Kitty. She had a little too much champagne last night. She kept introducing me to all her friends as Frank Williams, too. But I thought she gave you my full name."

"She may have," agreed Miss Gundersen. "I had trouble hearing a lot of what she said. These damned Mexican telephones. Anyway you're obviously a Pan Am pilot, and part of your name is Frank William, so you must be the one."

As instructed, I had stopped and obtained two passport-sized photographs. I gave those to Miss Gundersen, and walked out of the consulate building fifteen minutes later with a temporary passport in my pocket. I went back to the airport and changed into a suit and bought a ticket for London at the British Overseas Airways counter, paying cash.

I was told the flight was delayed. It wouldn't depart until seven that evening.

I changed back into my pilot's uniform and spent six

hours papering Mexico City with my decorative duds. I was $6,500 richer when I flew off to London, and the Mexican *federales* joined the posse on my tail.

In London I checked into the Royal Gardens Hotel in Kensington, using the name F. W. Adams and representing myself as a TWA pilot on furlough. I used my alternate alias on the premise that London police would soon be receiving queries on Frank W. Abagnale, Jr., also known as Frank Williams, erstwhile Pan Am pilot.

I stayed only a few days in London. I was beginning to feel pressure on me, the same uneasiness that had plagued me in the States. I realized in London that leaving the U.S. hadn't solved my problem, that Mexican police and Scotland Yard officers were in the same business as cops in New York or Los Angeles—that of catching crooks. And I was a crook.

Given that knowledge, and the small fortune in cash I had stashed away in various places, it would have been prudent of me to live as quietly and discreetly as possible under an assumed name in some out-of-the-way foreign niche. I recognized the merits of such a course, but prudence was a quality I didn't seem to possess.

I was actually incapable of sound judgment, I realize now, driven by compulsions over which I had no control. I was now living by rationalizations: I was the hunted, the police were the hunters, ergo, the police were the bad guys. I had to steal to survive, to finance my continual flight from the bad guys, consequently I was justified in my illegal means of support. So, after less than a week in England, I papered Piccadilly with some of my piccadillies and flew off to Paris, smug in the irrational assumption that I'd resorted to fraud again in self-defense.

A psychiatrist would have viewed my actions differently. He would have said I wanted to be caught. For now the British police began to put together a dossier on me.

Perhaps I was seeking to be caught. Perhaps I was subconsciously seeking help and my subliminal mind told me the authorities would offer that help, but I had no such conscious thoughts at the time.

I was fully aware that I was on a mad carrousel ride, a merry-go-round whirling ungoverned from which I seemed unable to dismount, but I sure as hell didn't want cops to stop the whirligig.

I hadn't been in Paris three hours when I met Monique Lavalier and entered into a relationship that was not only to broaden my venal vistas but, ultimately, was also to destroy my honey hive. Looking back, I owe Monique a debt of thanks. So does Pan Am, although some of the firm's officials might argue the point.

Monique was a stewardess for Air France. I met her in the Windsor Hotel bar, where she and several dozen other Air France flight-crew people were giving a party for a retiring captain pilot. If I met the honoree, I don't remember him, for I was mesmerized by Monique. She was as heady and sparkling as the fine champagne being served. I was invited to the party by an Air France first officer who saw me, dressed in my Pan Am attire, checking in at the desk. He promptly accosted me, hustled me into the bar, and my real protests evaporated when he introduced me to Monique.

She had all of Rosalie's charms and qualities and none of Rosalie's inhibitions. Apparently I affected Monique the same way she affected me, for we became inseparable during the time I was in Paris and on subsequent visits. Monique, if she had any thoughts of marrying me, never mentioned it, but she did, three days after we met, take me home to present me to her family. The Lavaliers were delightful people, and I was particularly intrigued with Papa Lavalier.

He was a job printer, operator of a small printing shop on the outskirts of Paris. I was immediately seized with an idea for improving upon my check-swindling scam involving phony Pan Am vouchers.

"You know, I have some good connections in the Pan Am business office," I said casually during lunch. "Maybe I can get Pan Am to give you some printing business."

Papa Lavalier beamed. "Yes, yes!" he exclaimed. "Anything you want done, we will try and do, and we would be most grateful, monsieur." Monique acted as an interpreter, for none of her family had the slightest command of English. That afternoon her father took me on a tour of his plant, which he operated with two of Monique's brothers. He employed one other young man, who, like Monique, spoke fractured English, but Papa Lavalier said he and his sons would personally perform any printing jobs I might secure for their little firm. "Whatever you want printed in English, my father and my brothers can do it," Monique said proudly. "They are the best printers in France."

I still had the actual Pan Am payroll check I'd cashed for the stewardess in Mexico. Studying it, I was struck by the difference between it and my imaginative version of a Pan Am check. My imitations were impressive, certainly, else I wouldn't have been able to pass so many of them, but one placed next to the real thing fairly shrieked "counterfeit!" I had been lucky to get by with passing them. Obviously the tellers who'd accepted them had never handled a real Pan Am check.

It occurred to me, however, that Pan Am checks might be very familiar to European bank tellers, since the carrier did the bulk of its business outside the continental United States. The thought had crossed my mind in London, even, when the teller in the one bank I'd bilked had seemed overly studious of my artwork.

"It's an expense check," I'd said, pointing to the bold black letters so stating.

"Oh, yes, of course," he'd replied, and had cashed the check, but with a trace of reluctance.

Now I had another thought. Maybe Pan Am had a dif-

145

ferent-type check, maybe a different-colored check, perhaps, for different continents. I thought it best to check on the theory before proceeding with my plan. The next morning I called Pan Am's Paris office and asked to speak to someone in the business office. I was connected with a man who sounded very young and very inexperienced, and soon proved he was the latter. I was becoming convinced that Lady Luck was my personal switchboard operator.

"Say, listen, this is Jack Rogers over at Daigle Freight Forwarding," I said. "I got a check here, and I think your company must have sent it to us by mistake."

"Uh, well, Mr. Rogers, why do you say that?" he inquired.

"Because I got a check here for $1,900, sent from your New York office, and I don't have an invoice to match the payment notation," I replied. "I can't find any record of having handled anything for you people. You got any idea what this check's for?"

"Well, not right offhand, Mr. Rogers. Are you sure the check's from us?"

"Well, it seems to me it is," I said. "It's a regular green check with Pan American in big letters across the top and it's made out to us for $1,900."

"Mr. Rogers, that doesn't sound like one of our checks," the fellow said. "Our checks are blue, and they have Pan Am—Pan Am—Pan Am in faded-out wording all over the face, along with a global map of the world. Does yours have that on it?"

I was holding the stewardess's check in my hand. He had described it perfectly, but I didn't tell him that. "You gotta Pan Am check there?" I demanded, in the tone of a man who wanted to remove all doubts.

"Well, yes, I do, but . . ."

I cut him off. "Who's it signed by? What's the comptroller's name?" I asked.

He told me. It was the same name appearing on the

check in my hand. "What's the string of little numbers across the bottom read?" I pressed.

"Why, 02 . . ." and he rattled them off to me. They matched the numbers on the stew's check.

"Nah, that's not the guy who signed this check and the numbers don't match," I lied. "But you people do bank with Chase Manhattan, don't you?"

"Yes, we do, but so do a lot of other companies, and you may have a check from some other firm operating under the name Pan American. I don't think you have one of our checks, Mr. Rogers. I suggest you return it and establish some sort of correspondence," he said helpfully.

"Yeah, I'll do that, and thanks," I said.

Monique flew the Berlin-Stockholm-Copenhagen run for Air France, a two-day turnaround trip, and then was off for two days. She had a flight that day. She was barely airborne when I appeared in her father's shop. He was delighted to see me, and we had no trouble conversing between the French I had learned from my mother and the English of his young printer.

I displayed the check I'd gotten from the Pan Am stewardess, but with her name and the amount of the check blocked out. "I talked to our business-office people," I said. "Now, we've been having these checks printed in America, a pretty expensive process. I told them I thought you could do the job as well and at a substantial savings. Do you think you can duplicate this check in payroll-book form?

"If you think you can, I am authorized to give you a trial order of ten thousand, provided you can beat the New York price."

He was examining the check. "And what is your printer's cost for these in New York, monsieur?" he asked.

I hadn't the faintest idea, but I named a figure I felt wouldn't offend New York printers. "Three hundred and fifty dollars per thousand," I said.

He nodded. "I can provide your company with a quality

product that will exactly duplicate this one, and at $200 per thousand," he said eagerly. "I think you will find our work most satisfactory."

He hesitated, seemingly embarrassed. "Monsieur, I know you and my daughter are close friends, and I trust you implicitly, but it is customary that we receive a deposit of fifty percent," he said apologetically.

I laughed. "You will have your deposit this afternoon," I said.

I went to a Paris bank, dressed in my Pan Am pilot's uniform, and placed $1,000 on the counter of one of the tellers' cages. "I would like a cashier's check in that amount, please," I said. "The remittor should be Pan American World Airways, and make the check payable to Maurice Lavalier and Sons, Printers, if you will."

I delivered the check that afternoon. Papa Lavalier had an inspection sample ready for the following day. I examined the work and had to restrain myself from whooping. The checks were beautiful. No, gorgeous. Real Pan Am checks, four to a page, twenty-five pages to the book, perforated and on IBM card stock! I felt on top of the mountain, and no matter it was a check swindler's pinnacle.

Papa Lavalier filled the entire order within a week, and I again acquired a legitimate cashier's check, purportedly issued by Pan Am, for the balance due him.

Papa Lavalier furnished me with invoices and receipts and was pleased that I was pleased. It probably never occurred to him, having never dealt with Americans before, that there was anything strange about our dealings. I was a Pan Am pilot. His daughter vouched for me. And the checks he received were valid checks, issued by Pan Am.

"I hope we can do more work for your company, my friend," he said.

"Oh, you will, you will," I assured him. "In fact, we're

so delighted with your work that we may refer others to you."

There were other referrals, all phony, and all handled personally by me, but Papa Lavalier never questioned anything I asked. From the time he delivered the 10,000 Pan Am checks, he was the printer of any spurious document I needed or desired, an innocent dupe who felt grateful to me for having opened the door of the "American market" to him.

Of course I had no need of 10,000 Pan Am checks. The size of the order was simply to avert any suspicion. Even Papa Lavalier knew Pan Am was a behemoth of the airline industry. An order for a lesser number of checks might have made him wary.

I kept a thousand of the checks and fueled the incinerators of Paris with the remainder. Then I bought an IBM electric typewriter and made out a check to myself for $781.45, which I presented to the nearest bank, garbed as a Pan Am pilot.

It was a small bank. "Monsieur, I am certain this check is a good one, but I would have to verify it before I cash it, and we are not allowed to make transatlantic calls at the bank's expense," he said with a wry smile. "If you would care to pay for the call . . ." He looked at me questioningly.

I shrugged. "Sure, go ahead. I'll pay whatever the call costs."

I hadn't anticipated such a precaution on the bank's part, but neither was I alarmed. And I had inadvertently chosen a time to cash the check when its worth as a counterfeit could be tested. It was 3:15 P.M. in Paris. The banks in New York had been open for fifteen minutes. It required about the same length of time for the teller to be connected with the bookkeeping department of the Chase Manhattan Bank. The French teller was proficient in English, although with an accent. "I have a check here, presented by a Pan

American pilot, drawn on your bank in the amount of $781.45, American dollars," said the teller, and proceeded to give the account number across the bottom left-hand corner of the sham check.

"I see, yes, thank you very much. . . . Oh, the weather here is fine, thank you." He hung up and smiled. "Every time I talk to America, they want to know about the weather." He handed me the check to endorse and commenced counting out the amount of the check, less $8.92 for the telephone call. All things considered, it was not an unreasonable service charge.

I showered Paris and its suburban environs with the bogus checks, and rented a safe-deposit box, for a five-year period paid in advance, in which to store my loot. Very rarely was a check questioned, and then it was only a matter of verification, and if the banks in New York were closed, I would return to the bank when they were open. Only once did I experience a tense moment. Instead of calling Chase Manhattan, one teller called Pan Am's business office in New York! Not once was my assumed name mentioned, but I heard the teller give the name of the bank, the account number and the name of the Pan Am comptroller.

Pan Am must have verified the check, for the teller paid it.

I was astonished myself at the ease and smoothness of my new operation. My God, I was now having my fictitious checks cleared by telephone and by Pan Am itself. I rented a car and while Monique was flying I drove around France, cashing the checks in every village bank and big-city treasury that loomed in sight. I have never verified the suspicion, but I often thought in later months and years that the reason I was so successful with those particular Pan Am checks was because Pan Am was paying them!

Papa Lavalier received a lot of business from me. I had him make me up a new Pan Am ID card, much more impressive than my own fraudulent one, after a real Pan Am pilot carelessly left his ID card on the bar in the Windsor. "I'll give it to him," I told the bartender. I did mail it to him, in care of Pan Am's New York offices, but only after I'd had Papa Lavalier copy it and substitute my own phony name, fake rank and photograph.

I had told the Lavaliers that I was in Paris as a special representative of Pan Am, doing public relations for the firm. A month after meeting Monique, however, I told her I had to return to flying status as a standby pilot, and caught a plane to New York. I arrived shortly before noon on a Tuesday and went immediately to the nearest branch of the Chase Manhattan Bank, where I purchased a $1,200 cashier's check, with "Roger D. Williams" as remittor and "Frank W. Williams" as payee.

I took a plane back to Paris that same day, checked into the King George V this time, and once in my room altered the Federal Reserve District number on the check so that, when cashed, it would be routed to San Francisco or Los Angeles.

Then I took the check to Papa Lavalier. "I need three hundred of these," I said.

I thought surely he would question the duplication of what was obviously a money order, but he didn't. I learned later that he never really understood what he was printing when he did jobs for me, but performed with a blind faith in my integrity.

I flew back to New York the day after receiving the three hundred duplicates, each an image of the original. There are 112 branches of Chase Manhattan in the New York metropolitan area alone. Over a period of three days I called at sixty of the branches, presenting one of the replicas in each bank. Only once in the sixty instances were there more than perfunctory words passed.

"Sir, I know this is one of Chase's checks, but it wasn't issued from this branch," she said apologetically. "I will have to call the issuing bank. Can you wait a minute?"

"Certainly, go ahead," I said easily.

She made her call within earshot of me. No part of the conversation surprised me. "Yes, this is Janice in Queens. Cashier's check 023685, can you tell me whom it was issued to, how much, when and what's the current status on it?" She waited, then apparently repeated what she'd been told. "Frank W. Williams, $1,200, January 5, currently outstanding. I must have it right here. Thank you very much."

"I'm sorry, sir," she said, smiling as she counted out the cash.

"That's all right," I said. "And you should never apologize for doing your job well." I meant it, too. That girl got stung, but she's still the kind banks should hire. And she saved Chase a bundle. I had intended to hit at least 100 Chase branches, but after she made her call, I pulled up on that particular caper.

I figured I couldn't afford another call to the bank that had issued the original check. I knew the odds favored me, but I couldn't chance the same bookkeeping clerk answering the phone if some other teller decided to go behind the check.

New York made me nervous. I felt I should head for a foreign clime again, but I couldn't decide whether to return to Paris and Monique or visit some new and exciting place.

While I was debating with myself, I flew to Boston, where I got myself flung into jail and robbed a bank. The former was a shock, like an unplanned pregnancy. The latter was the result of an irresistible impulse.

I went to Boston simply to get out of New York. I thought it would be as good as any place along the eastern seaboard as a point of embarkation, and it also had a lot of banks. On arrival, I stowed my bags in an airport rental locker, put the key in my ID folder and called at several of the banks, exchanging some of my Pan Am check facsimiles for genuine currency. I returned to the airport early in the evening, intending to catch an overseas flight as soon as possible. I had garnered over $5,000 in my felonious foray through Bean Town, and I stowed $4,800 of it in my bags before checking on what foreign flights were available that night.

I didn't have a chance to make my inquiries until late that night. Turning away from the locker, I encountered a pretty Allegheny Airlines stewardess from my embryo days as a pilot without portfolio.

"Frank! What a neat surprise!" she exclaimed. Naturally, we had to have a reunion. I didn't get back to the airport until after 11 P.M., and by then I'd decided to go to Miami and make an overseas connection from there.

I walked up to the Allegheny Airlines counter. "When's your next connecting flight to Miami?" I asked the ticket agent on duty, a man. I had changed into my pilot's uniform.

"You just missed it." He grimaced.

"Who's got the next flight, National, American, who?" I inquired.

"No one," he said. "You've missed any flight to Miami until tomorrow. Nothing flies out of here after midnight. Boston's got a noise-control ordinance, now, and no outgoing traffic is allowed after midnight. No airline can put a plane in the air until 6:30 A.M., and the first flight to Miami is National's at 10:15 A.M."

"But it's only 11:40 now," I said.

He grinned. "Okay. You want to go to Burlington, Vermont? That's the last flight out tonight."

All things considered, I declined. I walked over and sat down in one of the lobby chairs, mulling the situation. The lobby, like most large airport vestibules, was ringed with gift shops, newsstands, coffee shops, bars and various other shops, and I noted idly, while cogitating, that most of them were closing. I also noted, suddenly interested, that many of them were stopping at the night depository of a large Boston bank, situated near the middle of one exit corridor, and dropping bags or bulky enve-lopes—obviously their day's receipts—into the steel-faced receptacle.

My observation was interrupted by two chilling words: "Frank Abagnale?"

I looked up, quelling a surge of panic. Two tall, grim-visaged Massachusetts state troopers, in uniform, stood over me.

"You are Frank Abagnale, aren't you?" demanded the one in stony tones.

"My name is Frank, but it's Frank Williams," I said, and I was surprised that the calm, unflustered reply had issued from my throat.

"May I see your identification, please?" asked the one. The words were spoken politely, but his eyes said if I didn't promptly produce my ID, he was going to pick me up by the ankles and shake it out of my pockets.

I handed over my ID card and my fraudulent FAA pilot's license. "Look, I don't know what this is all about, but you're badly mistaken," I said as I tendered the docu-ments. "I fly for Pan American, and these ought to be proof enough."

The one studied the ID card and license, then passed them to his partner. "Why don't you knock off the bullshit, son? You're Frank Abagnale, aren't you?" said the second one, almost gently.

"Frank who?" I protested, feigning anger to cover my increasing nervousness. "I don't know who the hell you're after, but it's not me!"

The one frowned. "Well, we ain't gonna stand around here arguing with you," he growled. "Come on, we're taking you in."

They didn't ask where my luggage was, and I didn't volunteer. They took me outside, placed me in their patrol car and drove me directly to the state police offices. There I was ushered into the office of a harried-looking lieuten-ant, whom I assumed was the shift commander.

"What the hell is this?" he demanded in exasperated tones.

"Well, we think it's Frank Abagnale, Lieutenant," said one of the troopers. "He says he's a pilot for Pan Am."

The lieutenant eyed me. "You don't look very old to be a pilot," he said. "Why don't you tell the truth? You're Frank Abagnale. We've been looking for him for a long time. He's supposed to be a pilot, too. You fit his description—perfectly."

"I'm thirty years old, my name is Frank Williams and I fly for Pan Am, and I want to talk to my lawyer," I shouted.

The lieutenant sighed. "You ain't been charged with nothin' yet," he said. "Take him over to the city jail, book him for vagrancy and then let him call a lawyer. And call the feds. He's their pigeon. Let them straighten it out."

"Vagrancy!" I protested. "I'm no vagrant. I've got nearly $200 on me."

The lieutenant nodded. "Yeah, but you ain't proved you're gainfully employed," he said wearily. "Get 'im out of here."

I was taken to the county jail in downtown Boston, which had all the appearances of a facility that should have long ago been condemned, and had been, and I was turned over to the booking sergeant.

"Damn me, what did he do?" he queried, looking at me.

"Just book him for vagrancy. Someone will pick him up in the morning," said the one trooper.

"Vagrant!" bellowed the sergeant. "By damn, if he's a vagrant, I hope you guys never bring in any bums."

"Just book him," grunted the one trooper, and he and his partner left.

"Empty your pockets, lad," the sergeant said gruffly, pulling a form in triplicate from a drawer. "I'll give you a receipt for your goods."

I started placing my valuables before him. "Listen, can

I keep my ID card and pilot's license?" I asked. "Company regulations say I have to have them on me at all times. I'm not sure if being arrested is included, but I'd still like to keep them, if you don't mind."

The sergeant examined the card and the license and pushed them toward me. "Sure," he said kindly. "I'd say there's been some kind of mix-up here, lad. I'm glad I'm not involved."

A jailer took me upstairs and placed me in a dingy, rusty cell adjoining the drunk tank. "If you need anything, just holler," he said sympathetically.

I nodded, not replying, and slumped on the cot. I was suddenly depressed, miserable and scared. The game was over, I had to admit. The FBI would pick me up in the morning, I knew, and then it would be just one courtroom after another, I figured. I looked around the jail cell and hoped that prison cells were more tenable. Jesus, this was a rat hole. And I didn't have a prayer of getting out. But then no man has a prayer, I thought regretfully, when he worships a hustler's god.

Even a hustler's god, however, has a legion of angels. And one appeared to me now, preceded by a thin, wavering whistle, like a kid bolstering his courage in a graveyard. He hauled up in front of my cell, an apparition in a hideous, green-checked suit topped by a face that might have come out of a lobster pot, questioning lips punctuated by an odorous cigar and eyes that regarded me as a weasel might look on a mouse.

"Well, now, what the hell might you be doing in there?" he asked around the cigar.

I didn't know who he was. He didn't look like anyone who could help me. "Vagrancy," I said shortly.

"Vagrancy!" he exclaimed, examining me with his shrewd eyes. "You're a pilot with Pan Am, aren't you? How the hell can you be a vagrant? Did somebody steal all your planes?"

"Who're you?" I asked.

He fished in his pocket and thrust a card through the bars. "Aloyius James 'Bailout' Bailey, my high-flying friend," he said. "Bail bondsman par excellence. The cops bring 'em, I spring 'em. You're on their turf, now, pal. I can put you on mine. The street."

Hope didn't exactly spring eternal in my breast, but it crow-hopped.

"Well, I'll tell you the truth," I said cautiously. "There was this guy at the airport. He was getting pretty obnoxious with a girl. I racked his ass. They ran us both in for fighting. I should've stayed out of it. I'll probably lose my job when the skipper finds out I'm in jail."

He stared at me, unbelieving. "What the hell you sayin'? You ain't got nobody to bail you out? Call one of your friends, for Chris' sakes."

I shrugged. "I don't have any friends here. I flew in on a charter cargo job. I'm based in Los Angeles."

"What about the rest of your crew?" he demanded. "Call one of them."

"They went on to Istanbul," I lied. "I got time off due me. I was going to deadhead to Miami to see a chick."

"Well, goddamned! You have got your ass in a crack, haven't you?" said Aloyius James "Bailout" Bailey. Then he smiled, and his features suddenly took on the charm of a jolly leprechaun. "Well, my fighter-pilot chum, let's see if we can't get your butt out of this Boston bastille."

He disappeared and was gone for an agonizing length of time, all of ten minutes. Then he hove to in front of my cell again. "Goddamn, your bond is $5,000," he said in a surprised tone. "Sarge says you must have given the troopers a hard time. How much money you got?"

My hopes came to a standstill again. "Just $200, maybe not that much," I sighed.

He mulled the reply; his eyes narrowed. "You got any identification?" he asked.

"Sure," I said, passing my ID and pilot's license through the bars. "You can see how long I've been a pilot, and I've been with Pan Am seven years."

He handed back the documents. "You got a personal check?" he asked abruptly.

"Yeah, that is, the sergeant downstairs has it," I said. "Why?"

"Because I'm gonna take your check, that's why, Jet Jockey," he said with a grin. "You can write it out when the sarge lets you loose."

The sarge let me loose thirty-five minutes later. I wrote Bailey a check for the standard 10 percent, $500, and handed him a hundred in cash. "That's a bonus, in lieu of a kiss," I said, laughing with joy. "I'd give you the kiss except for that damned cigar!"

He drove me to the airport after I told him I was taking the first flight to Miami.

This is what happened later. I have it on unimpeachable sources, as the White House reporters are fond of saying. An ecstatic O'Riley, high enough with joy to require a pilot's license himself, showed up at the jail. "Abagnale, or whatever the hell name you've got him booked under, trot him out," he chortled.

"He made bond at three-thirty this morning," volunteered a jailer. The sergeant had gone home.

O'Riley flirted with apoplexy. "Bond! Bond! Who the hell bonded him out?" he finally shrieked in strangled tones.

"Bailey, 'Bailout' Bailey, who else?" replied the jailer.

O'Riley wrathfully sought out Bailey. "Did you post bond for a Frank Wiliams this morning? he demanded.

Bailey looked at him, astonishd. "The pilot? Sure, I went his bail. Why the hell not?"

"How'd he pay you? How much?" O'Riley grated.

"Why, the regular amount, $500. I've got his check right here," said Bailey, offering the voucher.

O'Riley looked at the check and then dropped it on

Bailey's desk. "Serves your ass right," he growled, and turned toward the door.

"What do you mean?" Bailey demanded as the FBI agent grasped the door handle.

O'Riley grinned wickedly. "Run it through your bank account, turd, and you'll find out what I mean."

Outside, a Massachusetts detective turned to O'Riley. "We can get out an APB on him."

O'Riley shook his head. "Forget it. That bastard's five hundred miles away. No Boston cop's gonna catch him."

A prudent man would have been five hundred miles away. I wasn't prudent. When you're hot, you're hot, and I had the cajones of a billy goat.

No sooner had Bailey dropped me at the airport, and was gone, than I grabbed a cab and checked in at a nearby motel.

The next morning I called the bank that had a branch at the airport. "Security, please," I said when the switchboard operator answered.

"Security."

"Yeah, listen, this is Connors, the new guard. I don't have a uniform for tonight's shift. My damned uniform got ripped up in an accident. Where can I get a replacement, lady?" I spoke in outrage.

"Well, we get our uniforms from Beke Brothers," the woman replied in mollifying tones. "Just go down there, Mr. Connors. They'll outfit you with a replacement."

I looked up the address of Beke Brothers. I also had my fingers do some walking through other sections of the Yellow Pages.

I went first to Beke Brothers. No one questioned my status. Within fifteen minutes I walked out with a complete guard's outfit: shirt, tie, trousers and hat, the name of the bank emblazoned over the breast pocket and on the right shoulder of the shirt. I stopped at a police-supply firm and picked up a Sam Browne belt and holster. I called at a gun shop and picked up a replica of a .38 police special.

It was harmless, but only an idiot would have ignored it were it pointed at him. I then rented a station wagon, and when I left my motel each door sported a sign proclaiming "SECURITY—BEAN STATE NATIONAL BANK."

At 11:15 P.M. I was standing at attention in front of the night-deposit box of the Bean State National Bank Airport Branch, and a beautifully lettered sign adorned the safe's depository: "NIGHT DEPOSIT VAULT OUT OF ORDER. PLEASE MAKE DEPOSITS WITH SECURITY OFFICER."

There was an upright dolly, with a large mail-type bag bulking open, in front of the depository.

At least thirty-five people dropped bags or envelopes into the container.

Not one of them said more than "Good evening" or "Good night."

When the last shop had closed, I secured the top of the canvas bag and began hauling the loot to the station wagon. I became stuck trying to get the dolly over the weather strip of the exit door. Try as I might, I couldn't get the damned thing across the little ridge. It was just too heavy.

"What's going on, buddy?"

I twisted my head and nearly soiled my drawers. They weren't the same ones, but a pair of state troopers was standing less than five feet away.

"Well, the box is out of order, and the truck broke down, and I've got the bank's station wagon out here and no goddamned hydraulic pulley, and I ain't exactly Samson," I said, grinning sheepishly.

The older one, a ruddy-faced redhead, laughed. "Well, hell, let us help you with it," he said, and stepped forward and grabbed the handle of the dolly. With three of us tugging, it came over the ridge easily. They helped me drag the dolly to the station wagon and assisted me in lifting the bulky, cumbersome cargo into the back of the vehicle. I slammed shut the tailgate and turned to the officers.

"I appreciate it, boys," I said, smiling. "I'd spring for

the coffee, but I've got to get this little fortune to the bank."

They laughed and one lifted a hand. "Hey, no sweat. Next time, okay?"

Less than an hour later, I had the booty in my motel room and was sorting out the cash. Bills only. I tossed the change, credit-card receipts and checks into the bathtub.

I netted $62,800 in currency. I changed into a casual suit, wrapped the haul in a spare shirt and drove to the airport, where I retrieved my bags. An hour later I was on a flight to Miami. I had a thirty-minute layover in New York. I used the time to call the manager of the airport in Boston. I didn't get him but I got his secretary.

"Listen, tell the Bean State Bank people they can get the majority of the loot from last night's depository caper in the bathtub of Room 208, Rest Haven Motel," I said and hung up.

The next day I winged out of Miami, bound for Istanbul.

I had an hour's layover in Tel Aviv.

I used it upholding my code of honor. In my entire career, I never yenched a square john as an individual.

I sought out a branch of an American bank. And laid a sheaf of bills on the counter before a teller.

"I want a $5,000 cashier's check," I said.

"Yes, sir. And your name?"

"Frank Abagnale, Jr.," I said.

"All right, Mr. Abagnale. Do you want this check made out to you?"

I shook my head. "No," I said. "Make it payable to Aloyius James 'Bailout' Bailey, in Boston, Massachu-setts."

CHAPTER EIGHT

A Small Crew Will Do—
It's Just a Paper Airplane

An entourage is expected of some peo-
ple. The President. Queen Elizabeth. Frank Sinatra. Mu-
hammad Ali. Arnold Palmer. Most celebrities, in fact.

And airline pilots.

"Where's your crew, sir?" asked the desk clerk in the
Istanbul hotel. It was a question I'd encountered before.

"I don't have a crew with me," I replied. "I just flew
in to replace a pilot who became ill." It was my standard
answer to such queries, which were much more numerous
in Europe and the Middle East than in the United States.
Continental hotels, obviously, were more accustomed to
catering to entire air crews. A lone pilot aroused curiosity.

And curiosity breeds suspicion.

I needed a crew, I mused that evening while dining in
a Turkish restaurant. I had doffed my uniform. Save on
special occasions, I now wore it only when checking in

and checking out of a hotel, passing a check or cadging a free ride.

The matter of a crew had entered my mind before. In fact, it entered my mind each time I saw a command pilot surrounded by his crew. His status was not only more believable than mine, but he also always seemed to be having much more fun than I. Stews, I had noticed, tended to act as handmaidens to the pilots. My life as a bogus birdman, on the other hand, was essentially a lonely existence. But then a man on the run is usually a forlorn figure. It's hard to play the social lion when you're moving like a scalded cat. My dalliances, by and large, had all the permanency of rabbits' relationships and about the same degree of satisfaction.

My fantasies of an aircrew of my own, of course, were motivated by more than just a desire for companionship. An aircrew—and I thought of an aircrew only in terms of stewardesses—would lend concrete validity to my role of airline pilot. I had learned that a solitary pilot was always subject to scrutiny. Conversely, a pilot trailing a squad of lovely stewardesses would almost certainly be above suspicion. If I had a beautiful bevy of flight attendants with me in my travels, I could scatter my valueless checks like confetti and they'd be accepted like rice at a wedding, I thought. Not that I was having any trouble passing them at present, but I was passing them one at a time. With a crew behind me, I could cash the sham checks in multiple numbers.

I left Istanbul after a week and flew to Athens. "Don't you have a crew with you, sir?" asked the hotel desk clerk. I gave him my usual reply, feeling harassed.

The next day I flew to Paris to visit the Lavaliers. "I wish you flew for Air France. I could be a member of your crew," Monique said at one point during the visit. The remark convinced me that an aircrew was a necessity.

But how did a pilot without portfolio, who didn't know

how to fly, go about assembling an aircrew? I could hardly gather a few girls at random and propose, "Hey, kids, wanna go to Europe? I've got this great scheme for passing worthless checks . . ." And since I had absolutely no connections in the underworld, American or European, I couldn't look for help there.

I was in West Berlin when a solution presented itself. It was long-range and fraught with risks, but it was also challenging. Pan Am's hives had always provided the bulk of my honey. If the carrier wasn't my parent company, I was in a sense its bastard child, and this was an issue demanding filial loyalty.

I'd let Pan Am furnish me a flight crew.

I flew to New York and on arrival called Pan Am's personnel office, representing myself as the placement director of a small western college, Prescott Presbyterian Normal. "I'm aware that you people send employment recruiting teams to various colleges and universities, and I wondered if you might possibly have our school on your schedule this year?" I said.

"I'm sorry, we don't," said the Pan Am personnel officer who took my call. "However, we will have a team on the University of Arizona campus during the last two weeks in October, interviewing students for various positions, and I'm sure they'd be glad to talk to any of your students who might be interested in a career with Pan Am. If you like, we can mail you some brochures."

"That would be nice," I said, and gave him a fictitious address for my nonexistent college.

Mine was a plan that demanded the boldness of a mountain climber. I donned my uniform and went to Pan Am's Hangar 14 at Kennedy. With my phony ID card dangling from my breast pocket, I had no trouble at all gaining entrance, and I spent a leisurely half hour roaming through the stores department until I had accumulated the supplies I needed: envelopes, large manila holders and stationery, all boasting Pan Am's letterhead, a pad of employment application forms and a stack of colorful brochures.

Back in my motel room, I sat down and composed a letter to the director of the University of Arizona placement office. Pan Am, I said, was initiating a new recruiting technique this year. In addition to the regular personnel recruiters who would visit the campus in October, the letter stated, Pan Am was also fielding pilots and stewardesses to interview prospective pilots and flight attendants, since actual flight personnel could offer a better perspective of what a flying position with Pan Am would entail and could also better evaluate the applicants.

"A pilot will be visiting your campus on Monday, September 9, and will be available for three days to interview stewardess applicants," the spurious letter stated. "Under separate cover, we are sending you some brochures and employment application forms which you might wish to distribute to interested students."

I signed the name of Pan Am's director of personnel to the letter and placed it in a Pan Am envelope. I packaged the brochures and application forms in one of the large manila holders. Then I went to Pan Am's office building, sought out the airline's mail room and dropped the missives off with a young clerk, brusquely ordering they be sent air mail.

I thought Pan Am's own postage meter, with its little Pan Am blurb, "World's Most Experienced Airline," would add a little class to the counterfeit mailings.

I dispatched the letter and the other material on August 18. On August 28 I called the University of Arizona and was connected with John Henderson, director of student placement.

"Mr. Henderson, this is Frank Williams, a co-pilot for Pan American World Airways," I said. "I am scheduled to visit your campus in a couple of weeks, and I'm calling to see if you received our material and if the dates are suitable."

"Oh, yes, Mr. Williams," enthused Henderson. "We're looking forward to your visit and we did receive your material. In fact, we've posted it about campus, and you should have a goodly number of applicants."

"Well, I don't know what was in the letter you received," I lied. "But I have been instructed by the flight supervisor to interview only juniors and seniors."

"We understand that, Mr. Williams," Henderson said. "In fact, all the inquiries I have received so far have been from juniors or seniors." He volunteered quarters on the campus for me, but I declined, saying I'd already made reservations with a hotel favored by the company.

I appeared on the University of Arizona campus at 8 A.M., Monday, September 9, and Henderson greeted me cordially. I was, of course, in uniform. Henderson had set aside a small room for my use during my stay. "We have thirty applicants to date, and I have scheduled them to appear in lots of ten each day," he said. "I know, of course, you'll be talking to them individually, and you can set your own daily schedule, if you wish. But the first ten will be here at 9 A.M."

"Well, I think I'll talk to them as a group at first, and then interview them individually," I said.

The first group of ten coeds was, collectively and individually, simply lovely. More than ever, looking at them, I saw the need for a crew of my own. The ten of them eyed me like I was Elvis Presley about to swing into action.

I affected a businesslike air. "First of all, ladies, I want you to know this is as new to me as it is to you. I'm more used to a cockpit than a classroom, but the company has assigned me this task and I hope I can carry it out successfully. With your help and understanding, I think I can.

"I say 'understanding' because I don't have the final say as to who will be hired and who will not. My job is just to select girls who I think would be most suitable as flight attendants and to make a recommendation in their behalf The personnel director has the authority to reject any or all of the candidates I offer. However, I can also say that you might be hired on my recommendation without your having to be interviewed by anyone else.

"There is also this—it's unlikely any of you will be hired by Pan Am before you graduate. But if you are selected as a future stewardess, it's our policy to give you some sort of assistance during your last year in school just so you won't be tempted to take some other job. Am I making myself clear?"

I was. The girls said so. I then dismissed them as a group and began interviewing them individually. I wasn't really sure of the type of girl I wanted in my "crew," but I was sure of the type I didn't want. I didn't want a girl who couldn't handle it if she learned she'd been conned into an elaborate scam.

Totally naïve and patently prudish candidates I crossed off immediately. Those who were personable and attractive, but superstraight (the kind of girl an airline would like as a stewardess), I marked as questionable. I put check marks after the names of girls who impressed me as easygoing, somewhat gullible, a little daring or devil-may-care, ultraliberal or not likely to panic in a crisis. I thought the girls who possessed such traits would be the best bets for my make-believe flight squad.

Henderson sat in during the morning sessions, but during the lunch break he led me to a file room behind his office and showed me an entrance near where I was interviewing the girls. He handed me a key to the door. "There's very rarely anyone on duty here, since our student records system is completely computerized," he said. "So you'll need this key. Now, I've pulled the files of all the applicants and put them aside on this desk here, in case you want to study the record of a particular girl. This way, you can operate pretty much on your own, although we'll be available to help you if you feel you need help, of course."

I was intrigued with the record-keeping system and Henderson obligingly showed me how the system worked before taking me to lunch as his guest.

I finished with the first ten applicants early in the afternoon and the following morning met the second batch of candidates. I gave them the same spiel, and like the first ten, they were equally amenable to my terms. The last girls, too, were exposed to the same con, and by the afternoon of the third day I had narrowed the field to twelve candidates.

I spent a couple of hours studying the files of the twelve on an individual basis, recalling my own interviews with them and my impressions of them, before settling on eight. I was leaving the records room when I was seized with an amusing whim, one that took me less than thirty minutes to satisfy. When I left the room, Frank Abagnale, Jr., a native of Bronxville, had transcripts in the files showing him to have earned both a bachelor's degree and a master's degree in social work.

The next morning I delivered my "thesis" to my eight finalists, since they were the lambs who had made possible my whimsical sheepskins.

The girls were excited when I assembled them, in the perfect mood for the con I put down. "Calm down, please, calm down," I implored them. "You haven't been hired as stewardesses. I think you ought to know that now."

The words achieved the desired multiple shock. And momentary total silence. Then I grinned and laid it on them. "That's because you're all juniors and we want you to finish your education before joining Pan Am," I said.

"I think I mentioned before that the company likes to assist approved stewardess candidates during their last year in school, and I've been authorized to make you eight girls an offer I think you'll find interesting.

168

"I have been informed that the company intends to hire a number of girls as summer interns for the coming year, and these girls will be sent to Europe in different groups to act as advertising representatives and public relations people. That is, they'll be used as models for photographs for Pan Am ads in various world publications—I'm sure you've all seen the kind I'm talking about—and some will be used as speakers at schools, civic group meetings, business seminars and that sort of thing. It's a show-the-company-flag type of tour and usually we use real stewardesses or professional models dressed up in flight-attendant uniforms.

"But this coming summer, we're going to use girls who've applied for stewardess positions and it will serve as sort of a pretraining period for them. I personally think it's a good idea for several reasons. One, it will allow our ad people to use pictures of our own personnel, depicted in cities we serve, and secondly, we won't have to pull actual stewardesses off the flight line when a photo situation calls for an actual stewardess. That's always made it tougher on the other stewardesses in the past, because summer months are our peak passenger months, and when we have to pull attendants off flight duty, other girls have to do their work.

"Now, if any or all of you would like to take part in the program this summer, I'm authorized to hire you. You'll have an expense-paid tour of Europe. You'll be paid the same salary as a starting stewardess, and you'll dress as stewardesses, but you won't be stewardesses. We'll supply your uniforms. Also, you'll be given a letter of employment, which is very important in this instance. It means that those of you who do decide to become stewardesses after graduation will be applying as former Pan Am employees, and you'll be given priority over all other applicants.

"Do I have any takers among you?"

They all volunteered. "Okay," I said, smiling. "Now,

you'll all need passports. That's your responsibility. I'll also need your addresses so the company can keep in touch with you. I'm sure you'll have your letters of employment within a month. That's it, ladies. I've certainly enjoyed meeting you all, and I hope that if and when you become stewardesses, some of you will be assigned to my crew."

I informed Henderson of the offer I'd made the girls, and he was as delighted as they had been. In fact, Henderson, his wife and the eight girls all hosted me that night at a delightful dinner party around the pool in the Hendersons' back yard.

I flew back to New York and rented a box with mail-answering service that had offices in the Pan Am Building. It was the perfect cover, since it allowed me to use Pan Am's own address in subsequent correspondence I had with the girls, but all their replies would be directed to my box with the mail-service firm.

After a week or so, I sent a "letter of employment" to each of them, along with a covering letter signed by myself (as Frank Williams) informing each of them that—surprise! surprise!—I had been assigned by the company to head up the European operation involving them, so they were to be my "crew" after all. I also enclosed a phony little form I'd made up, requesting all their measurements for purposes of having their uniforms made up. I directed each of them to address any future questions or information directly to me, in care of my box number.

Then I turned to getting ready for the tour myself. The passport I had was only a temporary one, and in my real name. I decided I needed a regular passport that I could use as Frank Williams and decided to take a chance that the passport office in New York was too busy for its employees to play cop.

I walked into the office one morning, turned in my temporary passport and ten days later was issued a regular passport. I was pleased to have the document, but it was, after all, issued to Frank W. Abagnale, Jr. It was not a passport that would serve "Pan Am First Officer Frank W. Williams," should the need ever arise. I started looking around and found what I needed in the hall of records of a large East Coast city. It was the death notice of Francis W. Williams, age twenty months, who had died at that young age on November 22, 1939. The archives disclosed the infant had been born on March 12, 1938, in a local hospital. I obtained a certified copy of the birth certificate for $3.00 by presenting myself to one of the clerks as the same Francis W. Williams. It seemed logical to me, and I'm sure it would make sense to anyone else, that anyone named "Francis" would prefer to be called "Frank."

I took the copy of the birth certificate to the passport office in Philadelphia, together with the necessary photos, and two weeks later had a second passport, one that matched my Pan Am uniform. I was now ready to "command" my crew, if nothing occurred in the next several months to upset my Arizona apple cart.

I spent those months knocking around the country, keeping a low profile in the main, but occasionally dropping a few phony Pan Am checks or counterfeit cashier's checks.

At one point I ended up in Miami, staying in the penthouse suite of a Miami Beach hotel, the Fontainebleau, under the guise of a California stock broker, complete with a briefcase full of $20s, $50s and $100s, and a rented Rolls-Royce, which I had leased in Los Angeles and driven to Florida.

It was all part of a grand scam I had in mind, which was to drop some really big counterfeit cashier's checks on some of the Miami banks and some of its more elite hotels after establishing a reputable front. I earned the reputable front in large part sheerly by accident. I had made it a point to acquaint myself with some of the hotel's top man-

171

agement people, and one of them stopped me in the lobby one afternoon and introduced me to a Florida broker, one whose financial genius was known even to me.

A staunch Floridian, he had the true Floridian's thinly disguised contempt for California, and I gathered from most of his remarks during our casual encounter that he didn't hold California stockbrokers in any esteem, either. He was so blatantly rude and arrogant at times that the hotel executive was patently embarrassed. After a few minutes I excused myself, he was so hostile. He grasped my arm as I was leaving.

"What's your opinion on the Saturn Electronics offering?" he asked with a supercilious smirk. I'd never heard of the company and in fact didn't know any such firm existed. But I regarded him blandly, then dropped one eyelid. "Buy all of it you can get your hands on," I said and walked off.

A few days later I encountered the man again as we were both waiting for our cars to be brought to the front entrance. He greeted me with grudging respect, which surprised me. "I should have listened to you on that Saturn stock," he said. "How the hell did you know Galaxy Communications was going to take over the company?"

I just grinned and gave him another wink. Later I learned that Saturn Electronics, after its acquisition by Galaxy, had closed from five to eight points up on each of the previous four days.

That evening I was accosted at the elevator by a well-groomed man in his thirties who introduced himself as a prominent city official.

"Rick [one of the hotel executives] told me about you, Mr. Williams," he said. "He said you might be setting up an office here and perhaps make your home in Miami during part of the year."

I nodded. "Well, I'm thinking about it seriously," I said, smiling. "I'll probably make up my mind within a few weeks."

"Well, perhaps I can help you," he said. "My wife and I are giving a party tonight and some of the city's and the state's top government and business leaders are going to be there, including the mayor and some people from the governor's staff. I'd like to invite you, if you'd consider coming. I think it would be an enjoyable evening for you, and like I say, you might meet some people who will help you make up your mind."

I accepted his invitation, because he was right, in a way. It was quite possible some of his guests could help me. By letting me fleece them.

It was a black-tie affair, but I had no trouble finding a tuxedo rental shop that was open and which could fit me on such short notice. I also had no trouble locating the city father's home, which proved to be uncomfortably close to a certain banker's home. I hoped she wasn't a guest also, but I had the parking attendant position my car for a quick getaway, just in case.

She wasn't a guest, but the most stunning and attractive blonde I've ever encountered, before and since, was a guest. I noticed her moments after I joined the throng of guests, and she kept attracting my attention all evening. Oddly enough, although she seemed always to be the center of a circle of admirers, she didn't seem to be with any one of the men paying her court. My host confirmed the fact.

"That's Cheryl," he said. "She's a standard decoration at parties like this. She's a model and she's been on the covers of several magazines. We have a pretty good arrangement with her. She lends excitement to our parties and we make sure she gets mentioned in all the society columns. Come on, I'll introduce you."

She made it immediately known that she'd been curious about me also. "I saw you arrive," she said, extending her hand. "That's a lovely Rolls. Is it yours or did you borrow it for the occasion?"

"No, it's one of mine," I said.

Her eyebrows arched. "One of yours? Do you have more than one Rolls-Royce?"

"I have several," I replied. "I'm a collector." I knew from the gleam in her eyes that I'd made a dear friend. She was obviously impressed by wealth and material possessions. In fact, I was continually surprised throughout the remainder of the evening that such a beautiful exterior masked such a venal and covetous interior. However, I wasn't interested in her lack of virtues. I was attracted by her obvious vices. She was avariciously gorgeous.

We weren't together the entire evening. We would part occasionally and go prowling separately, like two leopards seeking prey in the same jungle. I found the prey I was hunting, a couple of fat and juicy bank pigeons. She also found her prey. Me.

I took her aside about 2:30 A.M. "Look, this party's about dead," I proposed. "Why don't we go back to my penthouse and have some breakfast?"

Her reply was a blow to my ego. "What's it worth to you for me to go back to your hotel with you?" she asked, eying me provocatively.

"I thought you were a model," I blurted, surprised.

She smiled. "There're different kinds of modeling. Some modeling jobs come higher than others," she said.

I had never paid a girl to go to bed with me. The world of professional sex was an unknown realm. To my knowledge, I'd never before met a hooker or a call girl. But apparently I had now. However, I still wanted her in my bed, and having established her true calling, I made an attempt to establish her price. What the hell, I had plenty of money. "Uh, $300?" I ventured.

She grimaced prettily and shook her head. "No, I'm afraid $300 isn't enough,' she said.

I was astonished. Obviously I'd been cavorting in luxury for years without knowing the value of the wares I'd enjoyed. "Oh, all right, let's double it and say $600," I said.

She gave me a coolly speculative look. "That's closer," she said. "But for a man of your means, I should think it would be higher."

I looked at her and was irritated. I had established and followed a certain felonious code of ethics since taking up crime as a profession. Among other things, I'd never diddled an individual. For instance, I'd never purchased a wardrobe or any other personal item with a hot check. Too many department stores and business firms held an individual salesperson responsible for bogus checks. If a salesman took a check for a suit, and the check bounced, the cost of the suit came out of the clerk's salary. My targets had always been corporate targets—banks, airlines, hotels, motels or other establishments protected by insurance. When I splurged on a new wardrobe or anything else of a personal nature, I always hit a bank or a hotel for the needed cash.

It suddenly occurred to me that Cheryl would make a lovely exception to my rule. "Look, we could stand here all night and argue price," I said. "I hate quibbling. Instead of going to my place, why don't we go to your apartment, spend an hour or so there, and I'll give you $1,000."

She reached for her purse. "Let's go," she agreed. "But I don't have an apartment at the moment. I lost my lease and I'm staying at a hotel in Miami Beach." She named the hotel, which was one not too far from mine, and we were there within thirty minutes.

She was inserting her key into the door of her suite when I turned, saying, "I'll be right back."

She grabbed my arm. "Hey, where're you going?" she asked, somewhat agitated. "You're not going to back out, are you?"

I took her hand off my arm. "Look, you don't think I carry $1,000 in my pocket, do you?" I said. "I'm going downstairs and cash a check."

"At three-thirty in the morning!" she exclaimed. "You're

175

not going to get a check cashed for that amount at this hour. You couldn't get one cashed for $100."

I smiled loftily. "I think so. I know the owners of this hotel. Besides, this is a certified cashier's check, drawn on the Chase Manhattan Bank in New York. It's like gold here. I cash them all the time."

"Let me see it," she asked. I reached inside my jacket pocket and extracted one of the Chase Manhattan counterfeits I'd acquired before coming to Miami. It was in the amount of $1,400. She examined the voucher and nodded. "It is like gold," she agreed. "Why don't you just endorse it over to me?"

"Uh-uh," I declined. "This check is for $1,400. We agreed on $1,000, and while $400 isn't that important, a deal is a deal."

"I agree," she said. "So endorse it. I'll give you the $400." She dug in her purse and came up with a thin sheaf of $100s, from which she took four and handed them to me. I endorsed the check and handed it to her.

I have the sequel from what reporters call "reliable sources." Several days later, when her bank informed her the cashier's check was a counterfeit, she called the Dade County Sheriff's Department, furious. She eventually was contacted by O'Riley.

"Why'd he give you this check?" asked O'Riley.

"That doesn't matter," she snapped. "He gave it to me, and it's bad, and I want the bastard caught."

"I know," said O'Riley. "But I also need to know how this man thinks, so I can catch him. Your description fits Frank Abagnale, but he's never given any bad paper to an individual. He doesn't even pass bad paper in retail stores. Why, all of a sudden, is he giving a square john, and a beautiful woman at that, a worthless check for $1,400? What was the purpose?"

O'Riley is something of a con artist himself. He obtained the full story from her. "I don't mind his getting a free piece," she concluded bitterly. "Hell, I've given it away before. But that bastard conned me out of $400 cash. That I resent."

I have always agreed with O'Riley's assessment of the matter. We both got screwed.

However, her session with me was probably more delightful and less costly than the encounters I had with the two bankers before leaving Miami. I ripped them off for more than $20,000 each. I also flimflammed the Fontainebleau by paying my bill with a counterfeit cashier's check that yielded me several hundred dollars change.

I put the Rolls in a storage garage and sent a telegram to the California leasing firm informing them of its whereabouts. Cheryl was right. It was a lovely car and deserved better than being abandoned to the elements and vandals.

I holed up in Sun Valley, keeping a low profile and an honest demeanor, for the winter. As spring approached, I flew back to New York, set myself up in a brownstone flat in an elegant section of Manhattan and dropped "reminder" notes to each of my prospective "stews." The replies I received assured me that my fictional status as a Pan Am promotional executive was still believed, so I proceeded to fulfill my fleshly fantasy. I knew the name of the Hollywood firm that designed and manufactured all of the stewardess uniforms for Pan Am. I flew to Hollywood and, wearing my Pan Am pilot's garb, called on the fashion firm. I presented a phony letter of introduction to the woman in charge of Pan Am's account, detailed the fictional public relations tour of Europe and had my explanation accepted at face value. "We'll have the ensembles ready in six weeks," she said. "I presume you also want luggage for each of the girls?"

"Of course," I said.

I stayed in the Los Angeles area while the girls' clothing was being fashioned, attending to other facets necessary to the escapade. I paid a call to the Pan Am stores department at the Los Angeles Airport, dressed as a pilot, and picked up all the hat and uniform emblems they'd need.

I'd had all the girls send me one-inch-square color photographs of themselves. I used the photographs to make up fake Pan Am ID cards, similar to mine, and listing the status of each as "flight attendant."

When the uniforms were ready, I picked them up personally, driving a rented station wagon with counterfeit Pan Am logos on the doors, and paid for the uniforms by signing an invoice for them.

In late May I sent each of the girls a letter, enclosing an airline ticket for each—tickets I'd bought and paid for with cash—and telling them to assemble in the lobby of the Los Angeles airport on May 26.

The gathering of my eaglets was one of the boldest and more flamboyant productions of my poseur performances. I went to one of the more luxurious inns surrounding the airport and booked a room for each of the girls, and also engaged, for the day after their arrival, one of the hotel's conference rooms. I made all the bookings in Pan Am's firm name, although I paid cash for the facilities. I satiated the curiosity of the assistant manager who handled the transaction by explaining this was not regular Pan Am business but a "special feature" of the airline's promotion department.

On the morning the girls were to arrive, I donned my Pan Am pilot's uniform and visited Pan Am's operational department at the airport, seeking out the manager of the carrier's car pool.

"Look, I've got eight stewardesses coming in at two P.M. today on a special assignment, and I need some transportation to get them to the hotel," I said. "You think you can help me out?"

"Sure," he said. "I've got a regular crew wagon available. I'll pick them up myself. You gonna be there?"

"I'll just meet you here at one-thirty and go with you," I said. "You need me to sign anything?"

"Nah, I got you covered, Jetman." He grinned. "Just have one my size."

The girls showed up on time and were duly impressed with the gleaming Pan Am crew wagon, which was actually just an oversized station wagon. The pool chief and I loaded their luggage and he drove us all to the hotel, where he again assisted in unloading their luggage and getting the girls situated. I offered to buy him a drink after we were through, but he declined. "I like your kind of duty," he said, grinning. "Just call on me anytime."

The next morning I assembled the girls in the conference room, where I passed out their ID cards and presented them with their uniforms and luggage. They squealed with delight as they inspected the ensembles and the luggage, each piece of which was monogrammed with the owner's name and Pan Am's logo.

There were more squeals of joy as I outlined our itinnerary: London, Paris, Rome, Athens, Geneva, Munich, Berlin, Madrid, Oslo, Copenhagen, Vienna and other European spas. I quieted them down and took on the air of a stern father.

"Now, this sounds like a lot of fun, and I hope it will be, but we're on serious business, and I won't put up with any nonsense," I told them. "I have the authority to discharge any one of you for misconduct or for goofing off, and I will send you home if I have to. Let's get one thing straight—I'm the boss and you will live by my instructions and follow the policies I outline. I think you'll find my rules eminently fair, and you should have no trouble following them, and therefore no trouble at all.

"First off, you'll notice that each of you is identified as a stewardess on your ID card. As far as the personnel of the hotels where we'll be staying, and the photographers with whom we'll be working are concerned, you are stewardesses. But we will all travel as civilians, and that includes flying or driving, and I will tell you when you are to wear the uniforms. You're on a very desirable tour, duty that could cause some dissension and jealousy among our regular cadre of flight attendants, male and female. So if you do have occasion to mingle with regular flight crews, just say you're with our New York public relations office, on a special assignment, and answer as few questions about your actual status as possible. If anyone presses, refer him or her to me.

"Now, you'll be paid every two weeks, a regular company paycheck. It's very difficult to cash a check in Europe, so when I give you your paycheck, if you'll just endorse it, I'll cash it at the local Pan Am office or at one of the banks or hotels with which we've made arrangements.

"Now I know some of you are wondering why you can't just send your checks home to be deposited. There're two reasons. First, the checks will probably be issued on one of our foreign accounts. The company likes the checks to be cashed in Europe. Second is the exchange rate. If you cash a check yourself, it will be cashed at the current exchange rate and you'll usually end up losing money. So I'll cash your checks, give you the cash and then if you want to send any money home, you can send a money order or a cashier's check home. Does anyone have any questions?"

No one did. I smiled. "Okay, then, you're on your own for the rest of the day and the night. But get a good night's sleep. We leave tomorrow for London."

We did, too, using tickets that had cost me a small fortune in cash. We landed in London in a clammy, predawn rain and I instructed the girls to change into their stewardess uniforms before we went to the hotel.

I was, understandably, nervous and apprehensive at the outset of my scheme, but I plunged ahead recklessly. I even checked us in at the Royal Gardens in Kensington, gambling that none of the employees would associate

TWA Pilot Frank Adams with Pan Am First Officer Frank Williams. I hired a van to take us from the airport to the hotel, and the registration clerk, to my relief, was a total stranger to me.

"We're Pan Am Flight 738," I said. "We were diverted from Shannon and I don't know if anyone made reservations for us or not."

"No problem, Captain," said the clerk. "That is, if the girls don't mind doubling up. We've only five rooms available."

The girls slept until nearly noon. Then I loosed them on the town by themselves, telling them I had "set up a photo session" with the local Pan Am office. What I did was to go through the London telephone book until I found what I was looking for, a commercial photography firm. I called the company and identified myself as a Pan Am public relations representative.

"I've got eight girls at the Royal Gardens, stewardesses, and what we need is some color and black and white shots suitable for advertisements and promotion brochures— you know, candid stuff of the girls at Piccadilly, some of them at the Thames bridges, that sort of thing," I said. "Do you think you can handle it?"

"Oh, quite!" enthused the man to whom I spoke. "Why don't I have one of our boys pop right over with some samples of our work? I'm sure we can do business, Mr. Williams."

The firm's representative and I had lunch and worked out a deal. I'd picked one of the better firms in London, it seemed. They'd even done some work in the past for Pan Am.

"Well, this is a little different, something new we're trying," I said. "One thing you'll like, I'm sure, is that you'll be paid in cash at the end of each day. Just give me an invoice for the amount."

"What about the proofs?" asked the camera firm's rep.

"Well, chances are we'll be long gone to another city—

we've got a hectic schedule—so just send them to the public relations and advertising department of Pan Am in New York," I said. "If they decide to use any of your pictures, you'll be paid again at your normal commercial rate for each picture selected."

He whistled and raised his glass of beer. "That is a different way of doing things, and I like it," he said, grinning contentedly.

The next morning, a three-man camera crew in a passenger van loaded with photographic equipment called at the hotel and picked up my eight fledglings. I didn't go with them, but simply told the chief cameraman to use his own judgment and imagination and return the girls in a reasonably sober and presentable condition.

"Gotcha, guv'nor." He laughed and shepherded the girls into the van.

I had business of my own to conduct. I had embarked on this illicit odyssey well provisioned with sinful supplies: counterfeit cashier's checks (products of my own handiwork), Pan Am expense checks and regular paychecks (Papa Lavalier's unwitting artwork) and Pan Am reimbursement authorization forms (pilfered from Pan Am's own stores department), the last more for bluff than effect.

There were a lot of factors weighing in my favor. London, and most of the other major cities on out itinerary, was dotted with branches of major American banks.

The next morning I gathered the girls in my room and explained the hotel policy on airline crews, then spread out eight phony Pan Am "expense checks" for them to endorse. Each check, of course, was for much more than the hotel bill. "I'll need your ID cards, too, and while I'm settling the bill, you'll all have to stand in sight of the cashier," I said. Not one of them questioned the amount of the check she signed, if any one of them bothered to notice.

The scam went off flawlessly. The girls clustered in a group in the lobby, in view of the cashier, and I presented the nine fake checks in payment for our lodging and other charges. The cashier raised the only question.

"Oh, these are rather high, Captain, I'm not sure I have enough American dollars to make change," she said, inspecting her cash drawer. "In fact, I don't. You're going to have to take pounds in change, I'm afraid."

I acted miffed, but accepted the decision, knowing the cashier would probably make a profit, or thought she would. The pounds she gave me, however, were real. The Pan Am checks weren't.

We flew to Rome that afternoon, where, over the next three days, the procedure was repeated. The hotel cashier in Rome, too, questioned the amount of the expense checks, but was satisfied with my explanation.

"Well, I'm sorry about that," I said. "But we're on an eighteen-day tour of Italy, and, of course, you can give me change in lira if you like."

He liked, since it meant a personal profit of some fifty American dollars for him.

I decided against jaunting around Europe by air, not because of the expense but because it would have exposed the girls constantly to other airline crews. That was my biggest problem in implementing my scheme—shielding the girls from other airline people. As I previously pointed out, airline people like to talk shop, especially if they work for the same carrier.

There was, naturally, some unavoidable contact with other flight crews, since the success of my check-cashing scam demanded we stay at hotels which catered to airline personnel. There was always the risk that one of the girls, while in uniform, would encounter another, actual, Pan Am stewardess, and a disastrous dialogue would ensue.

Actual stew: "Hi, I'm Mary Alice, out of L.A. Where are you based?"

My girl: "Oh, I'm not based anywhere. I'm just over here on a P.R. thing."

Actual stew: "You're not a stewardess?"

My girl: "Not really. There're eight of us, and we're doing some photographic modeling for promotion and advertising purposes."

Actual stew (to herself): "Like hell. I've been with Pan Am for five years and I never heard of any such work. I'd better report this to the chief and see if these people are for real."

I wanted to avoid any such scenario, so I would frequently reinforce my instructions to the girls with repeat lectures. "Look, when you're out in civilian clothes and you meet a Pan Am flight attendant in uniform, don't say you fly for Pan Am, too, because you don't," I'd warn them.

"If you're in uniform and you encounter another Pan Am stewardess, just say you're here on vacation if your status is questioned. You may feel that's being deceptive, and it is, but we have a reason. We don't want other airlines to find out about this venture, because they'd most likely, with some justification, put the word out in the industry that Pan Am isn't using real stewardesses in our travel ads or promotional brochures. And we don't really want our line stewardesses to know, as I've told you, because it would likely cause dissension. For a working stewardess, this would really be a choice assignment."

The girls cooperated splendidly in that respect. And I rented a comfortable, almost luxurious Volkswagen bus for our meandering around Europe. At times my scheme seemed more like a leisurely vacation than a felonious venture, for we often spent days, sometimes a week or more, in colorful little out-of-the-way spots in this country or that one and during such detours I curbed my crooked activities. It was not part of my plan to shaft the peasants.

But my scam got back on the track in major cities. Before entering such a metropolis, we'd stop and change into our airline uniforms, and, on our arrival at the hotel of my choosing, the scheme would pick up steam and begin operating again.

Every two weeks I paid the girls with a counterfeit payroll check, then had them endorse the checks over to me in return for cash. Since I was paying all their expenses (although each thought Pan Am was picking up the tab), most of them purchased money orders and sent them home to their parents or their bank.

The girls were entirely guiltless, of course. Not one, during the summer, ever had an inkling she was involved in a criminal venture. Each thought she was legitimately employed by Pan Am. They were completely duped by my con.

Mine was an idyllic intrigue, but often hectic and taxing. Riding herd on eight lovely, vivacious, exuberant, energetic girls is akin to a cowboy riding herd on a bunch of wild steers while mounted on a lame horse—damned near impossible. I had determined at the outset of the scheme that there would be no personal involvement with any of the girls, but my resolve was endangered a score of times during the course of the summer. Each of them was an outrageous flirt, and I, of course, was a prince of philanderers, and when one of the girls was inclined to make a sexual advance (and each of them did on several occasions), I was hardly prone to fend her off. But I always managed.

I did not lead a celibate life during the summer. I had ample opportunities to engage in side liaisons with the girls of whatever localities we were frequenting, and I took advantage of each and every opportunity.

Monique was not one of the liaisons. When we visited Paris and I sought her out, she informed me our relationship was finished. "I'll still be your friend, Frank, and I hope you'll still help Papa in his business, but I want to settle down and you don't," she said. "I've met another man, a pilot for Air France, and we're pretty serious about our future."

I assured her of my understanding and, in fact, was somewhat relieved. I also affirmed that her father would continue to get "Pan Am business," although that statement was a lie. I was beginning to feel some guilt concerning my duplicitous use of Papa Lavalier, and had opted to release him as a pawn in my scurrilous game. Anyway, he'd already provided me with enough supplies to drain a dozen bank vaults if I used them all.

The girls and I ended our tour of Europe in Copenhagen, where I put them on a plane for Arizona. I dispatched them back to the States with their arms laden with roses and a flowery speech designed to allay any suspicions that might arise in their minds in coming weeks.

"Keep your uniforms, keep your ID cards and keep your check stubs [I'd always returned a check stub when I cashed a check]," I instructed them. "If the company wants the uniforms and IDs returned, you'll be contacted. As far as employment goes, just return to school, because we're not going to hire you on a permanent basis until you graduate, and then you'll be contacted by a company representative. It probably won't be me, because I've been ordered back to flight duty. But I hope you'll all end up as part of my crew again, for I've had a wonderful time with you this summer."

I had had a wonderful time, all things considered. If the girls put a lot of gray strands in my hair, they also, unwittingly, put a lot of green stuff in my pockets. Something like $300,000 in all.

The girls did hear from Pan Am, as a matter of fact. After three months of a steady stream of photographs, from dozens of European cities and all showing the same eight girls in Pan Am stewardess costumes, advertising executives of Pan Am launched an investigation. Eventually the entire matter ended up in O'Riley's hands and he deftly sorted it out and put it into focus for the carrier's officers and also for the girls.

I understand all eight of them took it gracefully, if with some vivid and descriptive language.

I stayed in Europe for several weeks after parting with the girls, then returned to the States, where I wandered around like a gypsy for several weeks, never staying in one place for more than two or three days. I was becoming moody again, nervous and edgy, and the knowledge that I would probably always be a man on the move, a fox perpetually hunted by the hounds, was beginning to weigh on my conscience, affecting my conscious life.

I virtually ceased my check-swindling activities, fearful the hounds were close enough and reluctant to create additional spoor. Only rarely was I challenged to display my creative criminality.

One such time was in a large midwestern city. I was sitting in the airport restaurant after arrival, enjoying lunch, when I became interested in the conversation in the adjoining booth, an exchange between an elderly, stern-faced man and a very young, servile companion, apparently an employee. I gathered from the conversation that the older man was a banker, en route to a convention in San Francisco, and from the remarks he made to the young man it was clear he expected his bank to make money in his absence. He was cool, crusty, arrogant and obviously proud of his lofty status, and when he was paged on the airport intercom I learned his name. Jasper P. Cashman.

That afternoon I did some discreet digging into Jasper P. Cashman's background, utilizing a local newspaper's library. J. P. Cashman was a prominent man in his community, a self-made tycoon. He'd started as a teller in his bank when the financial house had assets of less than $5 million. He was president now and the bank's assets exceeded $100 million.

I scouted the bank the following day. It was a new building, still boasting its expansion motto on the large front window. The interior was roomy and pleasing. Tellers on one side, junior officers scattered across an opposite

187

wall. Senior officers in airy, glassed-in offices. Cashman's offices on the third floor. J. P. Cashman didn't believe in close contact with the underlings.

I rented a car, drove to a modest city 175 miles distant and opened a checking account for $10,000 with a counterfeit cashier's check. Then I returned to Cashman's town and the next day called at his bank. I wasn't really interested in the money involved in my swindle. Cashman's manner had irked me, and I simply wanted to sting him.

I was the picture of the affluent businessman when I entered the bank. Gray three-piece suit. Alligators, luster-shined. Countess Mara tie. A leather brief-case, slim and elegant.

Cashman's companion at the airport was one of the junior officers. His desk was neat and tidy. His nameplate sparkled with newness. He obviously was newly promoted. I dropped into the chair in front of his desk.

"Yes, sir, can I help you?" he asked, patently impressed by my dress and bearing.

"Yes, you can, as a matter of fact," I said easily. "I'm Robert Leeman from Junction, and I need to cash a check, a rather large one. I've all the proper identification and you can call my bank for verification, but I don't think that'll be necessary. J. P. Cashman knows me, and he'll verify the check. You can call him. No, I'll do it myself, since I need to talk to him anyway."

Before he could react, I reached over, picked up his telephone and dialed Cashman's correct extension. Cashman's secretary answered.

"Yes, Mr. Cashman, please. . . . He isn't. . . . Oh, yes, he mentioned that last week and it slipped my mind. Well, listen, would you tell him when he returns that Bob Leeman dropped by, and tell him Jean and I are looking forward to seeing him and Mildred in Junction for the hunt. He'll know what I mean. . . . Yes, thank you."

I replaced the telephone and stood up, grimacing. "Doesn't look like my day," I said ruefully. "I needed the cash, too. I can't get to Junction and back in time for this deal. Well, good day, sir."

I started to turn and the young officer stopped me. "Uh, how big is the check you wanted to cash, Mr. Leeman?"

"Pretty good sized," I said. "I need $7,500. Do you think you can take care of it? I can give you the number of my bank in Junction." Without waiting for a reply, I dropped back into the chair, briskly wrote out a check for $7,500 and handed it to him. As I figured, he didn't call the bank in Junction. He stood up and turned toward one of the glassed-in offices. "Sir, I'll have to have Mr. James, the vice president, okay this, which I'm sure he will. I'll be back in a moment."

He walked into James's office and said (as I later learned) exactly what I'd conditioned him to say. "Sir, there's a Mr. Leeman here from Junction and he needs to cash this rather large check. He's a personal friend of Mr. Cashman, and he wanted to see Mr. Cashman, but as you know Mr. Cashman's in San Francisco."

"A personal friend of the old man's?"

"Yes, sir, business and social, I understand."

"Cash it. We sure as hell don't want to irritate any of the old man's associates."

A minute later the young officer was handing the phony check to a teller. "Cash this for the gentleman, please. Mr. Leeman, I'm glad I could help you."

I wasn't too well pleased with the Pavlov's-dog swindle. In fact, I didn't enjoy it at all. I left town that day and several days later stopped in a remote Vermont village to do some meditating. Mine were gloomy cogitations. I was no longer living, I decided, I was merely surviving. I had accumulated a fortune with my nefarious impersonations, swindles and felonies, but I wasn't enjoying the fruits of my libidinous labors. I concluded it was time to retire, to go to earth like a fox in a remote and secure lair where I could relax and commence building a new and crime-free life.

I reviewed the places I had been on the atlas of my mind. I was mildly astonished at the extensiveness of my travels, recalling my journeys of the past few years. I had crisscrossed the globe from Singapore to Stockholm, from Tahiti to Trieste, from Baltimore to the Baltics, and to other places I had forgotten I'd visited.

But one place I hadn't forgotten. And its name kept popping into my thoughts as I sought a safe haven. Montpellier, France.

Montpellier. That was my safe haven, I finally decided. And having made the decision, I didn't give it a second thought.

I should have.

CHAPTER NINE

Does This Tab Include the Tip?

Quantitatively, the vineyards of Bas Languedoc produce more wine than the other three great French wine departments combined. Qualitatively, with one or two exceptions, the wine of Languedoc has all the bouquet, body and taste of flat root beer. The considerate host serves an ordinary Languedoc wine only with leftover meat loaf, and preferably to guests whom he'd rather not see again.

It is, in the main, really bad juice.

Fortunately for France, the vintners, grape pickers, bottlers and the vast majority of the rest of the population consume the bulk of Languedoc's wines. France exports only its great wines from the vineyards of Burgundy, Bordeaux and Champagne, which are justly famous for quality and excellence.

I learned all about viniculture in Montpellier. The first

thing I learned was not to drink the local *vins du pays*.

I was probably the only water drinker in town. However, I didn't go to Montpellier for either the wine or the water. I was there to hide. Permanently, I hoped. I had reached the pinnacle of a criminal mountain and the view wasn't that great. Now I wanted an honest valley to shelter me in its hollow.

I had passed through Montpellier, driving from Marseille to Barcelona, during one of my first bad-check forays through Europe. Outside of town I had parked beneath a huge olive tree and picnicked on cheese, bread, sausages and soft drinks I'd picked up in the city. Close at hand, pickers swarmed like ants through a vast grape orchard and far away the snow-tipped peaks of the Pyrenees glistened in the sun. I felt comfortable, at ease, almost happy. As if I were home.

In a sense, I was. This part of southern France was my mother's native land. She had been born here and after she married my father, and following the breakout of guerrilla warfare in Algiers, her parents had returned here with their other children. My maternal grandparents, several uncles and aunts and a covey of cousins still lived within an hour's drive of the olive tree. I quelled an impulse to turn aside and visit my mother's people and drove on to Spain.

I had never forgotten that tranquil, enjoyable interlude near Montpellier. And when, at the ripe old age of twenty, I decided to retire from my life as a counterfeit person, dealing in counterfeit wares, I chose Montpellier as my retreat. I was not happy that I had to return there behind yet another counterfeit identity, but I had no choice.

Montpellier, in many ways, was ideal for my purpose. It was not a tourist attraction. It was situated too far inland from the Mediterranean to lure the Riviera set, yet close enough that a seashore outing was available at the end of a short drive.

It was large enough (80,000 population) that an American taking up residence would not excite undue curiosity, yet too small to command a major airport or to entice large hotel operators. There were no Hiltons or Sheratons in Montpellier and its tiny air facility served only light aircraft. The lack of air service or swank hotels weighed in my favor. There was very little chance of my encountering a pilot, a stewardess or a hotel employee who might recognize me.

I presented myself in Montpellier as Robert Monjo, a successful author and screenwriter from Los Angeles, "successful" in order to explain the sizable account I opened in one of the local banks. At that, I didn't deposit all the moneys I took with me to Montpellier. Had I done so, it might have aroused some curiosity as to my actual livelihood. I retained treble the amount in cash, hidden away in my luggage. As a matter of fact, the people of Montpellier were not prone to pry. I was asked only the necessary and perfunctory questions as I went about the business of becoming an expatriate citizen of the town.

I bought a small cottage, a charming and gracious little house with a tiny back yard shielded by a high board fence, where the previous owner had cultivated a minuscule garden. The operator of the store where I bought furnishings for the house lent me the services of his wife, a skilled interior decorator, in selecting the proper furniture and arranging the decor. I fixed up one room as a study and library, reinforcing my image as a writer engaged in research and literary creation.

I bought a Renault, one of the more comfortable models but not luxurious enough to attract attention. Within two weeks I felt at home, secure and content in my new surroundings.

And if God had shorted the Mediterranean Languedoc on good grapes, He made up for it in the people. They were a sturdy, amiable, courteous and gregarious populace in the main, quick to smile and to offer any assistance. The housewives in my neighborhood were always knocking on my door with gifts of pastry, fresh baked bread or a serving from their dinner pots. My immediate neighbor, Armand Perigueux, was my favorite. He was a huge, gnarled man of seventy-five and he still worked as an overseer in a vineyard, commuting to and from work on a bicycle.

He called the first time bearing two bottles of wine, one red and one white. "Most of our wines do not suit American palates," he said in his booming, yet gentle, voice. "But there are a few good wines in the Languedoc, and these two are among them."

I am not a tastevin, but having drunk of the good wines I determined never to sample the others. But the people of Montpellier drank more wine than any other liquid. A lunch or dinner was not served without wine. I have even seen wine consumed at breakfast.

From Armand I learned that God actually had nothing to do with Languedoc's poor record as a producer of quality wines. Nearly one hundred years past, he said, an insect, the phylloxera, had ravaged all the vineyards of France, almost dealing a death blow to the wine industry. "I have heard that this pest was brought to France attached to the roots of vines imported from America," said Armand. "But I do not know that to be true."

However, Armand told me, he did know it to be truth that the great bulk of France's grape vines were of American rootstock, immune to the wine bug, onto which French plants had been grafted. And, he said slyly after I had gained his confidence, Americans and other nationals probably consumed more Languedoc wines than they were aware of.

Almost daily, he informed me, tanker trucks filled with the cheap wines of the Languedoc chugged northward to the great wine districts, where their cargoes were blended with the choice wines of Burgundy and Bordeaux. "It is called stretching, like adding water to whiskey," said Armand. "I do not think it is honest."

Montpellier was a good place to learn about wines, he said. "We have the Wine University of France right here in our city," he said proudly. "You can go there and study."

I never visited the university. Since I had no taste for wine, although I drank it on social occasions, I had no yen to acquire a knowledge of wine. I was satisfied with the bits and pieces of information imparted by Armand. He was a good teacher. He never gave tests and he never graded me.

It was difficult for me to stay busy. Loafing is hard work. I spent a lot of time driving around. I would drive to the coast and spend a few days exploring the sand dunes. Or I would drive to the Spanish border and spend hours hiking in the foothills of the Pyrenees. Occasionally I visited Armand's vineyard or the orchard of another wine-grower. At the end of the first month, I drove to the small village where my grandparents lived and spent three days with them. My grandmother corresponded regularly with my mother, and she was aware of all the happenings at home. I wormed them out of her discreetly, for I did not want her to know I had exiled myself from my family. My mother was well, as were my sister and brothers. My father was still courting my mother, which my grandmother found amusing. My mother had apparently told my grandmother that I was "hitchhiking" around the world, seeking a goal and attempting to decide my future, and I fostered that impression during my visit.

I did not tell my grandparents that I was living in Montpellier. I told them I was on my way to Spain, with the thought in mind of enrolling in one of the Spanish universities. I visited them a second time during my stay in Montpellier. I told them on that occasion that I hadn't found a Spanish college that challenged me and was returning to Italy to explore the universities there.

195

As I became more satisfied with my life in Montpellier, I actually contemplated resuming my education. Montpellier is the seat of one of France's twenty academic districts and a small but fine state university was located in the city. I visited the campus and learned that several courses were available to foreigners, although none was taught in English. However, that was no bar to me, since French was a second tongue for me, acquired from my mother.

I also started thinking about getting a job or opening some kind of small business, perhaps a stationery store, since I was growing sleek and plump in the idle, luxurious life I was leading. Even Armand remarked on my increasing stoutness. "There is not much exercise in writing, eh, Robert?" he said, poking me in the stomach.

"Why don't you come to work for me in the vineyards, and I will make you lean and tough." I declined the offer. Physical labor is not my forte. Nor could I force myself to exercise.

I was still mulling the thought of registering at the university, and the idea of finding some useful employment, when both issues were rendered moot. Four months after taking up residence in Montpellier, I learned a bitter truth: when the hounds have help, there is no safe place for a fox to hide.

I shopped regularly at a small (by American standards) market on the outskirts of Montpellier, a grocery Armand had recommended. I went to the store twice weekly to supply my larder, or whenever I needed something. This occasion was one of my scheduled shopping trips and the store clerk was sacking my groceries when I remembered I needed milk. I told the boy to set my foodstuffs aside (there were others in line) and strolled to the back of the store for the milk. Returning to the check-out counter, I walked around a shelf of canned goods and saw four men at the checker's stand, now devoid of customers and clerk.

One had a shotgun, another had what appeared to be

a short-barreled machine gun and the other two had pistols. My first thought was that bandits were robbing the store and that the employees and customers were on the floor.

But as I wheeled to seek cover behind the shelves, one of the men shouted, "Abagnale!"

I ducked behind the shelves only to be confronted by three uniformed gendarmes, all pointing pistols at me. They came at me from all sides then, men in uniform, men in plainclothes and all pointing a pistol, shotgun, machine gun or rifle at me. Orders cracked around my ears like whip pops.

"Hands up!"

"Hands on your head!"

"Up against the shelves, spread-eagle!"

"Face down on the floor!"

I had my hands up. I didn't know which of the other commands to obey, but I sure as hell didn't want to be shot. And some of the officers were handling their weapons in a manner that scared me. As a matter of fact, they were scaring their fellow officers.

"For God's sake, don't shoot," I shouted. "One of you tell me what you want me to do and I'll do it."

A tall, lean man with austere features pointed his pistol at me. "Get on the floor, facedown!" he barked. I did as he instructed, helped by several less-than-gentle hands. Rough hands twisted my arms up behind my back and other uncaring hands clamped steel circlets tightly around my wrists.

I was then hauled unceremoniously to my feet and, surrounded by Sûreté detectives, Interpol agents, gendarmes and God knows what other kind of fuzz, I was hustled out of the store and rudely shoved into the back seat of an unmarked sedan. I can't say French police are brutal, but I will say they handle suspects with undue firmness. I was driven directly to the Montpellier police station. No one said a word en route.

At the station, the austere detective and two other officers, also Sûreté agents, ushered me into a small room. French policemen have a wide latitude in the handling of criminals, especially in interrogations of suspects. They get right to the point, dispensing with the reading of any rights a criminal may have. I don't think a crook has any rights in France.

"My name is Marcel Gaston, of the Sûreté," said the lean officer in curt tones. "You are Frank Abagnale, are you not?"

"I'm Robert Monjo," I said in indignant tones. "I'm a writer from California, an American. I'm afraid you gentlemen have made a very serious mistake."

Gaston slapped me, a sharp, stinging blow. "Most of the mistakes I make, monsieur, are serious mistakes, but I have not made a mistake in this instance. You are Frank Abagnale."

"I am Robert Monjo," I said doggedly, searching their faces for a hint of doubt.

One of the other Sûreté agents stepped forward, his hand balled into a fist, but Gaston put out an arm and stopped him, without releasing me from his fixed stare. Then he shrugged.

"We could beat it out of you, but that isn't necessary," he said. "I have all the time in the world, Abagnale, but I don't intend to waste too much of it on you. We can hold you until doomsday, or at least until we have located witnesses to identify you. Until then, unless you choose to cooperate, I am going to place you in the cell for common drunks and petty criminals. You can stay there for a week, two weeks, a month, it makes no difference to me. However, you will not be fed and you will have no water until you decide to confess. Why don't you just tell us what we want to know right now? We know who you are. We know what you have done. You will only inconvenience yourself.

"One other thing, Abagnale. If you force us to go to a

lot of trouble to get the information you could give us at this moment, I will not forget it. And you will always remember the consequences, I promise you."

I looked at Gaston and knew he meant every word he had spoken. Marcel Gaston was one tough bastard.

"I'm Frank Abagnale," I said.

I never really gave them the kind of confession they wanted. I never volunteered any details on any of the offenses I'd committed in France. But if they knew of a particular caper and outlined it for me, I'd nod and say, "That's about the way it happened, all right," or, "Yes, that was me."

Gaston made up a document, setting down a lot of my crimes, the circumstances of my arrest and my interrogation, and let me read it. "If that is essentially correct, you will help yourself by signing it," he said.

I couldn't quarrel with the instrument. He'd even included the fact that he'd slapped me. I signed it.

The affidavit also disclosed how I'd been caught. Major airlines didn't serve Montpellier, but it was visited frequently by stewardesses and other flight personnel. An Air France flight attendant, visiting relatives in Montpellier, had spotted me shopping a couple of weeks past and had recognized me. She had seen me get into my car and had jotted down the license number. On her return to Paris, she had sought out her captain and told him of her suspicions. She was positive enough about her identification that her captain called the police.

"I'm positive it's him. I dated him," she insisted.

I never learned which Air France stewardess put the finger on me. No one would tell me. I had dallied with several, over the years. I hoped it wasn't Monique, but to this day I still don't know the informant's identity. I don't think it was Monique, however. Had she seen me in Montpellier, she would have confronted me.

I was kept six days in Montpellier, during which time several lawyers appeared to offer their services. I selected a middle-aged man whose mannerisms and appearance reminded me of Armand, although he frankly stated he didn't think he could win me my freedom. "I have gone over all the police documents, and they have you dead to rights," he commented. "The best we can hope for is a light sentence."

I told him I'd settle for that.

Scarcely a week after my arrest, to my astonishment, I was removed to Perpignan and the day after my arrival there I was brought to trial in a court of assizes, made up of a judge, two assessors (prosecutors) and nine citizen jurors, all of whom would jointly decide my guilt or innocence.

It wasn't much of a trial, really, lasting less than two days. Gaston listed the charges against me and the evidence he'd gathered to support the accusations. There were ample witnesses available to appear against me.

"How does the defendant plead?" inquired the judge of my attorney.

"My client will offer no defense against these charges," replied the lawyer. "In the interest of time, we would like to sum up our position now."

He then launched into an eloquent and impassioned plea for leniency in my behalf. He cited my youth—I was still not twenty-one—and portrayed me as an unfortunate and confused young man, the product of a broken home "and still more of a delinquent than a criminal." He pointed out that a dozen other European nations where I had perpetrated similar crimes had placed formal demands for extradition, once my debt to France was paid.

"This young man will, in all probability, never see his native land for many, many years, and even when he does return home, he will return in chains and only to face prison there," argued the lawyer. "I need not point out to this court the harshness of the prison life this young man will have to endure here. I ask the court to take that into account in setting a penalty."

I was adjudged guilty. But at the time I thought jubilantly that my attorney, if he'd lost a battle, had won the war. The judge sentenced me to only one year in prison.

I was remanded to Perpignan's prison, the "House of Arrest," a gloomy, forbidding stone fortress constructed in the seventeenth century, and not until I had been there for a few days did I realize just how lenient the judge had been.

I was received by two guards who brusquely ordered me to strip and who then escorted me, still naked, to an upper floor where I was marched down a narrow corridor devoid of cells as such. On either side were only stone walls set with solid steel doors. The guards halted before one of the metal portals and one unlocked and opened the door. It screeched open with a sound reminiscent of a horror movie, and the other guard shoved me inside the dark cubicle. I stumbled and fell forward, striking my head against the back of the cell, for the cell was a sunken one. I had not noted the two steps leading to the floor. I was never actually to see the steps.

I was in total darkness. A damp, chilling, breath-stifling, frightening darkness. I stood up to grope around for the light switch and cracked my head against the steel ceiling.

There was no light switch. There was no light in the cell. There was, in fact, nothing in the cell but a bucket. No bed, no toilet, no wash basin, no drain, nothing. Just the bucket. The cell was not a cell, actually, it was a hole, a raised dungeon perhaps five feet wide, five feet high and five feet deep, with a ceiling and door of steel and a floor and walls of stone. The ceiling and door were chill to the touch. The walls wept chilly tears constantly.

I waited for my eyes to adjust to the darkness. No light filtered into the cell from any source. There were no cracks in the overhead or walls. The ancient door to my steel and stone box seemed to blend itself into its aperture like a hermetic seal. My eyes did not adjust. The eyes do not adjust to total darkness.

There was air entering the cell. Periodically a cold draft explored my skin like clammy fingers, raising goose bumps as much from the eerie sensation as from the chill. I wondered whence it came. Whatever its channels, they also were dark.

I slumped on the floor, shivering and feeling like I'd been entombed alive. Panic added to my shaking. I sought to calm myself by rationalizing my situation. Surely, I told myself, this was not to be the cell I would occupy during the entire year. Probably I was in here for observation. I discarded the theory immediately. Anyone observing me in this cell would have to have X-ray eyes. All right, then, I was being given a taste of what could happen to me if I misbehaved. I clung to the second supposition. Yes, this treatment was calculated to ensure my good behavior once I was released among the general prison population. After all, only unruly prisoners were confined in solitary under such harsh conditions, weren't they? Certainly no civilized country would permit such cruel and inhumane punishment to be meted out by its prison warders without cause.

France does. Or did.

I was not fed my first day in Perpignan's prison. I had been placed in my grim cell late in the afternoon. Several hours later, exhausted, cold, hungry, bewildered, frightened and desolate, I laid down on the hard floor and fell asleep. I slept curled in a ball, for I am six feet tall.

The screeching of the door awakened me. I sat up, wincing from the soreness and cramps caused by my uncomfortable sleeping position. The dim form of a guard loomed in the doorway. He was placing something on the steps inside my crypt. I was galvanized into action as he straightened and started to close the door.

"Wait! Wait!" I shouted, scrambling forward and placing my hands against the inside of the door, trying to restrain its closing.

"Why am I being kept in here? How long will I stay in here?"

"Until you have completed your sentence," he said, and shoved shut the door. The words clanked on my ears with the metallic finalness of the door slamming against the stone jamb.

I fell back, stunned by the ghastly truth. A year? I was to live in this black coffin a year? Without light? Without bedding? Without clothing? Without toilet facilities? And without God knows what else? It was impossible, I told myself. No man could live in such a dark void, under such conditions, for a year. He would die, and his death would be slow and torturous. It would have been better had I been sentenced to the guillotine. I loved France. But what kind of country was it that countenanced such punishment for such a crime as mine? And if the government was ignorant of such prison conditions, the people unknowing, what manner of men were the French penologists, into whose hands I had been delivered? Depraved monsters, madmen, perverts, undoubtedly.

I was suddenly scared, actually fearful. I did not know how, or if, I could survive a year in this Stygian vault. I still have nightmares from my stay in Perpignan's House of Arrest. Compared to Perpignan prison, the Black Hole of Calcutta was a health spa, Devil's Island a vacation paradise.

I had not expected prison life to be easy. My one experience behind bars, and then for only a few hours, had convinced me that jails and prisons were not nice places to reside. But nothing I had ever read, heard or seen had ever indicated that imprisonment could be as brutal and heartless as this.

I felt around and located the food the guard had brought. It was a quart container of water and a small loaf of bread. The simple breakfast had not even been brought on a tray. The guard had simply set the container of water on the top step and had dropped the bread beside it on the stone. No matter, I wolfed down the loaf of bread and gulped down the water in one swig. Then I huddled miserably against the wet granite wall and contemplated the machinations of French Justice.

Mine was not a term in prison, it was an ordeal designed to destroy the mind and body.

The menu in Perpignan prison never varied. For breakfast, I was served bread and water. Lunch consisted of a weak chicken soup and a loaf of bread. Supper was a cup of black coffee and a loaf of bread. The monotonous diet varied only in the time it was served or in the order it was served. I had no means of telling time and I soon lost track of the days, and the guards who served the meals further confused my attempts to keep a mental timetable and calendar by alternating the schedule of my meager rations. For instance, for several days breakfast, lunch and dinner might be served regularly at seven, noon and five, but then, abruptly, dinner would be served at ten A.M., supper at 2 P.M. and breakfast at 6 P.M. I am estimating the times. I really never knew at what hour I was fed, or whether it was day or night. And not infrequently I was fed only one or two times daily. Occasionally I wasn't fed at all during the span of the day.

I never left the cell. Not once during my stay in the hoary jail was I permitted outside for exercise or recreation. If the prison had a day room where prisoners might read, write letters, listen to the radio, watch television or play games, I was not among those privileged to share the facility. I was not allowed to write letters, and if any of my relatives knew I was jailed at Perpignan and wrote me, I did not receive the mail. My requests, made of the guards who served the meals, to contact my relatives, my attorney, the Red Cross, the warden or the American consular authorities were ignored save once.

On that occasion, the guard smacked me alongside the head with his huge hand. "Don't talk to me," he growled. "It is not permitted. Don't talk, don't sing, don't whistle, don't hum, don't make any sound or you will be beaten." He slammed the heavy door shut on further pleas.

The bucket was my latrine. I was not given any toilet paper, nor was the bucket removed after use. I soon adapted to the stench, but after a few days the bucket overflowed and I had to move around and sleep in my own fecal matter. I was too numbed, in body and spirit, to be revolted. Eventually, however, the odor became too nauseating for even the guards to endure, apparently. One day, between meals, the door creaked open and another convict scurried in with the furtiveness and manner of a rat, grabbed the bucket and fled. It was returned, empty, a few minutes later. On perhaps half a dozen other occasions during my time in the tiny tomb, the procedure was repeated. But only twice during my imprisonment were the feces cleaned from the floor of the cell. Each time a guard stood by at the door while an inmate hosed out the cell and then picked up the accumulated water in the hole with a mop. Both times I managed a makeshift shower in the spray of the hose, daring the wrath of the guard. Both times the cleaning was performed in absolute silence.

Those were the only times I was able to cleanse myself to any extent during my term, although occasionally I used a portion of my water ration to rinse my hands or to anoint my face.

I was not allowed to shave nor was I ever given a haircut. I am hirsute by heritage, and without the means to curb their growth, my hair and beard sprouted prodigiously. My hair was soon below my shoulders, a tangled, sodden skein, and my beard brushed my chest. Both hair and beard were oiled and perfumed with excrement, for I could not avoid soiling myself in my own wastes.

Lice and other insects small enough to gain admittance to the fetid cell nested in my body hair and feasted on my flesh. I developed sores from my scratching and these became infected from contact with the always present filth. My body soon became a mass of scabs, a living petri dish for the culture of myriad forms of bacteria. In the cramped confines of the hole, shrouded in blackness, I lost my sense of balance and fell often as I attempted to move about, stretch myself or perform simple exercises, nicking or bruising myself against the rough walls or the hard floor and further adding to my wounds.

I weighed 210 pounds when I was received at Perpignan. The tedious diet did not contain enough nutrients or calories to maintain me. My body began to feed upon itself, the muscles and tendons devouring the stored fats and oily tissues in order to fuel the pumps of my heart and my circulatory system. Within weeks I was able to encircle my biceps with my fingers.

I was not alone in my misery. I soon concluded that most if not all of the steel doors in Perpignan prison sealed a wretched inmate.

The stone walls between the cells were too thick to permit talk between adjoining prisoners, but they were by no means soundproof. Unintelligible shouts and curses, screams of pain and anguish, and muffled groans and cries washed softly along the corridor outside almost constantly, sometimes ceasing abruptly only to start again within minutes. The sounds, always laden with despair, permeated the walls of my dank box, filtering through the stone and seeping up from the floor like the sighs and sobs of some beleaguered banshee. Sometimes, however, the sounds had the qualities of rage and anger, reminiscent of the distant howl of a hunting wolf or the defiant yipping of a hurt coyote.

Sometimes the sounds were my own, for in my loneliness I often talked to myself just to hear the sound of a human voice. Or I would stand stooped before the door and scream at the guards to let me out or demand that I be treated like a human being, with dignity and consideration if not respect. I cursed them. I cursed myself. I ranted and raved, wept and screamed, chanted and sang, laughed and bellowed, shouted and banged the bucket against the walls, splattering excrement all over my crate-like cell. I felt I was going mad.

I had no doubt that many of the men in Perpignan were mad, reduced to lunacy by the maniacal manner in which they were treated. I was certain after a few weeks that I would lose my own sanity. I lost the ability to distinguish between that which was real and that which was unreal, and began to hallucinate. I would find myself back in the Royal Gardens, surrounded by my lovely "crew," dining sumptuously on lobster or roast beef, or strolling along the golden beaches of the Costa Brava, my arm around Monique. Only to regain my reason in the damp dungeon that was reality, wallowing in my own excreta and cursing the fates that had condemned me to Perpignan.

I think that I actually would have gone mad and died a lunatic in Perpignan prison had it not been for my vivid imagination. The creative ability that had enabled me to concoct the brilliant swindles I'd perpetrated over the years, and which had resulted in my present plight, now served as a lifeguard.

If I were going to hallucinate, I determined, mine would be planned hallucinations, and so I began to produce my own fantasies. I would sit on the floor, for instance, and recall the image I presented in my airline uniform and pretend that I was a real pilot, commander of a 707. And suddenly the cramped, vile and oozy pit in which I was prisoner became a sleek, clean jet liner, crowded with joyful, excited passengers attended by chic, glamorous stewardesses. I employed all the airline jargon I'd acquired over the years as I pretended to taxi the plane away from the terminal, obtain takeoff clearance from the tower and jockey the great machine into the air, leveling off at 35,000 feet.

Then I'd pick up the PA mike. "Ladies and gentlemen, this is your captain speaking. Welcome aboard Flight 572 of Abagnale Airlines, Seattle to Denver. We're presently cruising at 575 miles per hour and we expect good weather, and thus a good flight, all the way to Denver. Those of you seated on the starboard side—that's the right side of the aircraft—should have a good view of Mount Rainier below and off in the distance. Mount Rainier, with an elevation of 14,410 feet, is, as you probably know, the highest peak in Washington State . . ."

Of course I was a hero at times, fighting my huge plane through terrible storms or overcoming dire mechanical disasters to deliver my human cargo safely and to bask in the gratitude of the passengers. Especially the women. Especially the pretty women.

Or I would imagine I was a tour bus driver, displaying the splendors of the Grand Canyon or the enchantments of San Antonio, New Orleans, Rome, New York City (I actually remembered that New York City had enchantments) or some other historic city to a group of rapt tourists, entertaining them with my rapid, witty spiel. "Now, the mansion on your left, ladies and gentlemen, is the home of J. P. Greenstuff, one of the city's founders. He made big money most of his life. Trouble is, he made it too big, and now he's spending the rest of his life in a federal prison."

In my fantasies, I was anyone I wanted to be, much as I'd been during the five years before my arrest, although I added to and amplified my Perpignan impersonations. I was a famous surgeon, operating on the President and saving his life with my medical skills. A great author, winning the Nobel Prize for literature. A movie director, making an Oscar-winning epic. A mountain guide, rescuing hapless climbers trapped on a dangerous mountain face. I was tinker, tailor, Indian chief, baker, banker and ingenious thief. For I sometimes restaged some of my more memorable capers. And some of my more memorable love scenes too.

But always the curtain had to come down on my plays, and I returned to reality, but knowing I'd been on a make-believe journey, in my chill, gloomy, dark and loathsome cell.

Walter Mitty in durance vile.

One day the door grated open at an unexpected time and a guard tossed something into my cell. It was a thin, dirty, evil-smelling mattress, hardly more than a tick, but I spread it out on the floor and curled up on it, reveling in its comfort. I fell asleep wondering what model deportment I had exhibited that deserved such a luxurious reward.

I was awakened by the mattress's being jerked savagely from beneath me by a burly guard, who laughed jeeringly as he slammed the steel door shut. I do not know what time it was. It was long before I was served breakfast, however. Sometime after dinner, the door shrieked open again and the mattress was dumped on the steps. I grabbed it and fell on its softness, fondling it like it was a woman. But again I was rudely awakened by a guard's removing the tick forcefully from under me. And yet again, at some unknown hour later, the mattress was plopped onto the steps. The truth dawned. The guards were playing a game with me, a cruel and barbaric game, but a game nonetheless. Some of their other mice have died, I told myself, and I ignored the bedding. My body had become accustomed to the smooth stone floor, or at least as accustomed to it as any blending of soft flesh and hard rock. I never used the tick again, although the guards continued providing it each night, in hopes, I supposed, that I would again use it and furnish them more sport.

In my fifth month in Perpignan's House of Arrest (a fact established later) there was a tap on the outside of my cell door and then a portion of it slid open, admitting a weak, filtered light. I was astonished, for I had been unaware the door had a sliding panel, so cunningly was it contrived.

"Frank Abagnale?" asked a voice unmistakably American.

I floundered to the door and peered out. Standing on the outer side of the corridor, where he had recoiled from the stench, was a tall, skinny man with an equally bony face, in the act of putting a handkerchief over his mouth and nostrils.

"I'm Frank Abagnale," I said eagerly. "Are you an American? Are you with the FBI?"

"I'm Peter Ramsey, and I'm from the American Consulate in Marseille," replied the thin man, removing the handkerchief from his face. "How are you doing?"

I stared at him, astonished. My God, he acted like we were talking over a glass of wine in some Marseille sidewalk cafe. Words suddenly started cascading from my mouth like gravel from a sluice.

"How am I doing?" I repeated his query in near hysterical tones. "I'll tell you how I'm doing. I'm sick, I'm sore, I'm naked, I'm hungry and I'm covered with lice. I don't have a bed. I don't have a toilet. I don't have a wash basin. I'm sleeping in my own shit. I have no light, no razor, no toothbrush, no nothing. I don't know what time it is. I don't know what day it is. I don't know what month it is. I don't even know what year it is, for Christ's sake. . . . I'm being treated like a mad dog. I'll probably go mad if I stay in here much longer. I'm dying in here. That's how I'm doing!"

I slumped against the door, exhausted from my tirade.

Ramsey's features, save for an obvious reaction to the odor emanating from my cell, did not change. He nodded impassively when I finished.

"I see," he said calmly. "Well, perhaps I should explain my visit. You see, I make the rounds of my district about twice a year, calling on Americans in this district, and I learned only recently that you were here. Now, before you get your hopes up, let me tell you now that I am powerless to assist you. . . . I am aware of the conditions here and of the way you're being treated.

"And it's precisely because of that treatment that I can't do anything. You see, Abagnale, you're being treated ex-

210

actly the same as every Frenchman who's confined here is treated. They're not doing anything to you that they're not doing to the man on either side of you, to the man in each cell in the prison, in fact. Each of them has the same accommodation as you. Each is living in the same filth. Each is eating the same food. Each is denied the privileges you're denied.

"You haven't been singled out for especially harsh treatment, Abagnale. And as long as they treat you as they treat their own, I can't do a damn thing about your predicament, not even complain.

"The minute they discriminate against you, or treat you differently because you're an American, a foreigner, then I can step in and complain. It may not do any good, but I could, then, intervene in your behalf.

"But as long as they mete out the same punishment to you as they do to their own, that's it. French prisons are French prisons. It's always been like this, to my knowledge, and it'll always be like this. They don't believe in rehabilitation. They believe in an eye for an eye, a tooth for a tooth. In short, they believe in punishment for a convicted criminal and you're a convicted criminal. You're lucky, really. It used to be worse than this, if you can believe it. Prisoners were once beaten daily. As long as you're not being specifically abused by someone, there's nothing I can do."

His words fell on my ears like whip strokes across my back. I felt like a death sentence had been pronounced on me. Then Ramsey, with the ghost of a grin, handed me a reprieve.

"It is my understanding that you only have another thirty days or so here," he said. "You won't be freed, of course. I am told that authorities from another country, which one I don't know, are coming to take you into custody for trial in that country. Wherever you go, you're bound to be treated better than this. Now, if you'd like me to write your parents and let them know where you are, or if you want me to get in touch with anyone else, I'll be glad to do so."

His was a generous gesture, one he didn't have to make, and I was tempted, but only momentarily. "No, that won't be necessary," I said. "Thank you, anyway, Mr. Ramsey."

He nodded again. "Good luck to you, Abagnale," he said. He turned and seemed to disappear in a radiant explosion. I jumped back, shielding my eyes and screaming with pain. It was only later that I knew what had happened. The lights in the corridor were variable power lights. When a cell door was opened or a peephole broached, the lights were dimmed, low enough to avoid damage to the eyes of the prisoner who lived like a mole in his lightless hole. When a visitor like Ramsey appeared, the lights were turned up, so he might see his way. Once he halted in front of my cell, the lights had been dimmed. When he left, a guard had hit the bright switch prematurely. A concern for their sight was the only consideration accorded prisoners in Perpignan's House of Arrest.

After Ramsey left, I sat down against the wall and, after the pain in my eyes had subsided, mulled the information he'd imparted. Was my sentence nearly over? Had it really been eleven months since I was shoved into this awful crypt? I didn't know, I had lost all sense of time, but I felt he had told me the truth.

I tried to keep count of the days thereafter, to tally thirty days on the almanac of my mind but it was impossible. You simply can't keep a calendar in a feculent vacuum, void of light, where any segment of time, if such existed, was devoted to surviving. I am sure it was only a few days before I returned to just holding on to my sanity.

Still, time passed. And one day the panel in the door opened, admitting the dim light that, with the one exception, was the only light I knew.

"Turn around, face the back of your cell and shut your

212

eyes," a voice ordered gruffly. I did as instructed, my heart hammering. Was this the day of my release? Or was something else in store for me.

"Do not turn around, but open your eyes slowly and let them get accustomed to the light," the voice instructed. "I will leave this open for an hour, then I'll be back."

I slowly opened my eyes and found myself surrounded by a bright, golden glow, too bright for my weak orbs. I had to shut them against the glare. Gradually, however, my pupils adjusted to the illumination and I was able to look around me without squinting and without pain. Even so, the cell was still gloomy, like twilight on a rainy day. An hour later the guard returned, or at least the voice sounded the same.

"Close your eyes again," he instructed. "I am going to turn up the lights further." I did so, and when he instructed me to do so, I opened my eyes slowly and cautiously. The tiny cubicle was flooded with a luminous glare, causing me to squint again. The radiance ringed the cell like a nimbus around a dark star, illuminating fully for the first time the interior of the tiny vault. I was appalled and sickened as I looked around. The walls were moist and crusted with slimy mold. The ceiling, too, glistened with moisture. The floor was filthy with excrement, and the bucket, unemptied for some time, teemed with maggots. The odious worms were also slithering around the floor.

I vomited.

It was perhaps another hour before the guard returned. This time he opened the door. "Come with me," he ordered. I scrambled from the foul cave without hesitation, experiencing shooting pains in my neck, shoulders, arms and legs as I straightened up for the first time since my arrival. I had difficulty walking, but I waddled after the guard like a half-drunk duck, sometimes steadying myself by putting a hand against the wall.

He led me downstairs and into a sparsely furnished room.

"Stand here," he ordered, and disappeared through an open door that led to another chamber. I turned, inspecting the room, marveling at its size and spaciousness after so long in my moldy burrow, and then stopped as I suddenly confronted the most hideous creature I had ever encountered.

It was a man. It had to be a man, but God in heaven, what manner of man was this? He was tall and emaciated, his head crowned by a dirty, unkempt thatch of hair that spilled to his waist, his face hidden by a filthy, matted beard that fell to his belly. Spittle drooled from the slash that was his mouth, and his eyes were wildly glowing coals in their sunken sockets. He was naked and his flesh was coated with filth, sores and scabs, lending it a leprous appearance. The nails of his fingers and toes were grown out, elongated and curved like the talons of a vulture. Indeed, he looked like a vulture. I shuddered as I regarded the apparition. I shuddered again as recognition loomed.

I was facing myself in a mirror.

I was still horrified at my appearance when the guard returned, clothing draped over his arm and a pair of shoes in his hand.

I recognized the apparel as mine, the clothes I was wearing when I was received in the prison. "Put these on," said the guard brusquely, handing me the garments and dropping the shoes on the floor. "Can't I shower and shave first, please?" I asked.

"No, put on the clothes," he said, giving me a malevolent look. I hurriedly garbed my filthy frame in the clothes, which were now several sizes too large for me. My belt was missing. I clutched the trousers around my wasted stomach and looked at the guard. He stepped into the next room and returned with a length of cotton rope. I cinched the waist of my trousers with that.

214

Almost immediately two gendarmes appeared one of them carrying an array of restraints. One of them cinched a thick leather belt with a ringbolt in the front around my waist while the other fastened heavy shackles around my ankles. I was then handcuffed and a long, slender steel chain was looped around my neck and the handcuff chain, threaded through the ringbolt and fastened with a lock to the chain connecting my leg irons. Neither officer said a word as they trussed me. One then pointed toward the door and gave me a light shove as his partner led the way through the exit.

I shuffled after him, unable to walk because of the leg irons and fearful of my destination. I had never been chained like this before. I considered such restraints only for violent, dangerous criminals.

"Where are we going, where are you taking me?" I asked, squinting in the late afternoon sunlight. It was even more brilliant than the lights inside. Neither of them bothered to answer me.

Silently, they placed me in the back seat of an unmarked sedan and one climbed behind the wheel as the other seated himself beside me.

They drove me to the railroad station. The afternoon light, even sheltered as I was in the car, made me dizzy and nauseous. The nausea was not all due to my sudden exposure to daylight after all these months, I knew. I'd been ill—feverish, vomiting, diarrhea and racked at times by chills—for the past month or so. I had not complained to the guards in Perpignan. They would have ignored me, as they had ignored all my other pleas and protests.

At the railroad station I was taken from the car and one of the gendarmes snapped one end of a light chain onto my belt. He wrapped the other end around his one hand, and, leashed like a dog, I was led and dragged through the people assembled at the depot and shoved onto the train. The conductor showed us to a glassed-in compart-

215

ment containing two benches, the door of which was adorned with a sign stating the booth was reserved for the Ministry of Justice. The other passengers looked at me in horror, shock or revulsion as we passed among them, some falling back in disgust as they detected my odor. I had long since lost all olfactory sensitivity to my own feculence, but I could sympathize with them. I had to smell like a convention of outraged skunks.

The compartment was large enough to accommodate eight persons and as the train filled and all the seats were occupied, several sturdy peasants, at various times, appeared and sought permission to ride in the compartment with us. They seemed oblivious to my malodorous condition. Each time, the gendarmes waved them on with a curt refusal.

Then three vivacious, pretty American girls appeared, dressed in a minimum of silks and nylon and festooned with shopping bags laden with souvenirs and gifts, wines and foods.

They reeked delightfully of precious perfumes, and with a broad smile, one gendarme rose and gallantly seated them on the opposite bench. They immediately tried to engage the officers in conversation, curious as to who I was and what my crime had been. Obviously, ensnared in chains as I was, I was some notorious, terrible murderer, on a par at least with Jack the Ripper. They seemed more fascinated than frightened, and animatedly discussed my offensive stench. "He smells like they've been keeping him in a sewer," remarked one. The others laughingly agreed.

I did not want them to know I was an American. I felt degraded and ashamed of my appearance in their presence. The gendarmes finally made the three young women understand that they neither spoke nor understood English, and the three fell to talking among themselves as the train pulled out of the station.

I did not know where we were going. I had no sense of direction at the moment and I thought it would be useless to again seek my destination from the gendarmes. I huddled miserably between the officers, ill and despondent, occasionally looking out at the passing landscape or covertly studying the girls. I gathered from their conversational comments that they were schoolteachers from the Philadelphia area and were in Europe on a vacation. They'd been to Spain, Portugal and the Pyrenees and were now journeying to some other enchanted area. Were we en route to Paris, I wondered?

As the miles passed I grew hungry, despite my feeling of sickness. The girls took cheeses and breads from their bags, canned pâtés and wine, and began to eat, sharing their repast with the gendarmes. One attempted to feed me a small sandwich (my hands were restrained so that I could not have eaten had I been allowed), but one gendarme grasped her wrist gently.

"No," he said firmly.

At some point, some hours after we left Perpignan, the young women, convinced that neither I nor the gendarmes could understand English, commenced discussing the amorous adventures they'd been having on vacation, and in such intimate detail that I was astonished. They compared the physical attributes, prowess and performance of their various lovers in such vivid language that I actually felt embarrassed. I'd never heard women engage in such locker-room tales, replete with all the four-letter words and lewd comments. I concluded I still had a lot to learn about women and at the same time I speculated as to my own standing had I been a participant in their sexual Olympics. I made a mental note to try out for their games should we ever meet again.

Our destination was Paris. The gendarmes hauled me to my feet, made their farewells to the ladies and hustled me off the train. But not before I'd said my own good-bye.

As I was pulled through the door of the compartment, I twisted my head and smiled lasciviously at the three young teachers.

"Say hello to every one in Philly for me," I said in my best Bronx voice.

The expressions on their faces buoyed my sagging ego.

I was driven to the *préfecture de police* jail in Paris and turned over to the *préfet de police*, a plump, balding man with sleek jowls and cold, remorseless eyes. Nonetheless, those eyes registered shock and disgust at my appearance, and he set about promptly remedying my image. An officer escorted me to a shower, and after I had washed myself clean of my accumulated filth an inmate barber was summoned to snave my beard and shear my mane. I was then escorted to a cell, a small and austere little cubicle in reality, but sheer luxury compared to my previous prison accommodations.

There was a narrow iron cot with a wafer of a mattress and coarse, clean sheets, a tiny wash basin and an honest-to-john toilet. There was also a light, controlled from the outside. "You may read until nine o'clock. The light goes out then," the guard informed me.

I didn't have anything to read. "Look, I'm sick," I said. "Can I see a doctor, please?"

"I will ask," he said. He returned an hour later bearing a tray on which reposed a bowl of thin stew, a loaf of bread and a container of coffee. "No doctor," he said. "I am sorry." I think he meant it.

The stew had meat in it and was a veritable feast for me. In fact the meager meal was too rich for my stomach, which was unaccustomed to such hearty fare. I vomited the food within an hour after dining.

I was still unaware of my circumstances. I didn't know whether I would be brought to trial again in Paris, whether I was to complete my term here or be handed over to some other government. All my queries were rebuffed.

I was not to stay in Paris, however. The following morning, after a breakfast of coffee, bread and cheese which I managed to keep inside me, I was taken from my cell and again shackled like a wild animal. A pair of gendarmes placed me in a windowed van, my feet secured by a chain to a bolt in the floor, and started on a route that I soon recognized. I was being driven to Orly Airport.

At the airport I was taken from the van and escorted through the terminal to the Scandanavian Airlines Service counter. My progress through the terminal attracted a maximum of attention and people even left cafes and bars to gawk at me as I shuffled along, my chains clinking and rattling.

I recognized the one clerk behind the SAS counter. She'd once cashed a phony check for me. I couldn't now remember the amount. If she recognized me, she gave no indication of it. However, the man she'd cashed a check for had been a robust two-hundred-pounder, tanned and healthy. The chained prisoner before her now was a sick, pallid-faced skeleton of a man, stooped and hollow-eyed. In fact, after one look at me, she kept her eyes averted.

"Look, it won't hurt for you to tell me what's going on," I pleaded with the gendarmes, who were scanning the human traffic in the vicinity of the ticket counter.

"We are waiting for the Swedish police," one said in abrupt tones. "Now, shut up. Don't speak to us again."

He was suddenly confronted by a petite and shapely young woman with long blond hair and brilliant blue eyes, smartly dressed in a tailored blue suit over which she wore a fashionably cut trench coat. She carried a thin leather case under one arm. Behind her loomed a younger, taller Valkyrie, similarly attired, also holding an attaché case tucked under an arm.

"Is this Frank Abagnale?" the smaller one asked of the gendarme on my left. He stepped in front of me, holding up his hand.

"That is none of your business," he snapped. "At any rate, he is not allowed visitors. If this man is a friend of yours, you will not be allowed to talk to him."

The blue eyes flashed and the small shoulders squared. "I will talk to him, Officer, and you will take those chains off him, at once!" Her tone was imperiously demanding. Then she smiled at me and the eyes were warm, the features gentle.

"You are Frank Abagnale, are you not?" she asked in perfect English. "May I call you Frank?"

CHAPTER TEN

Put Out an APB—
Frank Abagnale Has Escaped!

The two gendarmes were transfixed in amazement, two grizzly bears suddenly challenged by a chipmunk. I myself stood gaping at the lovely apparition who demanded that I be released from my chains and who seemed determined to take me from my tormentors.

She extended a slender hand and placed it on my arm. "I am Inspector Jan Lundström of the Swedish police, the national police force," she said, and gestured to the pretty girl behind her.

"This is my assistant, Inspector Kersten Berglund, and we are here to escort you back to Sweden, where, as I am sure you are aware, you face a criminal proceeding."

As she talked, she extracted a small leather folder from her pocket and opened it to display to the French officers her credentials and a small gold badge.

The gendarme, perplexed, looked at his partner. The

221

second gendarme displayed the sheaf of papers. "He is her prisoner," he said with a shrug. "Take off the chains."

I was unshackled. The crowd applauded, an ovation accompanied by a whistling and stamping of feet. Inspector Lundström drew me aside.

"I wish to make some things perfectly clear, Frank," she said. "We do not normally use handcuffs or other restraints in Sweden. I never carry them myself. And you will not be restrained in any way during our journey. But our flight makes a stop in Denmark and my country has had to post a bond to ensure your passage through Denmark. It is a normal procedure in these cases.

"We will be on the ground only an hour in Denmark, Frank. But I have a responsibility to the French Government, to the Danish Government and to my own government to see that you are brought to Sweden in custody, that you do not escape. Now, I can assure you that you will find Swedish jails and prisons far different from French prisons. We like to think our prisoners are treated humanely.

"But let me tell you this, Frank. I am armed. Kersten is armed. We are both versed in the use of our weapons. If you try to run, if you make an attempt to escape, we will have to shoot you. And if we shoot you, Frank, we will kill you. Is that understood?"

The words were spoken calmly and without heat, much in the manner, in fact, of giving directions to a stranger, cooperative but not really friendly. She opened the large purse she carried on a shoulder strap. Bulking among its contents was a .45 semiautomatic pistol.

I looked at Inspector Berglund. She smiled angelically and patted her own purse.

"Yes, I understand," I said. I really thought she was bluffing. Neither of my lovely captors impressed me as an Annie Oakley.

Inspector Lundström turned to the clerk behind the ticket counter. "We're ready," she said. The girl nodded and summoned another clerk, a young man, from a room behind her. He led us through an office behind the counter, through the baggage area, through operations and to the plane's boarding stairwell.

Save for the shabby clothing I was wearing, we appeared to be just three more passengers. And from the lack of interest in my appearance, I was probably regarded as just another hippie.

We were fed on the plane before we landed in Copenhagen. It was the usual meager airline meal, but deliciously prepared, and it was the first decent meal I'd had since being committed to prison. For me, it was a delightful feast and I had to force myself to refuse my escorts' offer of their portions.

We had a longer layover in Denmark than was expected, two hours. The two young officers promptly escorted me to one of the terminal's restaurants and ordered a lavish lunch for the three of us, although I'm sure they couldn't have been hungry again. I felt it was strictly an attempt to appease my still ravenous hunger, but I didn't protest. Before we boarded the plane again, they bought me several candy bars and some English-language magazines.

Throughout the trip they treated me as if I were a friend rather than a prisoner. They insisted I call them by their given names. They conversed with me as friends, inquiring about my family, my likes, my dislikes and other general subjects. They probed only briefly into my criminal career, and then only to ask about my horrible treatment in Perpignan prison. I was surprised to learn I had served only six months in that hellhole. I had lost all track of time.

"As a foreigner, you were not eligible for parole, but the judge had discretion to reduce your term, and he did so," said Jan. I was suddenly grateful to the stern jurist who'd sentenced me. Knowing that I had served only six months, I realized I would not have lasted a full year in Perpignan. Few prisoners did.

The plane landed in Malmo, Sweden, thirty minutes after leaving Copenhagen. To my surprise, we disembarked in Malmo, retrieved our luggage, and Jan and Kersten led the way to a marked police car, a Swedish black-and-white, parked in the terminal lot, a uniformed officer at the wheel. He helped load our luggage—the girls' luggage, really, since I had none—into the trunk and then drove us to the police station in the village of Klippan, a short distance from Malmo.

I was intrigued by the Klippan police station. It seemed more like a quaint old inn than a police precinct. A ruddy-faced, smiling sergeant of police greeted us, Jan and Kersten in Swedish, me in only slightly accented English. He shook my hand as if he were greeting a guest. "I have been expecting you, Mr. Abagnale. I have all your papers here."

"Sergeant, Frank needs a doctor," said Jan in English. "He is very ill, I'm afraid, and needs immediate attention."

It was nearly 9 P.M, but the sergeant merely nodded. "At once, Inspector Lundström," he said, beckoning to a young uniformed officer who stood watching the scene. "Karl, please take the prisoner to his quarters."

"Ja, min herre," he said and grinned at me. "If you will follow me, please." I followed him in somewhat of a daze. If this was the treatment accorded criminals in Sweden, how did they treat honest folk?

He led me down the hall to a huge oaken door, which he unlocked, opened and then stood aside for me to enter. I was stunned when I stepped inside. This was no cell, it was an apartment, a huge, spacious room with a great picture window overlooking the village, a large bed with carved head and footboard and a colorful spread, rustic furniture and a separate bathroom with both a tub and a shower. Prints of gallant scenes from Sweden's past decorated the walls, and tasteful drapes, drawn at the moment, afforded privacy from outside passersby.

"I hope you will be well soon, *min herre*," said Karl in his accented English before closing the door.

"Thank you," I replied. I didn't know what else to say, although I wanted to say more. After his departure, I inspected the room closely. The windows were thick plate glass and could not be opened and the door also could not be opened from the inside, but no matter. I had no thoughts of escape from this prison.

I didn't get to sleep in the bed that night. Within minutes the door opened again to admit Jan and a balding, amiable but very efficient, doctor. "Strip, please," he said in English. I hesitated, but Jan made no move to leave, so I peeled my scant attire, really embarrassed to stand naked before her. Her face mirrored nothing but concern, however. Nudity, I learned, is sexual only under the circumstances with the Swedes.

The doctor poked, prodded, looked and listened, using a variety of instruments, and tapped, felt and pressed, all in silence, before he put away his instruments and stethoscope and nodded. "This man is suffering from severe malnutrition and vitamin deficiency, but worst of all, he has, in my opinion, double pneumonia," he said. "I suggest you call an ambulance, Inspector."

"Yes, Doctor," said Jan and ran from the room.

Within thirty minutes I was ensconced in a private room in a small, clean and efficient hospital. I was there a month, recuperating, a uniformed officer outside my door at all times but seeming more a companion than a guard. Each day, either Jan or Kersten, the sergeant or Karl visited me, and each time they brought me something, a bouquet, candy, a magazine or some other little gift.

Not once during my hospital stay was I questioned about my alleged crimes, nor was any reference made to my upcoming trial or the charges against me.

I was returned to my "cell" at the end of the month, before lunch, and at noon Karl brought me a menu. "We do not have a kitchen," he said apologetically. "You may order what you wish from this, and we will bring it from the cafe. It is very good food, I assure you."

It certainly was. Within a month I was back nudging two hundred pounds.

The day following my release from the hospital, Jan called on me, accompanied by a thin man with sprightly features.

"I am Inspector Jan Lundström with the Swedish National Police," she said formally. "It is my duty to tell you that you will be held here for a period of time, and that it is also my duty to interrogate you. This is a minister, and he will act as interpreter. He speaks perfect English and is familiar with all of your American slang and idioms."

I was flabbergasted. "Aw, come on, Jan, you speak perfect English yourself," I protested. "What is this?"

"Swedish law requires that an interpreter fluent in the language of a prisoner be present when that prisoner is questioned, if he or she is a foreigner," said Jan, still speaking in correct tones as if she had never seen me before.

"The law also says you have the right to an attorney, and your attorney must be present at all times during your interrogation. Since you have no funds to retain a lawyer, the government of Sweden has appointed you a counsel. Her name is Elsa Kristiansson and she will meet with you later today. Do you understand everything I have told you?"

"Perfectly," I said.

"I will see you tomorrow, then," she said, and left.

An hour later there was a knock on my door and then the portal opened. It was one of the guards with my supper, a bountiful and tasteful meal, which he arranged on a portable table as if he were a waiter and not a jailer.

When he returned to gather up the dishes, he grinned at me. "Would you like to take a walk?" he asked. "It will only be in the building, as I make my rounds, but I thought perhaps you might be getting tired of being shut inside."

I accompanied him to the kitchen, where a waiter from a nearby restaurant took the tray and used dishes from him. The kitchen was not really a kitchen, just a nook where the guards could brew coffee for themselves. He then led me on a tour of the jail, a two-story affair that could accommodate only twenty prisoners. At each cell, he knocked before opening the door, greeted the occupant pleasantly and inquired of the prisoner's needs. He bade each a cheery good night before closing and locking the door.

When I returned to my cell, Elsa Kristiansson was waiting for me, as was the interpreter, Rev. Carl Greek. I wondered at his presence until he explained that Mrs. Kristiansson did not speak any English at all. Nor did she spend any time inquiring about my case. She merely acknowledged the introduction and then told me she would be on hand the next morning when Jan commenced her interrogation.

She was a tall, handsome woman of about forty, I judged, serene and courteous, but I had misgivings about her acting as my lawyer. Still, I had no choice. I had no funds to hire an attorney of my choice. The French police had seized all my assets in France, or so I presumed. They had not mentioned anything about my loot following my arrest or during my detention, and they certainly hadn't returned any money to me on my release. And, here in Sweden, I had no way of getting funds from one of my many caches.

Jan appeared the next morning with Mrs. Kristiansson and Herre Greek. She commenced immediately to question me about my criminal activities in Sweden, with Bergen translating her queries for Mrs. Kristiansson, who sat silent, merely nodding now and then.

I was evasive with Jan during the first two interrogative

sessions. Either I refused to answer or I would reply "I don't remember" or "I can't say."

On the third day Jan became exasperated. "Frank! Frank!" she exclaimed. "Why are you so defensive? Why are you so evasive? You're here, you're going to go to trial, and it would be much better for you if you are honest with me. We know who you are and we know what you've done, and you know we have the evidence. Why are you so reluctant to talk?"

"Because I don't want to go to prison for twenty years, even if it is a nice prison like this one," I replied bluntly.

Bergen translated for Mrs. Kristiansson. The reaction of all three was totally unexpected. They burst into laughter, the loud, tear-producing peals of laughter usually provoked only by fine slapstick comedy. I sat looking at them in amazement.

Jan calmed herself somewhat, but still shaking with delight, she looked at me. "Twenty years?" she gulped.

"Or five years, or ten years, or whatever," I replied defensively, irritated at their attitude.

"Five years? Ten years?" Jan exclaimed. "Frank, the maximum penalty for the crime you are charged with is one year, and I will be very surprised if you receive that much time, since you are a first offender. Frank, murderers and bank robbers rarely receive over ten years on conviction in this country. What you did is a very serious offense, but we consider a year in prison a very serious punishment, and I assure you that is the maximum sentence you face."

I gave her a complete confession, detailing what I could recall of my transactions in Sweden. A week later I was brought to trial in Malmo before a jury of eight men and women who would determine both my guilt and my punishment, my confession having excluded any question of innocence.

Yet I almost beat the rap. Or Mrs. Kristiansson did. She surprised me by challenging the whole proceedings at the close of testimony against me. The charge against me was "serious fraud by check," she told the presiding judge.

"I would point out to the court that the instruments introduced here today are not checks, as defined by Swedish law," she contended. "They are instruments he made up himself. They never were checks. They are not checks at this time.

"Under Swedish law, Your Honor, these instruments could never be checks, since they are utter counterfeits. Under the law, Your Honor, my client has not really forged any checks, since these instruments are not checks, but merely creations of his own, and therefore the charges against him should be dismissed."

The charges weren't dismissed. But they were reduced to a lesser felony, the equivalent of obtaining money under false pretenses, and the jury sentenced me to six months in prison. I considered it a victory and rendered my enthusiastic thanks to Mrs. Kristiansson, who was also pleased with the verdict.

I was returned to my cell in the Klippan jail, and the next day Jan appeared to congratulate me. However, she also had disquieting news. I was not to serve my time in my comfortable and homey little hostelry in Klippan, but was to be transferred to the state institution in Malmo, located on the campus of Lund University, the oldest college in Europe. "You will find it very different from the prisons in France. In fact it is very different from any of your American prisons," Jan assured me.

My misgivings evaporated when I was delivered to the prison, known on the campus as "The Criminal Ward." There was nothing of a prison atmosphere about the ward— no fences, no guard towers, no bars, no electronic gates or doors. It blended right in with the other large and stately buildings on the campus. It was, in fact, a completely open facility.

I was checked in and escorted to my quarters, for I no longer looked on Swedish detention rooms as cells. My room in the ward was slightly smaller, but just as comfortable, and with similar furnishings and facilities, to those of the one in which I'd been lodged at Klippan.

The prison rules were relaxed, the restrictions lenient. I could wear my own clothes, and since I had only the one set, I was escorted to a clothing store in the city where I was outfitted with two changes of clothes. I was given unrestricted freedom to write and receive letters or other mail, and my mail was not censored. Since the ward housed only one hundred prisoners, and it was not deemed economical to maintain a kitchen, food was brought to prisoners from outside restaurants and the prisoner prepared his own menu within reason.

The ward was a coed prison. Several women were housed in the institution, but sexual cohabitation was prohibited between inmates. Conjugal visits were allowed between a man and wife, a wife and husband or between an inmate and his/her boy/girl friend. The prisoners had the freedom of the building between 7 A.M. and 10 P.M., and they could receive visitors in their quarters between 4 P.M. and 10 P.M. daily. The inmates were locked into their rooms at 10 P.M., curfew time in the ward.

The ward housed no violent criminals. Its inmates were check swindlers, car thieves, embezzlers and similar nonviolent criminals. However, prisoners were segregated, in multiroomed dormitories, by age, sex and type of crime. I was lodged in a dormitory with other forgers and counterfeiters of like age.

Swedish prisons actually attempt to rehabilitate a criminal. I was told I could, during my term, either attend classes at the university or work in a parachute factory situated on the prison grounds. Or I could simply serve my time in the ward. If I attended classes, the Swedish Government would pay my tuition and furnish my supplies. If I chose to work in the parachute factory, I would be paid the prevailing free-world wage for my job classification.

Escape would have been easy, save for one factor. The Swedes, at an early age, are issued identity cards They are rarely required to produce the card, but a policeman has a right to ask a citizen to display his or her identity card. And display of the ID is required for any border crossing, or international train or plane journey. I didn't have one. I also didn't have any money.

It really didn't matter. Escape never entered my mind. I loved it at Malmo prison. One day, to my astonishment, one of my victims, a young bank clerk, appeared to visit me, bringing a basket of fresh fruit and some Swedish cheeses. "I thought you might like to know that I did not get into any trouble because of your cashing checks at my station," said the young man. "Also, I wanted you to know I have no ill feelings toward you. It must be very difficult to be imprisoned."

I had really conned that kid. I had made him my friend, in fact, even visiting in his home, in order to perpetrate my swindle. His gesture really touched me.

I both worked in the parachute factory and attended classes, which seemed to please the ward's supervisors. I studied commercial art, although I was more adept in some of the techniques taught at Lund than the instructors.

The six months passed swiftly, too swiftly. During the fourth month, Mrs. Kristiansson appeared with alarming news. The governments of Italy, Spain, Turkey, Germany, England, Switzerland, Greece, Denmark, Norway, Egypt, Lebanon and Cyprus had all made formal requests to extradite me on completion of my sentence, and had been accorded preference in that order. I would be handed over to Italian authorities on completion of my term, and Italy would determine which country would get me after I settled my debt with the Italians.

One of my fellow inmates in the ward had served time in an Italian prison. The horror tales he recounted convinced me that Italian prisons were as bad as, if not worse

231

than, Perpignan's jail. Mrs. Kristiansson, too, had heard that conditions in Italian penal units were extremely harsh and brutal. She also had information that Italian judges and juries were not noted for leniency in criminal cases.

We launched a determined campaign to prevent my extradition to Italy. I bombarded the judge who had presided at my trial, the Minister of Justice and even the King himself with petitions and pleas for sanctuary, asking that I be allowed to stay in Sweden after my release or at the worst that I be deported to my native United States. I pointed out that no matter where I went, if I was denied refuge in Sweden, I would be punished again and again for the same crime, and conceivably I could be shunted from prison to prison for the rest of my life.

Each and every one of my pleadings was rejected. Extradition to Italy seemed inevitable. The night before Italian authorities were to take me into custody, I lay in my bed, unable to sleep and mulling over desperate plans for escape. I didn't feel I could survive any amount of imprisonment in Italy if penal conditions there were as terrible as I had been told, and I actually felt it would be better for me to be killed in an escape attempt than to die in a hellhole similar to Perpignan's.

Shortly before midnight, a guard appeared. "Get dressed, Frank, and pack all your belongings," he instructed me. "There're some people here to get you."

I sat up, alarmed. "What people?" I asked. "The Italians weren't supposed to pick me up before tomorrow, I was told."

"They aren't," he replied. "These are Swedish officers."

"Swedish officers!" I exclaimed. "What do they want?"

He shook his head. "I don't know. But they have the proper papers to take you into custody."

He escorted me out of the ward and to a marked police car parked at the curb. A uniformed officer in the back seat opened the door and motioned for me to get in beside him. "The judge wants to see you," he said.

They drove me to the judge's home, a modest dwelling

in an attractive neighborhood, where I was admitted by the judge's wife. The officers remained outside. She led me to the judge's study and gestured toward a large leather chair. "Sit down, Mr. Abagnale," she said pleasantly. "I will bring you some tea, and the judge will be with you shortly." She spoke perfect English.

The judge, when he appeared a few minutes later, was also fluent in English. He seated himself opposite me after greeting me and then regarded me in silence for a few minutes. I said nothing, although I wanted to ask a dozen or more questions.

Finally the judge started speaking, in a soft, deliberate manner. "Young man, I've had you on my mind for the past several days," he said. "I have, in fact, made many inquiries into your background and your case. You are a bright young man, Mr. Abagnale, and I think you could have made a worthwhile contribution to society, not only in your own country but elsewhere, had you chosen a different course. It is regrettable that you have made the mistakes that you have made."

He paused. "Yes, sir," I said meekly, hopeful that I was here for more than a lecture.

"We are both aware, young man, that if you are returned to Italy tomorrow, you might very well face a prison sentence of up to twenty years," the judge continued. "I have some knowledge of Italian prisons, Mr. Abagnale. They are very much like French prisons. And when you have served your sentence, you will be handed over to Spain, I understand. As you pointed out in your petition, young man, you could very well spend the rest of your life in European prisons.

"And there's very little we can do about that, Mr. Abagnale. We have to honor Italy's request for extradition just as France honored ours. The law is not something we can flout with impunity, sir." He paused again.

"I know, sir," I said, my hopes receding. "I would like to stay here, but I understand I cannot."

He rose and began to pace around the study, talking

the while. "What if you had a chance to start your life anew, Mr. Abagnale?" he asked. "Do you think you would choose a constructive life this time?"

"Yes, sir, if I had the chance," I replied.

"Do you think you've learned your lesson, as the teachers say?" he pursued.

"Yes, sir, I really have," I said, my hopes rising again

He seated himself again and looked at me, finally nodding. "I did something tonight, Mr. Abagnale, that surprised even myself," he said. "Had someone told me two weeks ago that I would take this action, I would have questioned his sanity.

"Tonight, young man, I called a friend of mine in the American Embassy and made a request that violates your rights under Swedish law. I asked him to revoke your U.S. passport, Mr. Abagnale. And he did."

I gazed at him, and from his slight grin I knew my astonishment was visible. I was really puzzled at his action, but not for long.

"You are now an unwelcome alien in Sweden, Mr. Abagnale," the judge said, smiling. "And I can legally order your deportation to the United States, regardless of any extradition requests pending. In a few minutes, Mr. Abagnale, I am going to order the officers outside to take you to the airport and place you on a plane for New York City. All the arrangements have been made.

"Of course, you should know that police of your own country will be waiting to arrest you when you debark from the aircraft. You are a wanted criminal in your own country, too, sir, and I felt it only proper that they be notified of my actions. The FBI has been informed of your flight number and the time of your arrival.

"I'm sure you will be tried in your own country. But at least, young man, you will be among your own people and I'm sure your family will be present to support you and to visit you in prison, if you are convicted. However, in case you aren't aware, once you have served your term in America, none of these other countries can extradite you. The law in the United States prohibits a foreign nation from extraditing you from the land of your birth.

"I have taken this action, young man, because I feel it is in the best interests of all concerned, especially yourself. I think, when you have settled your obligations in your own country, that you can have a fruitful and happy life. . . . I am gambling my personal integrity on that, Mr. Abagnale. I hope you don't prove me wrong."

I wanted to hug and kiss him. Instead I wrung his hand and tearfully promised him that I would make something worthwhile of my future. It was a promise I was to break within eighteen hours.

The officers drove me to the airport, where, to my delight, Jan was waiting to take charge of me. She had a large envelope containing my passport, my other papers and the money I had earned in the prison parachute factory. She gave me a $20 bill for pocket money before handing over the envelope to the pilot. "This man is being deported," she told the plane commander. "Officers of the United States will meet the plane in New York and will take him into custody. You will turn over this property to them."

She turned to me and took my hand. "Good-bye, Frank, and good luck. I hope your future will be a happy one," she said gravely.

I kissed her, to the astonishment of the pilot and a watching stewardess. It was the first overture I had made toward Jan, and it was a gesture of sincere admiration. "I will never forget you," I said. And I never have. Jan Lundström will always be a fine and gracious person, a lovely and helpful friend, in my thoughts.

It was a nonstop flight to New York. I was seated up front, near the cockpit, where the crew could keep an eye on me, but otherwise I was treated as just another passenger. In flight I had the freedom of the passenger sections.

I do not know when I began thinking of eluding the waiting officers, or why I felt compelled to betray the judge's trust in me. Perhaps it was when I started thinking of my short sojourn in the Boston jail, with its sordid tanks and cells. Certainly it was luxurious when compared to Perpignan's prison, but if American prisons were comparable, I didn't want to do time in one. My six months in the Klippan jail and the ward had spoiled me.

The jet was a VC-10, a British Viscount, an aircraft with which I was very familiar. A BOAC pilot had once given me a detailed tour of a VC-10, explaining its every structural specification, even to construction of the johns.

From past flight experiences, I knew the jet would land on Kennedy's Runway 13 and that it would require approximately ten minutes for the aircraft to taxi to the terminal.

Ten minutes before the pilot was to make his landing approach, I rose and strolled back to one of the lavatories and locked myself inside. I reached down and felt for the snap-out knobs I knew were located at the base of the toilet, pulled them out, twisted them and lifted out the entire toilet apparatus, a self-contained plumbing unit, to disclose the two-foot-square hatch cover for the vacuum hose used to service the aircraft on the ground.

I waited. The plane touched down with a jolt and then slowed as the pilot reversed his engines and used his flaps as brakes. At the end of the runway, I knew, he would come to almost a complete stop as he turned the jet onto the taxi strip leading to the terminal. When I judged he was almost at that point, I squeezed down into the toilet compartment, opened the hatch and wriggled through, hanging from the hatch combing by my fingers, dangling ten feet above the tarmac. I knew when I opened the hatch that an alarm beeper would sound in the cockpit, but I also knew from past flights that the hatch was often jarred open slightly by the impact of landing and that the pilot, since he was already on the ground, usually just shut off the beeper as the hatch being ajar posed no hazard.

I really didn't care whether this pilot was of that school or not. We had landed at night. When the huge jet slowed almost to a stop, I released my hold on the combing and lit running.

I fled straight across the runway in the darkness, later learning that I had escaped unnoticed, the method of my escape unknown until an irate O'Riley and other FBI agents searched the plane and found the lifted-out toilet.

On the Van Wyck Expressway side of the airport, I scaled a cyclone fence and hailed a passing cab. "Grand Central Station," I said. On arrival at the station, I paid the cabbie out of the $20 bill I had and took a train to the Bronx.

I didn't go home. I felt both my mother's apartment and my father's home would be under surveillance, but I did call Mom and then Dad. It was the first time in more than five years that I had heard their voices, and in each instance, both Mom and I and Dad and I ended up blubbering with tears. I resisted their entreaties to come to one of their homes and surrender myself to officers. Although I felt ashamed of myself for breaking my promise to the Malmo judge, I felt I'd had enough of prison life.

Actually, I went to the Bronx to see a girl with whom I'd stashed some money and some clothing, one suit of which contained a set of keys to a Montreal bank safe-deposit box. She was surprised to see me. "Good lord, Frank!" she exclaimed. "I thought you had disappeared for good. A few more days and I was going to spend your money and give your clothes to the Salvation Army."

I did not stop to dally. I wasn't sure how many of my girl friends and acquaintances the FBI had been able to identify, or which ones, but I knew some had been ferreted out. I grabbed my clothes, gave her all but $50 of the money and grabbed a train for Montreal.

I had $20,000 stashed in a Montreal safe-deposit box. It was my intention to pick up the money and take the soonest flight to São Paulo, Brazil, where I intended to go to earth. You pick up some interesting information in prison, and in the ward I had learned that Brazil and the United States had no extradition treaty. Since I hadn't committed any crimes in Brazil, I felt I would be safe there and that Brazilian authorities would refuse extradition even if I were caught in that country.

I picked up the money. I never made the flight. I was waiting in line at the Montreal airport to purchase a ticket when someone tapped me on the shoulder. I turned to face a tall, muscular man with pleasant features, in the uniform of the Royal Canadian Mounted Police.

"Frank Abagnale, I am Constable James Hastings, and you are under arrest," said the Mountie with a friendly smile.

The next day I was driven to the New York–Canada border and handed over to the U.S. Border Patrol, who turned me over to FBI agents, who took me to New York City and lodged me in the federal detention facility there.

I was arraigned before a U.S. commissioner who bound me over for trial under a $250,000 bond and remanded me to the detention house pending a decision on the part of prosecutors as to where to bring me to trial.

Two months later the U.S. attorney in the Northern District of Georgia prevailed, and U.S. marshals took me to the Fulton County, Georgia, jail to await my trial.

The Fulton County Jail was a pest hole, a real roach pit. "It's bad news, man," said another prisoner I met in the day room of our cruddy cellblock. "The only decent facility in the joint is the hospital, and you have to be dying to get in there."

The only decent facility in the day room was a pay telephone. I plopped a dime in and dialed the desk sergeant. "This is Dr. John Petsky," I said in authoritative tones.

"You have a patient of mine as a prisoner, one Frank

Abagnale. Mr. Abagnale is a severe diabetic, subject to frequent comas, and I would appreciate it, Sergeant, if you could confine him in your medical ward where I can visit him and administer proper treatment."

Within thirty minutes a jailer appeared to escort me to the hospital ward, leaving the other inmates who had heard my conversation grinning in admiration.

A week later a U.S. marshal appeared, took me into custody and transferred me to the Federal Detention Center in Atlanta to await trial. It was from this prison that I perpetrated what has to be one of the most hilarious escapes in the annals of prison history. At least I thought it was funny, and I'm still amused by the episode, although there're several others who still hold an opposite view.

Actually, mine wasn't so much an escape as it was a cooperative eviction, made possible by the time and the circumstances. I was ensconced in the detention facility during a period when U.S. prisons were being condemned by civil rights groups, scrutinized by congressional committees and investigated by Justice Department agents. Prison inspectors were working overtime, and undercover, and earning the enmity and hostility of prison administrators and guards.

I was brought into this atmosphere under exactly the right circumstances. The U.S. marshal who delivered me to the facility had no commitment papers for me, but did have a short temper.

The admissions officer to whom I was offered had a lot of questions for the U.S. marshal. Who was I? Why was I being lodged here? And why didn't the marshal have the proper papers?

The marshal blew his cool. "He's here under a court order," he snapped. "Just put him in a damned cell and feed him until we come after him."

The admissions officer reluctantly accepted custody of me. He really had no choice. The marshal had stormed out. I think I could have followed him without anyone's stopping me, in light of what I learned. "Another damned prison inspector, eh?" murmured the guard who escorted me to my cell.

"Not me, I'm here awaiting trial," I replied truthfully.

"Sure you are," he scoffed, slamming the cell door. "You bastards think you're slick, don't you? You people got two of our guys fired last month. We've learned how to spot you."

I wasn't issued the white cotton uniform the other inmates sported. I was allowed to keep my regular clothing. I noted, too, that the cell in which I was placed, while not posh, was exceedingly livable. The food was good and the Atlanta papers were brought to me daily, usually with a sarcastic remark. I was never called by name, but was addressed as "fink," "stoolie," "007" or some other derisive term meant to connote my assumed status as a prison inspector. Reading the Atlanta papers, which twice the first week contained stories relating to conditions in federal penal institutions, I realized the personnel of this facility really did suspect I was an undercover federal agent.

Had I been, they would have had no worries, and I was puzzled as to why large numbers of influential people thought American prisons were a disgrace to the nation. I thought this one was great. Not quite up to the standards of the Malmo ward, but much better than some motels in which I'd stayed.

However, if the guards here wanted me to be a prison inspector, that's what I'd be. I contacted a still loyal girl friend in Atlanta. The prison rules were not overly lenient, but once a week we were allowed to use the telephone in privacy. I got her on the phone when it was my turn.

"Look, I know what it usually takes to get out of here," I told her. "See what you have to do to get in, will you?"

Her name was Jean Sebring, and she didn't have to do much to get in to see me. She merely identified herself as my girl friend, my fiancée, in fact, and she was allowed to visit me. We met across a table in one of the large visiting rooms. We were separated by a three-foot-high pane of glass perforated by a wire-mesh aperture through which we could talk. A guard was at either end of the room, but out of earshot. "If you want to give him something, hold it up and we'll nod if it's permissible," one guard instructed her.

I had concocted a plan before Jean arrived. It might prove to be merely an intellectual exercise, I knew, but I thought it was worth a try. However, I first had to persuade Jean to help me, for outside assistance was vital to my plot. She was not difficult to persuade. "Sure, why not?" she agreed, smiling. "I think it would be funny as hell if you pulled it off."

"Have you met an FBI agent named Sean O'Riley or talked to him?" I asked.

She nodded. "In fact, he gave me one of his cards when he came around asking about you," she said.

"Great!" I enthused. "I think we're in business, baby."

We really were. That week, Jean, posing as a free-lance magazine writer, called at the U.S. Bureau of Prisons in Washington, D.C., and finagled an interview with Inspector C. W. Dunlap, purportedly on fire safety measures in federal detention centers. She pulled it off beautifully, but then Jean is not only talented, she is also chic, sophisticated and lovely, a woman to whom any man would readily talk.

She turned at the door as she left. "Oh, may I have one of your cards, Inspector, in case some other question comes to mind and I have to call you?" she asked.

Dunlap promptly handed over his card.

She laughingly detailed her success during her next visit, in the course of which she held up Dunlap's card, and when the one guard nodded, she passed it over the barrier to me.

Her visits only bolstered the guards' belief that I was a Bureau of Prisons prober. "Who is she, your secretary, or is she a prison inspector, too?" one guard asked me as he returned me to my cell.

"That's the girl I'm going to marry," I replied cheerfully.

Jean visited a stationery print shop that week. "My father just moved into a new apartment and has a new telephone number," she told the printer. "I want to present him with five hundred new personal cards as a housewarming gift. I want them to look exactly like this, but with his new home telephone number and his new office number inserted." She gave the printer O'Riley's card.

O'Riley's new telephone numbers were the numbers of side-by-side pay telephones in an Atlanta shopping mall.

The printer had Jean's order ready in three days. She passed me one of the cards on her next visit, and we finalized our plans. Jean said she'd enlisted the aid of a male friend just in case. "I didn't fill him in on anything, of course; I just told him we were pulling a practical joke," she said.

"Okay, we'll try it tomorrow night," I said. "Let's hope no one wants to use those phones around 9 P.M."

Shortly before 9 P.M. the following day, I hailed the cellblock guard, whom I had cultivated into a friendly adversary. "Listen, Rick, something's come up and I need to see the lieutenant on duty. You were right about me. I am a prison inspector. Here's my card." I handed him Dunlap's card, which bore only his Washington office number. If anyone decided to call the Bureau of Prisons, they'd be told the offices were closed.

Rick scanned the card and laughed. "By God, we knew we were right about you," he chortled. "Combs is gonna like this. Come on." He opened the cell door and led me to Lieutenant Combs' office.

The lieutenant was equally pleased to learn, as he also had suspected, that I was a prison inspector. "We had you figured all along," he growled amiably, tossing Dunlap's card on his desk after looking at it.

I grinned. "Well, it would have all come out Tuesday

anyway," I said. "And I'll tell you now that you people don't have anything to worry about. You're now running a clean, tight ship, the kind the bureau likes to brag about. You'll like my report."

A pleased look began to spread across Combs' face and I plunged ahead with my gamble. "But right now I've got some urgent business to take care of," I said. "I need to get hold of this FBI agent. Can you get him on the horn for me? He'll still be at his office, I'm sure." I handed over the doctored card bearing O'Riley's name, his position with the FBI and the two phony telephone numbers.

Combs didn't hesitate. He picked up his telephone and dialed the "office" number. "I've read about this guy O'Riley," he remarked as he dialed. "He's supposed to be hell on wheels for nabbing bank robbers."

The "office" phone started ringing. Jean answered on the second ring. "Good evening, Federal Bureau of Investigation. May I help you?"

"Yes, is Inspector O'Riley in?" Combs said. "This is Combs at the detention center. We've got a man here who wants to talk to him."

He didn't even wait for "O'Riley" to answer. He just passed the phone to me. "She said she'll get him for you," Combs told me.

I waited an appropriate few seconds and then launched into my act. "Yes, Inspector O'Riley? My name is Dunlap, C. W. Dunlap, with the Bureau of Prisons. If you've got your list handy, my authorized code number is 16295-A. . . . Yes, that's right. . . . I'm here now, but I've told these people who I am. . . . I had to. . . . Yes. . . ."

"Listen, Inspector O'Riley, I've come up with some information on that Philly case you're working, and I need to get it to you tonight. . . . No, sir, I can't give it to you over the telephone . . . it's too sensitive . . . I have to see you, and I have to see you within the hour. . . . Time is important. . . . Oh, you are. . . . Well, look these guys won't blow your cover. . . . No, it'll only take ten minutes.

... Wait a minute, let me talk to the lieutenant, I'm sure he'll go along."

I covered the mouthpiece of the telephone and looked at Combs. "Boy, these J. Edgar Hoovers are really way out. He's working undercover on something and doesn't want to come inside . . . some kind of Mustache Pete job or something," I told Combs. "If he parks out front, can I go out and talk to him in his car for about ten minutes?"

Combs grimaced. "Hell, why don't you call your people and spring yourself right now?" he asked. "You ain't needed here anymore, are you?"

"No," I said. "But we have to do these things by the book. A U.S. marshal will come for me Tuesday. That's the way my boss wanted it done, and that's the way it'll be done. And I'd appreciate it if you people wouldn't let on that I blew my own cover. But I had to. This is too big."

Combs shrugged. "Sure, we'll let you meet O'Riley. Hell, spend an hour with him, if you like."

I went back to the telephone. "O'Riley, it's okay. . . . Yeah, out front . . . . a red-over-white Buick. . . . Got it. . . . No, no problem. These guys are okay. I really don't know why you're being so damned cautious. They're on our team, too, you know."

Rick brought me a cup of coffee and stood by the window while I sipped the brew and chatted with Combs. "Here's your Buick," Rick said fifteen minutes later. Combs rose and picked up a large ring of keys. "Come on," he said. "I'll let you out myself."

There was an elevator, used by guards only, behind his office. We rode it down and he escorted me past the guard in the small foyer and unlocked the barred doors. I walked through as the guard looked on curiously but without comment, and strolled down the walkway leading to the curb and the parked car. Jean was behind the wheel, her hair hidden under a man's broad-brimmed hat and wearing a man's coat.

She giggled as I climbed in beside her. "Hot dog! We did it!" she gurgled.

I smiled. "See how fast you can get the hell away from here," I said, grinning from sheer jubilation.

She peeled out of there like a drag racer, burning rubber and leaving tire marks on the pavement as a memento. Away from the center, she slowed to avoid attracting the attention of any cruising radio patrolman, and then drove a meandering course through Atlanta to the bus station. I kissed her good-bye there and took a Greyhound to New York. Jean went home, packed and moved to Montana. If she was ever connected with the caper, no one was inclined to press charges.

It was a very embarrassing situation for the prison officials. It is a matter of record in FBI files that Combs and Rick sought to cover themselves, when they realized they'd been had, by reporting I had forcibly escaped custody. However, the truth, as the sage observed, soon outed.

I knew I would be the subject of an intense manhunt, and I resolved again to flee to Brazil, but I knew I would have to wait until the hunt for me cooled. For the next few days, I was certain, all points of departure from the United States would be under surveillance.

My escape made the front page of one New York paper. "Frank Abagnale, known to police the world over as the Skywayman and who once flushed himself down an airline toilet to elude officers, is at large again . . ." the story commenced.

I didn't have a stash of money in New York, but Jean had loaned me enough to live on until the hunt for me died down. I holed up in Queens and, two weeks later, took the train to Washington, D.C., where I rented a car and checked into a motel on the outskirts of the capital.

I went to Washington because I had several caches in banks across the Potomac in Virginia, and Washington seemed to offer a safe haven, with its huge and heterogeneous population. I didn't think I'd attract any attention there at all.

I was wrong. An hour after I checked into my room, I happened to glance out the window through a part in the drapes and saw several police officers scurrying to take up positions around this section of the motel. I learned that the registration clerk, a former airline stewardess, had recognized me immediately and had telephoned the police after an hour of fretting and wondering whether she should get involved.

Only one thing weighed in my favor, and I didn't know it at the moment. O'Riley, on being informed that I was cornered, had told the officers not to move in on me until he arrived to take charge. O'Riley, whom I had met briefly after my arraignment, wanted this collar himself.

But at the moment I was on the verge of panic. It was late at night, but both the front and back of this section of rooms was well lighted. I didn't think I could make it to the safety of the darkness beyond the lighted parking areas.

I knew, though, that I had to try. I slipped on my coat and fled out the back door, but held myself to a walk as I headed for the corner of the building. I had taken only a few steps, however, when two officers rounded the corner of the building. Both pointed pistols at me.

"Freeze, mister, police!" one barked in a command right out of a television police drama.

I didn't freeze. I kept walking, right at the muzzles of their guns, whipping out my billfold as I walked. "Davis, FBI," I said, surprised at my own coolness and the firmness of my voice.

"Is O'Riley here yet?"

The pistols were lowered. "I don't know, sir," said the one. "If he is, he's around front."

"All right," I said crisply. "You people keep this area covered. I'll check and see if O'Riley is here yet."

They stood aside as I passed them I didn't look back. I walked on into the darkness beyond the parking lot.

Epilogue

Not even the wiliest fox can elude the pack consistently, not if the hounds are persistent, and where Frank Abagnale was concerned the hounds of the law were not only persistent, they were exceedingly angry. Insult one policeman and you have insulted all policemen. Embarrass the Royal Canadian Mounted Police and you have embarrassed Scotland Yard. Humiliate a traffic cop in Miami and you have humiliated the California Highway Patrol. Frank Abagnale, for years, had insulted, embarrassed and humiliated police everywhere with regularity and maddening insouciance. And so police everywhere sought him day and night, without respite, and as much to vindicate themselves as to serve justice.

Less than a month after Abagnale evaded capture in Washington, D.C., two New York City detectives, munching hot dogs in their parked squad car, spotted him as he

247

walked past the unmarked vehicle and accosted him. Although he denied his identity, within two hours Abagnale had been positively identified and was given into custody of FBI agents.

Within weeks, Abagnale was inundated with state and federal complaints charging forgery, passing worthless checks, swindling, using the mails to defraud, counterfeiting and similar offenses, leveled by authorities in all fifty states. Various U.S. attorneys and state prosecutors vied for jurisdiction, each claiming to have the most damaging case or cases against the prisoner. All the liens against Abagnale had validity. Although the cleverness and intelligence Abagnale had exhibited in the course of his criminal career was undisputed, he had been more bold than deceptive, more overt than discreet. A multitude of witnesses was available to identify Abagnale in one or the other of his roles, to accuse him in one or the other of his transgressions. Had all the charges against Abagnale been tossed into the air and one caught at random, the evidence in that case would have been overwhelming.

Abagnale was not unaware of his predicament and the knowledge caused him undue mental anguish. He knew he was going to serve time in some state or federal prison, perhaps several terms in several different prisons. He could not expect any American prison to be as humane as Malmo Prison. His great fear was that he might be incarcerated in an American version of Perpignan's House of Arrest. His trepidations were not allayed when an arbitrary decision was made by federal authorities to bring him to trial in Atlanta, Georgia. More than in any other U.S. city where officials had cause to dislike him, Abagnale felt he was least popular in Atlanta.

However, he was represented by able counsel, and his lawyer struck a bargain with the United States Attorney that Abagnale eagerly endorsed.

In April 1971, Frank Abagnale appeared before a federal judge and pleaded guilty under Rule 20 of the United

States Penal Code, a plea that encompassed "all crimes, known and unknown," that Abagnale had committed in the continental United States, whether a violation of state or federal statutes. The presiding judge entered an order of *nolle prosequi* (no prosecution) in all but eight of the hundreds of charges pending against Abagnale, and sentenced Abagnale to ten years on each of seven counts of fraud, the terms to run concurrently, and to two years on one count of escape, the term to be served consecutively.

Abagnale was ordered to serve his twelve years in the Federal Correctional Institution in Petersburg, Virginia, where he was taken that same month. He served four years of his term, working as a clerk in one of the prison industries during those years at a "salary" of 20¢ per hour. Three times during that period, Abagnale applied for parole and each time was rejected. "If we do consider you for parole in the future, to what city would you like to be paroled?" Abagnale was asked at one point during his third appearance.

"I don't know," Abagnale confessed. "I would not like it to be New York, since I feel that would be an unhealthy environment for me, considering past events and circumstances. I would leave it to the parole authorities' discretion as to where I should be paroled."

Shortly thereafter, and for reasons Abagnale has never attempted to fathom, he was paroled to Houston, Texas, with orders to report to a U.S. parole officer there within seventy-two hours of his arrival and, if possible, to find gainful employment within the same period of time.

Frank Abagnale quickly learned, as do most freed prisoners, that there is a post-prison penalty society inflicts upon its convicts. For some, this penalty is simply a social stigma, but for the majority such post-prison punishment comprises much more than just slurs and slights. The ex-convict seeking employment invariably finds his quest much more difficult than does the hard-core unemployed, even though he may possess a needed or wanted skill (often acquired in prison). The employed ex-convict is the first to lose his job during economic downturns necessitating worker layoffs. Too often, the very fact that he is an ex-convict is sufficient reason for firing.

Abagnale's post-release problems were compounded by the fact that the bureaucrat selected to supervise his parole was hostile and antipathetic. The parole officer bluntly apprised Abagnale of his feelings toward his ward.

"I didn't want you here, Abagnale," the hard-nosed official told him. "You were forced on me. I don't like con men, and I want you to know that before we even start our relationship. . . . I don't think you'll last a month before you're headed back to the joint. Whatever, you had better understand this. Don't make a wrong move with me. I want to see you every week, and when you get a job, I'll be out to see you regularly. Mess up, and I'm sure you will, and I'll personally escort you back to prison."

Abagnale's first job was as a waiter, cook and managerial trainee in a pizza parlor operated by a fast-food chain. He did not inform his employer that he was an ex-convict when he applied for the job because he wasn't asked. The job was colorless, unexciting, and made even less appealing by the periodic visits of Abagnale's dour parole officer.

Although he was an exemplary worker, and one often entrusted with the banking of the firm's cash receipts, Abagnale was fired after six months when company officials, checking more closely into his background in preparation for naming him a manager of one of the chain's shops, learned he was a federal prison parolee. Abagnale within a week found employment as a grocery stocker with a supermarket chain, but again neglected to tell his employer that he was an ex-convict. After nine months, Abagnale was promoted to night manager of one of the firm's stores and top management officials began to pay personal attention to the well-groomed, handsome and personable young man who seemed so zealously dedicated to company affairs. Obviously he was an executive prospect, and the firm's directors commenced to prepare him as such. Abagnale's grooming as a grocery guru, however, abruptly ended when a security check disclosed his blighted past and he again was given the boot.

In ensuing months, the discouraging procedure became repetitively familiar to Abagnale, and he began to contemplate a return to his former illicit lifestyle, feeling now that he had a justifiable grudge against the establishment. Abagnale might actually have returned to his felonious career, as have so many ex-convicts frustrated by similar situations, save for two fortuitous circumstances. First, he was removed from the supervision of his antagonistic parole officer and placed in the hands of a more rational, unbiased steward. And second, Abagnale shortly thereafter took a lengthy and introspective look at himself, his situation and what the future might or might not hold for him.

"I was working as a movie projectionist at the time," Abagnale recalls today. "I was making good money, but there I was, five nights a week, sitting in this small room, with nothing to do, really, save to watch the same movie over and over again. I thought to myself that I was smarter than that, that I was ignoring and wasting real talents that I possessed."

Abagnale sought out his parole officer and broached a plan he had formulated in the lonely projection booth. "I think I have as much knowledge as any man alive concerning the mechanics of forgery, check swindling, counterfeiting and similar crimes," Abagnale told the officer. "I have often felt since I was released from prison that if I directed this knowledge into the right channels, I think I could help certain people a great deal. For instance, every time I go to the store and write a check, I see two or three mistakes made on the part of the clerk or cashier, mistakes that a bum check artist would take advantage of. I have concluded that it is simply a lack of training, and I know

I can teach people who handle checks or cash vouchers how to protect themselves against fraud and theft."

With the blessings of his parole officer, Abagnale approached a suburban bank director, outlined what he had in mind and detailed his background as a master bilker of banks. "At the moment I have no slide presentations or anything," said Abagnale. "But I'd like to give a lecture to your employees for one hour after closing. If you think my lecture is worthless, you owe me nothing. If you think it is beneficial, you pay me $50 and make a couple of calls to friends you have in other banks to tell them what you think about my talk and what I'm doing."

His first appearance as a "white-collar crime specialist" led to another appearance at a different bank, and then to another and yet another. Within months Abagnale was in widespread demand by banks, hotels, airlines and other businesses.

Today, three years later, Frank Abagnale is one of the nation's most popular crime authorities, with offices in both Houston and Denver, a highly-trained staff, and gross revenues approaching $3 million. He still leads a life on the fly, constantly criss-crossing the nation to present seminars, give lectures or to appear on various television panels. Frank Abagnale leads a very satisfying life.

More importantly, he now realizes why he first embarked on a criminal voyage and why he is not now adrift on that dismal cruise.

"If I did not do what I do today—if I had stayed a pizza cook, a grocery executive or a movie projectionist—I might very well be back in prison today," Abagnale muses. "Why? Because there's no glamour, no excitement, no adventure and nothing to fulfill my ego in those vocations.

"What I do today, on the other hand, fulfills all my needs. I get up in front of thousands of people, and I know they're listening to what I say. That's an ego trip. I appear on dozens of television programs annually. To me, that's a glamorous life. It's an adventuresome life, because I'm constantly being challenged by white collar criminals who come up with new gimmicks to defraud clients—and I know they're out to put me down as much as they are to make a bundle.

"Actually, I haven't changed. All the needs that made me a criminal are still there. I have simply found a legal and socially acceptable way to fulfill those needs. I'm still a con artist. I'm just putting down a positive con these days, as opposed to the negative con I used in the past. I have simply redirected the talents I've always possessed. Today, if I walked into a crowded room and wanted to impress the people therein, I could impress them more by saying, 'I'm Frank Abagnale, the impostor,' than if I were to be the old Frank Abagnale, posing as a pilot, a doctor or whatever."

Frank Abagnale, in reality, is still a bumblebee personality, flying where he isn't supposed to fly at all, and making a pot of honey on the side.